The Evolution

of the

Weird Tale

S. T. Joshi

Hippocampus Press

New York

Published by Hippocampus Press
P.O. Box 641, New York, NY 10156.
http://www.hippocampuspress.com

Cover art by Wallace Smith from *Fantazius Mallare*
by Ben Hecht (Covici-McGee, 1922).
Cover design by Barbara Briggs Silbert.
Hippocampus Press logo designed by Anastasia Damianakos.

First Edition
1 3 5 7 9 8 6 4 2

ISBN 0-9748789-2-8

Contents

Introduction...7

I. Some Americans of the Golden Age 11
   W. C. Morrow: Horror in San Francisco 13
   Robert W. Chambers: The Bohemian Weird Tale............................. 18
   F. Marion Crawford: Blood-and-Thunder Horror 26
   Edward Lucas White: Dream and Reality 39

II. Some Englishmen of the Golden Age...47
   Sir Arthur Quiller-Couch: Ghosts and Scholars 49
   Rudyard Kipling: The Horror of India.. 53
   E. F. Benson: Spooks and More Spooks.. 60
   L. P. Hartley: The Refined Ghost 64

III. H. P. Lovecraft and His Influence...75
   H. P. Lovecraft: The Fiction of Materialism.................................... 77
   Frank Belknap Long: Things from the Sea...................................... 98
   A Literary Tutelage: Robert Bloch and H. P. Lovecraft 107
   Passing the Torch: H. P. Lovecraft and Fritz Leiber...................... 124

IV. Contemporaries 137
   Rod Serling: The Moral Supernatural 139
   L. P. Davies: The Workings of the Mind.. 149
   Les Daniels: The Horror of History 166
   Dennis Etchison: Spanning the Genres 178
   David J. Schow and Splatterpunk.. 190
   Poppy Z. Brite: Sex, Horror, and Rock-&-Roll............................. 203

Bibliography...209

Introduction

Robert Bloch long ago remarked that "Lovecraft was my university." By this he meant that association with Lovecraft opened up to him many realms of enquiry that he might not otherwise have explored, so that, beyond the valuable assistance Lovecraft lent him in the actual writing of his weird fiction, his intellectual horizons were also vastly expanded. That same result can be had by anyone who approaches Lovecraft's work critically and analytically; in particular, his study *Supernatural Horror in Literature* (1927) provides tantalisingly brief discussions of authors of weird fiction the full range of whose work begs for exploration. In many ways, the essays in this volume are attempts to probe some of the writers Lovecraft found stimulating but whom he felt unable to study at length in his avowedly compressed monograph.

It should, however, not be assumed that, aside from the essays in Section II, my focus is in any sense upon the manner in which the writers in question influenced Lovecraft. That is something that can and should be the subject of separate enquiry. Instead, I have sought to examine the entirety of the weird output of these authors in an attempt to grasp their overall literary aims and purposes. My critical method is explicitly judgmental, as I consider it an essential component of the critic's function to pass an informed judgment upon the merits or demerits of a given work of literature, or of the author's work as a whole. Critics occupy a central function in the establishment of a literary canon, and they are important in counteracting the spurious impressiveness of mere popular appeal. But the key is not the mere expression of a judgment upon a given author or work, but a judgment informed by an exhaustive knowledge of the field and—that most intangible and indefinable of qualities—a keen critical sense that distinguishes the superficial from the profound, the meretricious from the sincere, and the obvious from the complex. It was, after all, Lovecraft who first identified the "modern masters" of weird fiction in Arthur Machen, Algernon Blackwood, Lord Dunsany, and M. R. James; and it was in conscious homage of this critical judgment that I chose, in *The Weird Tale* (1990), to discuss these four authors—along with Ambrose Bierce and Lovecraft himself—in greater detail than Lovecraft allowed himself to do.

I am unwavering in my acknowledgement of Philip Van Doren Stern's designation of the period roughly spanning the years 1880–1940 as the "Golden Age" of weird fiction. The leading figures of this period are too well-known to cite, but I have found substantial merit in several lesser authors who added their cumulative merits to this rich period, whether it be such Americans as W. C. Morrow or Robert W. Chambers or such Englishmen as E. F. Benson and Rudyard Kipling. In my researches I have been fortunate enough to have had the resources to unearth uncollected weird writings by these and other authors, so that the whole of their weird work could be assessed. Even such a highly regarded mainstream writer as L. P. Hartley has rarely been treated as a contributor to the literature of the weird; and further work could be done in relating his ghostly tales to his non-weird novels and stories.

Lovecraft is, in many senses, the linchpin of the twentieth-century weird tale, not only for his absorption of the best weird work of the past but for his nurturing of a fair proportion of the best work that followed him. Of the three disciples whose work I discuss here—Fritz Leiber, Robert Bloch, and Frank Belknap Long—Leiber is clearly preeminent, and is perhaps the only writer of the "Lovecraft Circle" who can bear comparison with Lovecraft himself in literary stature. Further study—elaborating upon Bruce Byfield's pioneering treatise, *Witches of the Mind: A Critical Study of Fritz Leiber* (Necronomicon Press, 1991)—ought to be done in explicating the whole of Leiber's substantial work.

In contemplating post-Lovecraftian weird fiction, it is difficult to resist concluding that we have entered a definite "Silver Age" that reveals a marked falling-off of quality and richness from the "Golden Age." This need imply no disrespect to such writers as Shirley Jackson or Ramsey Campbell—the two authors I treated exhaustively in *The Modern Weird Tale* (2001). Campbell, indeed, has now produced so extensive and meritorious a body of work as to challenge both Lovecraft and Blackwood for absolute preeminence in the field. But aside from such lamentably unprolific writers as T. E. D. Klein and Thomas Ligotti, the modern age seems to boast few figures who can rival the "modern masters," or even some of the more interesting lesser writers of the earlier period. My own fondness for Rod Serling, Les Daniels, and the exceedingly little-known L. P. Davies is perhaps largely a personal prejudice; but no one can deny that Dennis Etchison and David J. Schow belong somewhere within the canon of modern weird fiction. Of the merits of the popular Poppy Z. Brite I am a bit more sceptical.

None of the essays in this volume should be regarded as exhaustive or definitive; there is always more to say about any author of substance, and differing judgments as to the merits or flaws of a given writer can frequently stimulate thought and discussion. It is true that in most cases I am writing here as an advocate—as someone who is convinced of the worth of the writers he is treating and who hopes to convey that worth to others. But I trust that this approach does not blind me to these authors' faults, or commit me to the assumption that they occupy the very loftiest strata in the canon of weird fiction. It will be sufficient if what I say about them incites readers to seek out their work—difficult though it may be to locate, in some instances—and come to their own evaluative judgments as to their substance and interest.

—S. T. JOSHI

Acknowledgements

Some of the essays contained in this book began as introductions to collections of weird tales by the authors discussed. This includes the essays on W. C. Morrow (from Morrow's *The Monster Maker and Other Stories* [Midnight House, 2000]), Robert W. Chambers (from Chambers' *The Yellow Sign and Other Stories* [Chaosium, 2000]), Edward Lucas White (from White's *The Stuff of Dreams* [Hippocampus Press, forthcoming]), Sir Arthur Quiller-Couch (from Quiller-Couch's *The Horror on the Stair and Other Stories* [Ash-Tree Press, 2000]), and Rudyard Kipling (from Kipling's *The Mark of the Beast and Other Stories* [Dover, 2000]).

Several essays first appeared in *Studies in Weird Fiction*, including those on F. Marion Crawford (Winter 1998), Frank Belknap Long (Summer 2001), Robert Bloch (Winter 1995), Fritz Leiber (Winter 1999), Rod Serling (Spring 1990), Les Daniels (Fall 1990), Dennis Etchison (Summer 1994), and David J. Schow (Summer 1993). The essay on L. P. Hartley appeared in *Niekas* (1998). "H. P. Lovecraft: The Fiction of Materialism" appeared in *American Supernatural Fiction*, ed. Douglas Robillard (Garland, 1996). The essay on E. F. Benson was initially a review in *Necrofile* (Winter 1994), and the essay on Poppy Z. Brite was a review in *Worlds of Fantasy & Horror* (Winter 1996–97). The essay on L. P. Davies appeared in *Armchair Detective* (Spring 1991). All the essays have been revised—in some cases substantially—from their first appearances.

Bibliographical information on primary and secondary works cited in the text can be found in the Bibliography. In some instances I have found it necessary to include some bibliographical or explanatory information in notes, which can be found at the end of each essay.

I am grateful to my many colleagues—notably Stefan Dziemianowicz, Steven J. Mariconda, Scott D. Briggs, Douglas A. Anderson, and Darrell Schweitzer—for encouraging my work and stimulating my thought in regard to the authors discussed here. I am under an especial debt of gratitude to David E. Schultz for his assistance in bringing this book to fruition.

I. Some Americans of the Golden Age

W. C. Morrow: Horror in San Francisco

We are indebted to the pioneering work of the late Sam Moskowitz for much of the scanty biographical and bibliographical information we currently possess about William Chambers Morrow (1854–1923). Prior to Moskowitz's work, we were reliant upon the brief chapter on Morrow in Vincent Starrett's *Buried Caesars* (1923), where Morrow was shown to be a short story writer of unusual power and a fringe member of Ambrose Bierce's literary circle in California; and, of course, there was the evidence of his "famously obscure" story collection, *The Ape, the Idiot and Other People* (1897), a choice prize for the collector of weird and unusual fiction. Now, however, we can paint a much broader picture of Morrow the man and writer, although certain phases of his career remain frustratingly elusive.

Moskowitz has established that Morrow was born on 7 July 1854 (not 1853, as has usually been given in reference works and library catalogues), in Selma, Alabama. His family owned numerous slaves, and two of them were registered specifically in Morrow's own name as early as 1860, when he was only a child. This fact, however, helps to confirm Morrow's own statement, in the autobiographical vignette "Some Queer Experiences" (1891), that "my earliest mental development was largely the work of intelligent but highly superstitious negro women—slaves—serving as nurses and housekeepers." From childhood, then, Morrow was predisposed to write of the bizarre.

Morrow's father, although a Baptist minister, also owned a moderate-sized farm and a large hotel, the Gulf City Hotel, in Mobile. The Civil War, however, clearly crippled the family's finances—in no small measure because they lost their slaves—and the hotel evidently became their chief source of income. Morrow himself graduated in 1869, at the early age of fifteen, from Howard College (now Samford University) in Birmingham; but perhaps this was some kind of preparatory school, for Moskowitz has unearthed evidence that Morrow also attended the University of Alabama at Tuscaloosa sometime during the period 1869–79, although he did not receive a degree.

The young Morrow was clearly compelled to assist in the family hotel business rather than pursue higher education, for as early as 1876 Morrow himself, not his father, is listed as being in charge of the hotel. Possibly his father was ailing, for he died in 1879. A year previous, Morrow had apparently given up the Gulf City Hotel in Mobile and opened a smaller one in Meridian, Mississippi. And yet, the very next year, some months prior to his father's death in October, Morrow made the fateful decision to head west to California.

The record is blank as to what could have impelled Morrow to take so bold a step. We do not know if he had done any writing during his years in Alabama and Mississippi, but we have to assume that he must have done so; for he began selling his short stories to a variety of papers in the San Francisco area almost immediately upon his arrival there.

Some ambiguous evidence on the matter may be provided by the autobiographical "Some Queer Experiences." In the last of the brief accounts in this essay Morrow tells the tale of how he, "arriving at legal age" (i.e., the age of twenty-one, or around 1875), became bizarrely involved in the running of a weekly paper in conjunction with an "invisible partner" who had given him $50,000 to initiate the enterprise. This is odd enough, but Morrow goes on to relate how the paper would feature outrageously satirical squibs for whose appearance in the paper Morrow himself could not account, but which had evidently come from his own hand. Eventually Morrow separated himself from the paper, which folded shortly thereafter. It is difficult to know how seriously we are to take this soberly narrated account; Moskowitz makes no comment on it, and evidently no effort has been made to trace such a paper in Alabama. If true, it would be a most extraordinary initiation for a future weird writer!

In any event, Morrow found a ready home for his work when he reached California. One of his first published tales is "Awful Shadows," a grim tale of the lynching of an African American in Mississippi that clearly drew (in its general background, at any rate) upon Morrow's personal experiences. It appeared in the Argonaut for 19 July 1879. This weekly paper, founded in 1877 by Frank Pixley and Fred Somers, had also employed Ambrose Bierce as a columnist for the period 1877–79. Just at the time that Morrow's story was published, Bierce was severing his relations with the paper to join a short-lived gold-mining company in the Black Hills of South Dakota. No doubt Bierce and Morrow first became acquainted at this time.

Morrow published numerous other tales in the *Argonaut*, including two striking tales of the Civil War, "The Bloodhounds" (13 December 1879) and "The Three Hundred" (10 January 1880), both of them set in the South.[1] The first tale that might conceivably be termed weird was "A Glimpse of the Unusual," appearing in the *Californian* for April 1880. Although purely a tale of psychological horror, it already displays the features that would come to typify much of Morrow's later work: a crisp, tightly controlled prose style, penetrating psychological analysis of a disturbed mentality, and an unrelenting focus on the protagonist's psychological state—tantamount, in some later works, to a kind of proto-stream-of-consciousness. It would be difficult to find parallels for these tales in the entire range of nineteenth-century literature—except, perhaps, in the tales of Poe (clearly a dominant influence on Morrow), some of the later work of Guy de Maupassant (written after Morrow's early work), and the tales of Ambrose Bierce, who Moskowitz plausibly believes was actually influenced by Morrow's example in his own memorable Civil War tales and horror stories of the later 1880s.

In 1881 Morrow married Lydia E. Houghton. They had one child that was either stillborn or died in infancy. Around this time Morrow apparently felt the need for more regular employment, so he joined the staff of the *San Jose Mercury* as a reporter. During the period 1882–87 almost no short stories of his have been discovered. However, Morrow did publish his first novel, *Blood-Money* (1882), a searing indictment of the rapacity of the huge railroad companies that were dominating Californian politics and economy at this time. *Blood-Money* deals with the Mussel Slough affair, in which the Southern Pacific Railroad forced settlers off a tract of land they had worked hard to cultivate, leading to a gunfight in 1880 in which some settlers were killed. The novel was not widely reviewed, and sold poorly (Moskowitz conjectures that the railroads themselves conspired to suppress it); but today it is recognised as a significant work of social criticism.[2]

When William Randolph Hearst took over the operation of the *San Francisco Examiner* from his father in 1887, one of the writers he urged to contribute (probably on Bierce's recommendation) was W. C. Morrow. Now began a fruitful phase of Morrow's short-story writing, and some of his best work appeared in this newspaper. Morrow resumed contributions to the *Argonaut* as well, writing such tales as the grim tale of revenge "His Unconquerable Enemy" (11 March 1889), the tense detective thrillers as "The Woman of the Inner Room" (12 January 1891) and "The Red Strangler" (18 May 1891), the *conte cruel* "The Wrong Door" (9 February 1891), and the science-fiction/horror story "The Surgeon's Experiment" (15 October 1887), later to be titled "The Monster-Maker."

Incredibly, around 1891 Morrow actually accepted a position in the public relations department of the Southern Pacific Railroad. Possibly the nemesis of his *Blood-Money* period was trying to buy his silence. He stayed in the position for two years, then joined the staff of the *San Francisco News Letter.* Morrow also allowed himself to participate in several "stunts" in the *Examiner.* During 1891–92 he wrote a series of "Possible Solutions" of real-life murder cases in San Francisco. Then, in 1892, he wrote the beginning of a tale, "The Unfinished Story," and the paper offered prizes for the best conclusion sent in by readers.[3]

By 1896 Morrow evidently felt that he had enough tales to assemble a collection. In fact, by this time he had written enough to fill two or three volumes, and it is not entirely certain that he exercised sound judgment in the tales he decided to include in *The Ape, the Idiot and Other People.* Nevertheless, that volume, published by the Philadelphia firm of Lippincott, is a landmark for all lovers of the weird, the strange, and the unusual. Bierce himself sang its praises in his "Prattle" column:

> . . . I should like to pile in a lot of good words for Mr. W. C. Morrow's new book, "The Ape, the Idiot and Other People." It is capital reading, as every one familiar with this writer's stories in "The Examiner" would naturally expect it to be. Mr. Morrow has a taste for the shadow-side of life, and seldom gets far away from the "terminator" into the area of illumina-

tion. If he lived on Venus, which presents always the same side to the sun, the terrestrial telescope that could pick him up would need to be no less alert than strong. He knows that, curiously considered, the "more things" noted by Hamlet have a sharper and more insistent interest than the familiar phenomena saluted daily by "our philosophy"; and he is just the man curiously to consider them. At times, shaking ourselves free from the spell of his astonishing ingenuity, we feel that he has been taking a liberty with us—that by the sobriety of his narrative he has duped us into acceptance of the rank impossible, instead of the unbanned impossible that we rightly expected to get; but he bears our resentment with charity and soon has us again lapped in our pleasing dream of the fiveness of twice two.[4]

Strangely enough, after the publication of his seminal collection, Morrow appeared to lose interest in the short story as a form of expression. Only random tales—rarely in the weird or even the suspense mode—emerged from his pen over the next decade or so during which he was a practicing writer. Possibly economic concerns were a factor. By no later than 1899 Morrow had begun a school for beginning writers. Bierce, in a tart comment on Morrow's new occupation, suggests that it was indeed undertaken out of economic necessity: "Yes, it is a pity, that Morrow teaches others to write badly, instead of himself writing well. But I fancy we have no grievance therein, or if we have it is against the pig public, not against Morrow. He would write books, doubtless, if he could afford to, as I would do."[5] Perhaps the slim pamphlet that emerged around this time—*The Art of Writing for Publication* (1901)—was a product of Morrow's tutorial work.

Morrow's relatively few book publications of the first decade of the twentieth century suggest that he was either trying to capture the tastes of a more general readership or, in fact, had declined into hackwork. *A Man; His Mark: A Romance* (1900) and *Lentala of the South Seas* (1908) are adventure novels with romantic elements (something Morrow never handled very well in his short stories), while a work entitled *Bohemian Paris of To-day* (1900) is declared on its title page to be "Written by W. C. Morrow, from notes by Edouard Cucuel." A slim travel booklet, *Roads around Paso Robles* (1904), completes Morrow's book publications during his lifetime. No work published subsequent to 1909 has been located.

It is difficult to characterise Morrow's literary work—even his short stories—in small compass. Writing at a time when the rigid division of literature into well-recognised "genres" was unknown, Morrow chose to experiment at will in what would only later be termed mystery, suspense, weird, or even science fiction. In many ways, it is his seamless amalgamation of several of these modes within a single tale that lends it its distinctiveness.

It is worth noting that there may not be a single orthodox tale of the supernatural in Morrow's entire corpus. "The Monster-Maker" clearly relies upon a conjectural development of medical science—whether plausible or not—in its depiction of an anencephalous man; "The Woman of the Inner Room" advances a pseudo-scientific argument for a woman's ability to perceive a man's thoughts when she inserts a finger into a bullet wound in his head and touches his brain. Similar medical erudition is utilised in "The Permanent Stiletto" (first published as "A Peculiar Case of Surgery" in the *Argonaut* for 4 February 1889). The bizarre story "The Queen of the Red Devils"—published in the Christmas 1892 issue of the San Francisco weekly magazine, the *Wave* (later known for its publication of many of the tales of Frank Norris)—is a fantasy of sorts; but in spite of Moskowitz's high praise, I do not believe it an effective tale.

Had the field of mystery or detective fiction been more clearly defined in his day, Morrow could well have become a noted writer in this realm. As it is, aside from several fine tales in which ingenious strokes of deductive genius are featured, Morrow wrote a 55,000-word short novel, *A Strange Confession*, serialised in the *Californian* in 1880–81. This fast-paced, action-packed mystery/suspense novel is well worthy of book publication.

W. C. Morrow has waited far too long to gain his due as a writer of the strange. Even *The Ape, the Idiot and Other People* has been out of print for many years,[6] and his uncollected tales would, save for Sam Moskowitz's industrious work, have been consigned to the oblivion of the newspapers and magazines of more than a century ago in which they first appeared. But Morrow can now take his rightful place as a distinctive voice in the American literature of the later nineteenth century. His gripping tales—the products of a powerful and unusual imagination, a taut prose style, and an insight into aberrant psychology rarely displayed in his time—retain the power to fascinate and terrify.

Notes

1. Both stories are now reprinted in my anthology, *Civil War Memories* (Nashville, TN: Rutledge Hill Press, 2000).

2. See the discussion in George L. Henderson's *California and the Fictions of Capital* (New York: Oxford University Press, 1999).

3. Bierce, who regarded any kind of literary contests of this sort with great disdain, expressed his scorn of Morrow's action in a letter: "Morrow's recent performance with that 'unfinished' story surprised me, for Morrow can write. It struck me as disagreeable that he would be willing to make literature ridiculous with such a mountebank trick." Bierce to James Tufts, 16 April 1893 (ms., Colorado College).

4. Bierce, "Prattle," *San Francisco Examiner* (25 April 1897): 6.

5. Bierce to Herman Scheffauer, 7 September 1903 (ms., Bancroft Library, University of California).

6. Two of the stories from the volume were, however, published separately as pamphlets by the Book Club of California: *Over an Absinthe Bottle* (1936) and *The Ape and the Idiot* (1939).

Robert W. Chambers: The Bohemian Weird Tale

Chambers is like Rupert Hughes and a few other fallen Titans—equipped with the right brains and education, but wholly out of the habit of using them." Such was H. P. Lovecraft's harsh judgment of Robert W. Chambers shortly after discovering him in 1927 (Lovecraft 148). And if that judgment requires some small qualification, we must nevertheless agree with Frederic Taber Cooper's lugubrious assessment: "So much of Mr. Chambers's work exasperates, because we feel that he might so easily have made it better" (Cooper 81). The career of Robert W. Chambers—whether we consider only his fantastic writing or his output as a whole—is the sad tale of a man who, starting with a vivid and distinctive imagination and a seemingly natural gift for putting words to paper, discovered popularity too quickly and devoted the rest of his life to catering to popular whim. The best of Chambers' work can almost be measured by its very lack of popularity.

Of Chambers' life we know little. Born in Brooklyn on 26 May 1865, he entered the Art Students' League around the age of twenty, where the artist Charles Dana Gibson was his fellow-student. From 1886 to 1893 he studied art in Paris, at the Ecole des Beaux Arts and at Julian's, and his work was displayed at the Salon as early as 1889. Returning to New York, he succeeded in selling his illustrations to *Life*, *Truth*, and *Vogue* ("the three most frivolous and ephemeral publications of any commercial standing that New York has ever known," as John Curtis Underwood termed them), but for reasons still not entirely clear turned to writing and produced his first "novel," *In the Quarter* (1894), really a series of loosely connected character sketches of artist life in Paris. C. C. Baldwin (92) suggested that Chambers was inspired "to make use of his Latin Quarter experiences" by Henri Murger's *Scènes de la vie de Bohème* (1851; the novel upon which Puccini's *La Bohème* is based), and this may be right; although there is no way to ascertain whether it was so specific a literary influence as this, since Lovecraft in *Supernatural Horror in Literature* makes note of Chambers' "somewhat trivial and affected cultivation of the Gallic studio atmosphere made popular by Du Maurier's *Trilby*." That Chambers was not, in any case, sincerely interested in capturing his own experiences is testified by the fact that he completely dropped the "Gallic studio atmosphere" after *The Mystery of Choice* (1897), presumably because it no longer proved popular. With *The King in Yellow* (1895) Chambers' career as a writer was established—not because he had felt himself a born writer but because that collection of short stories was (probably in spite rather than because of the horror tales contained in it) successful. Chambers had somehow caught the public eye; he knew what the public wanted and gave it to them.

Although from time to time he returned to fantasy, Chambers never did so with the gripping and almost nightmarish intensity of *The King in Yel-*

low; nor did he ever again attempt a sincere and almost scathing depiction of the hollowness of American social and intellectual life as he did in the unsuccessful novel *Outsiders* (1898), which alone of his works may be of interest to the social historian. Instead, he wrote novels and tales which, while superficially dealing with a wide range of topics—the Franco-Prussian War; the American Revolution; modern New York society; World War I; the Civil War—all contained an unending procession of pompous and dim-witted fellows (usually of independent means and attemptedly cynical temperament) falling in love at the least provocation with an equally endless parade of simpering and virtuous women who, although capable of blushing instantly at the slightest suggestion of impropriety, nevertheless give themselves body and soul to their male pursuers after what proves to be a merely token resistance. Some passages in Chambers' works would probably have been considered salacious at the time of their writing, and the only fitting modern parallels are Harlequin romances. It is doubtful whether any of Chambers' work would serve even as raw material for historical or sociological analysis of the period, since even in his own day he was castigated for producing wooden and unrealistic characters; of his females in particular F. T. Cooper remarked: "They are all of them what men like to think women to be, rather than the actual women themselves." It is not, then, surprising that nearly the whole of Chambers' output—of which I have counted eighty-seven different volumes, including novels, tales, one volume of poems, one drama, juvenile books on nature, and even an opera libretto—has lapsed into obscurity and has yet to be resurrected by industrious academics always on the lookout for new dissertation topics.

There is not much to tell of Chambers' later life. At least two of his novels reached official best-seller status—*The Fighting Chance* (1906) and *The Younger Set* (1907), both selling some 200,000 copies—and Chambers settled into a luxurious and elegantly furnished mansion in Broadalbin, in upstate New York. Like Lord Dunsany, Chambers liked the "great outdoors," and was an ardent hunter and fisherman. He collected butterflies, Oriental rugs and vases, and—if the photograph of his study printed in Rupert Hughes' laudatory sketch of Chambers in *Cosmopolitan* is any guide—he was in no small way a bibliophile. He died, presumably in comfort and peace, on 16 December 1933.

Of the pleasantness of Chambers' character there seems no doubt: Hughes unhesitatingly said that "Bob Chambers is the salt of the earth," and Joyce Kilmer's interview with him in 1917 reveals him to be genial, completely lacking in the arrogance of success, and even fairly perceptive about writing and writers; his concluding advice to the would-be author ("Let him not take himself too seriously!") is surely a reference to himself. It is, however, ironic that Chambers' very popularity drove each of his works into obscurity as its successor emerged; and so early as 1927 August Derleth complained in a letter to H. P. Lovecraft[1] that even *The King in Yel-*

low—the most widely reprinted of Chambers' works both during and after his lifetime—was becoming difficult of access.

Chambers' fantastic writing is limited principally to five volumes—*The King in Yellow* (1895), *The Mystery of Choice* (1897), *In Search of the Unknown* (1904), *Police!!!* (1915), and the novel *The Slayer of Souls* (1920)—while several ancillary volumes contain weird matter in lesser degrees—*The Maker of Moons* (1896), *The Tracer of Lost Persons* (1906), and *The Tree of Heaven* (1907). This wide scattering of his fantastic writing shows that Chambers never considered himself a fantaisiste in the tradition of Poe and Bierce (although he was influenced by both), but seems to have written fantasy whenever the mood struck him. It is, of course, to be noted that three of the eight works listed date to Chambers' very early period; and future generations of fantasy readers have confirmed C. C. Baldwin's remark on Chambers' output: "Had I my choice I'd take the first three or four [of his books] and let the rest go hang" (Baldwin 90).

The inspiration for *The King in Yellow*—a collection of short stories of which only the first six are fantastic, and of these the first four are loosely interrelated—is, however, sufficiently obvious. Chambers must have read Ambrose Bierce's collection *Tales of Soldiers and Civilians* (1891)—or the English edition of 1892, *In the Midst of Life*—shortly after his return to America from France, for he adopts certain cryptic allusions and names coined in some of Bierce's tales and appropriates them for his own.[2] The focus of these first four tales in *The King in Yellow* is a mysterious drama (apparently in two acts) called *The King in Yellow*, which incites a peculiar fear and desperation upon reading. Chambers' descriptions of this odd volume may rank as some of his finest moments:

> This is the thing that troubles me, for I cannot forget Carcosa where black stars hang in the heavens; where the shadows of men's thoughts lengthen in the afternoon, when the twin suns sink into the Lake of Hali; and my mind will bear forever the memory of the Pallid Mask. I pray God will curse the writer, as the writer has cursed the world with this beautiful, stupendous creation, terrible in its simplicity, irresistible in its truth—a world which now trembles before the King in Yellow. ("The Repairer of Reputations")

It has, however, not been generally noticed that Chambers has apparently wilfully altered the components he derived from Bierce, and it is in any case not clear whether the Bierce influence really extends beyond these borrowed names. Bierce indeed created Carcosa, which he describes in "An Inhabitant of Carcosa" as some great city of the distant past. Chambers maintains this notion, but in Bierce Hali was simply a prophet who is "quoted" as the epigraphs for the tales "The Death of Halpin Frayser" and "An Inhabitant of Carcosa." Finally, Chambers borrows the term "Hastur" from Bierce; but whereas Bierce imagined Hastur as a god of the shepherds (see "Haïta the Shepherd"), Chambers regards Hastur alternately as a place or as a person. In "The Repairer of Reputations" Chambers creates another mythical book, *The Imperial Dynasty of America* (it is never again cited in later works), and cites the beginning of it: "Then from Carcosa, the Hyades, Hastur, and Aldebaran . . ." This itself seems to be derived from a sentence in Bierce's "Inhabitant of Carcosa": "I saw through a sudden rift in the clouds Aldebaran and the Hyades!" But in "The Demoiselle d'Ys" Hastur becomes one of the demoiselle's companions. (It is to be noted that Lovecraft, when mentioning such things as Carcosa, the Lake of Hali, and the like in his own tales, was consciously following Chambers, although he knew full well the Biercian origin of these terms. His one mention of Hastur in "The Whisperer in Darkness" is entirely inconclusive, and it seems rather irresponsible of August Derleth to elevate this bare citation into one of the major gods of his "Cthulhu Mythos.")

From the first four stories in *The King in Yellow* we learn a few more details about the contents of Chambers' mythical play: there are at least three characters, Cassilda, Camilla, and the King in Yellow himself; aside from places such as Hastur and the Lake of Hali, we learn of regions called Demhe, Yhtill, and Alar (the last also from Bierce); finally, there are other details such as the Pallid Mask and the Yellow Sign. It is obvious that Chambers intended to leave these citations vague and unexplained; he wished merely to provide dim hints as to the possible worlds of horror and awe to which his mythical book was a guide. Although in "The Silent Land" (in *The Maker of Moons*) Chambers twice makes mention of a "King in Carcosa," he never develops this "King in Yellow mythology" elsewhere.

The tales in *The King in Yellow* differ widely in tone, flavour, and quality. The first, "The Repairer of Reputations," is a bizarre tale of the future (its setting is New York in 1920) in which Chambers, aside from oddly predicting a general European war, imagines a quasi-utopia with euthanasia chambers for those who wish to slough off the burden of existence, while Chicago and New York rise "white and imperial" in a new age of architecture wherein the "horrors" of Victorian design are repudiated. Nevertheless, the tale cannot be called science fiction (on which see further below), since the futuristic setting does not in the end have any role in the story line, which concerns a demented young man who imagines that he is the King in Yellow and that his cousin is vying for the throne. Such a bald description cannot begin to convey the otherworldly, nightmarish quality of the tale, where the unexplained elements of Chambers' "King in Yellow mythology," along with a prose style bordering upon the extravagant and an intentionally chaotic exposition, create an atmosphere of chilling horror. "The Mask," in contrast, is an exquisitely beautiful tale set in France concerning a sculptor who has discovered a fluid capable of petrifying any plant or animal such that it resembles the finest marble. Several portions of the narration, especially toward the end, are pure poetry.

"The Yellow Sign" is generally considered to be the best tale in *The King in Yellow*, and deals horrifyingly with the nameless fate of an artist who has found the Yellow Sign. Lovecraft in *Supernatural Horror in Literature* has well described the loathsome hearse-driver who is a harbinger for the narrator's death—a soft, pudgy, wormlike creature who has one of his fingers torn off in a tussle and who, when found in the artist's studio at the end, is pronounced to have been dead for months. "The Demoiselle d'Ys," in spite of its inclusion of Hastur as a minor character, is not part of the "King in Yellow mythology," but is another hauntingly beautiful tale about a man who is supernaturally transplanted into the mediaeval age while hunting in the Breton countryside and falls in love with a lovely huntress three centuries dead. The rest of *The King in Yellow* contains a series of fine prose-poems ("The Prophets' Paradise") followed by several gripping tales dealing with the Franco-Prussian War.

The Mystery of Choice (1897) is an undeservedly forgotten collection, and—in its more refined and controlled prose style, greater unity of theme, and exquisite pathos—ranks close to *The King in Yellow* in quality. The first five stories are linked by a common setting—Brittany—and some recurring characters; and although the first ("The Purple Emperor") is an amusing parody on the detective story, the rest of the collection contains fine tales of fantasy and even science fiction. Here again Chambers can, when he chooses, create moments of heart-rending exquisiteness, and his powers of description are unexcelled:

> Then the daily repeated miracle of the coming of dawn was wrought before our eyes. The heavens glowed in rainbow tints; the shredded mist rising along the river was touched with purple and gold, and acres of meadow and pasture dripped precious stones. Shreds of the fading night-mist drifted among the tree tops, now tipped with fire, while in the forest depths faint sparkles came from some lost ray of morning light falling on wet leaves. Then of a sudden up shot the sun, and against it, black and gigantic, a peasant towered, leaning upon his spade. ("The White Shadow")

This is the art not only of the painter but of the etcher or engraver, and holds us breathless while it lasts.

In *Search of the Unknown* (1904) Chambers begins to take another tack—the mingling of weirdness, humour, and romance—and readers must judge for themselves how felicitous this union is. His conceptions are as fertile as ever (we are here concerned with a series of tales depicting successive searches for lost species of animals, including a loathsome half-man and half-amphibian called "the harbor-master," a group of invisible creatures apparently in the shape of beautiful women, and the like), but in every tale the narrator attempts to flirt with a pretty girl, only to lose her at the last moment to some rival. Chambers reprinted "The Man at the Next Table" (from *The Maker of Moons*) and "A Matter of Interest" (from *The Mystery of Choice*) into this work; a work that, though labelled a novel, is in fact a string of tales (actually published separately in journals) stitched together into a continuous narrative. Indeed, so many of Chambers' "novels" are of this sort that few can be termed other than episodic. A sequel to this volume is *Police!!!* (1915), a collection of tales where further searches are made into lost species— including mammoths in the glaciers of Canada, a group of "cave-ladies" in the Everglades, and the like. This book places still greater emphasis on humour than its predecessor, and several of the tales are quite amusing; but there also seems to be a slight decline in Chambers' fertility of invention: the amphibian man in "The Third Eye" too closely resembles the harbor-master, while in "Un Peu d'Amour" we encounter an irascible character obviously reminiscent of a similar character in the first segment of *In Search of the Unknown*. But even here there are some gripping moments: "Un Peu d'Amour" presents some horrifying glimpses of a gigantic worm burrowing beneath the fields of upstate New York, while another tale ("The Ladies of the Lake") discloses a school of huge minnows the size of Pullman cars.

The *Tracer of Lost Persons* (1906) is another episodic novel, somewhat more unified than many of Chambers' others. Most of the tales are rather flippant accounts of a mysterious gentleman, Westrel Keen, who assists young men in finding their true loves; but one haunting episode about the resurrection of an Egyptian woman suspended in a state of hypnosis for thousands of years is another remarkable fusion of beauty and horror. *The Tree of Heaven* (1907) is similarly not exclusively fantastic, but contains some very fine moments. The construction of the "novel" is ingenious: at the outset an odd mystic utters prophecies to a group of his friends, and the subsequent episodes are concerned with their fulfilment. For once the love-element is not extrinsic to the plot, and in several of these tales love is simply given a supernatural dimension that creates a profundity not often found in Chambers; even the non-fantastic romantic tales are handled with a seriousness and depth completely absent in other of Chambers' works. The superb atmosphere of delicate pathos and dream-fantasy maintained in some of these tales may place this volume only behind *The King in Yellow* and *The Mystery of Choice* as Chambers' finest. The various "chapters" in fact appeared previously as short stories: "The Carpet of Belshazzar" (as "The Tree of Heaven") in *Harper's Weekly* (10 December 1904); "The Sign of Venus" in *Harper's* (December 1903); "The Case of Mr. Helmer" in *Harper's* (October 1904); and "The Bridal Pair" in *Harper's* (December 1902). Probably the six other chapters in the volume were also published in magazines, but I have not located their appearances.

With *The Slayer of Souls* (1920), however, Chambers reaches the nadir of his career. Even if we could swallow the appallingly tasteless premise—that "Anarchists, terrorists, Bolshevists, Reds of all shades and degrees, are now believed to represent in modern times" the descendants of the devil-worshipping Yezidi sect of inner Asia, which is poisoning the minds of misguided leftists and labour unionists for the overthrow of good and the establishment of evil, whatever that means—there is no escaping the tedium of the whole work, which is concerned with the efforts of the U.S. Secret Service, along with a young woman who, although having lived for years with these evil Chinese, has now defected and converted to Christianity, to hunt down the eight leading figures of the sect and exterminate them. This happens with mechanical regularity, and it is no surprise that civilisation is saved in the end for God-fearing Americans. The novel—an elaboration of the title story of *The Maker of Moons* (1896), although that tale is handled far better and contains some delicate moments of shimmering fantasy—is further crippled by a ponderous and entirely humourless style, and with characters so moronic that they cannot reconcile themselves to the supernatural even after repeated exposure to it. And the crowning absurdity is that the origin of all these evils is a "black planet . . . not a hundred miles" from the earth! There is not a single redeeming element in this novel.

Some general remarks can now be made on Chambers' fantastic work. One of its most interesting features is a proto-science-fictional element that emerges in some works cheek by jowl with the overt supernaturalism of other tales. We have seen that "The Repairer of Reputations" is set in the future; but "The Mask" actually makes greater use of a science-fictional principle of great importance: the scientific justification for a fantastic event. Chambers never precisely explains the nature of the petrifying fluid used in the story, but we are led to believe that it would not be beyond the bounds of chemistry to encompass it. Similarly, in "A Matter of Interest" elaborate attempts are made at the outset to establish the veracity and accuracy of the narrative, which concerns the discovery of the last living dinosaur (the "thermosaurus"). Other segments of *In Search of the Unknown* are even more emphatic on the point, and one of the characters vigorously denies the supernatural character of the harbor-master: "'I don't think that the harbor-master is a spirit or a sprite or a hobgoblin, or any sort of damned rot. Neither do I believe it to be an optical illusion.'" Less scientific justification is presented for the creatures in *Police!!!*, but even here few strain credulity beyond the breaking-point. Even *The Slayer of Souls* enunciates the principle: "'We're up against something absolutely new. Of course, it isn't magic. It can, of course, be explained by natural laws about which we happen to know nothing at present.'" Unfortunately, in this case little effort is made to coordinate the bizarre events into a plausibly scientific framework.

The detective element in Chambers emerges in such parodies as "The Purple Emperor" and "The Eggs of the Silver Moon" (in *Police!!!*), but most concentratedly in the episodic novel *The Tracer of Lost Persons*. The central character is an enigmatic and seemingly omniscient figure who presents himself much in the model of Sherlock Holmes; although perhaps the parallel to Poe's C. Auguste Dupin would be closer, since the segment of the novel involves the decoding of a cipher in hieroglyphics which appears clearly derived from "The Gold Bug."

Finally, I have had frequent occasion to remark upon interrelations between Chambers' tales. Many of the short story collections use the same characters and setting, and are not much different from his episodic novels. Interrelations between entire works exist; *The King in Yellow* derives some of its characters from *In the Quarter;* some characters in *In Search of the Unknown* return in *Police!!!;* in *The Tree of Heaven* there is passing allusion to the central character of *The Tracer of Lost Persons.* Much of this seems to have been done in a spirit of fun, and need not imply any serious thematic connexion.

Chambers' influence on subsequent fantasy writing is difficult to judge; several leading fantaisistes of the next generation—Lovecraft, Clark Ashton Smith, A. Merritt—professed to have been impressed with his work (especially—and almost exclusively—*The King in Yellow*), but in Lovecraft's case at any rate the influence does not seem to extend much beyond the borrowing of names from Chambers' "King in Yellow mythology"; the general "cosmic" attitude of both Lovecraft and Smith was clearly established before they ever encountered its dim adumbration in Chambers. The best of Chambers was a product of the "Yellow Nineties," and gains its power in large part by capturing the languor and pathos of that distinctive period.

Robert W. Chambers is a decidedly frustrating writer—a man for whom writing seems to have come as easily as (on a far higher level) composition seems to have come for Telemann or Mozart; who could draw literary substance from his own experiences—as a painter in France; as a hunter and fisher in New York state; as a collector of butterflies and general dabbler in science—but who marred so many of his creations with flippancy, pseudo-sophistication, and catchpenny sentimentality; whose descriptive and imaginative powers were of a high order but who was too lulled by the favour of the mob to use them consistently and effectively; who has left us some immortal tales of horror and fantasy which must be laboriously sifted out from a plethora of trash appalling in its scope. Chambers was an intellectual dilettante, and wrote whatever came to mind; we are fortunate that he now and again turned his careless and free-flowing pen to the creation of a few weird tales of transcendent beauty and horror.

Notes

1. See Lovecraft to Derleth, 6 May 1927 and 16 May 1927; mss., State Historical Society of Wisconsin.

2. The stories by Bierce that influenced Chambers—"Haïta the Shepherd" and "An Inhabitant of Carcosa"—were originally collected in *Tales of Soldiers and Civilians,* but in later editions were transferred to the revised edition of *Can Such Things Be?,* whose original edition (1893) did not contain them, hence could not have been the volume that influenced Chambers. Since, however, it is these later editions that have subsequently been reprinted, the two tales can now be found in modern editions of *Can Such Things Be?* (e.g., Citadel Press, 1974).

F. Marion Crawford: Blood-and-Thunder Horror

Of the voluminous work of Francis Marion Crawford (1854–1909), the American novelist, short story writer, essayist, and historian, sadly little is read today. The writer who in his day was compared favourably to William Dean Howells and Henry James, and who may have been the most popular American novelist of the late nineteenth century, is now remembered for a few powerful weird tales and some novels where the weird enters fitfully; oblivion has—probably justifiably—overtaken his dozens of other historical and romantic novels, although the F. Marion Crawford Society tries valiantly to perpetuate the memory of his entire work.

Although supernaturalism is tangentially involved in several works—including *Mr. Isaacs: A Tale of Modern India* (1882) and *With the Immortals* (1886)—Crawford's weird work can rightly be restricted to four volumes, the novels *Zoroaster* (1885), *Khaled* (1891), and *The Witch of Prague* (1891), and, above all, the landmark posthumous story collection *Wandering Ghosts* (1911). This is all that anyone with an interest in fantasy need read of Crawford's work.

Zoroaster is, as the title proclaims unambiguously, a novel about the life of Zoroaster (the Greek name for Zarathustra), founder of Zoroastrianism. This description would seem to imply that the work is more properly to be categorised amongst Crawford's many historical novels; and although it is true that only the faintest touches of the supernatural are found in this novel, it is really what one might call an historical fantasy. In the first place, so little is definitely known about the life of Zoroaster that much imagination would be required to involve him in a narrative; in the second place, Crawford has evidently ignored or contradicted much of what is known about him.

The novel deals with the young Zoroaster, who is raised in the court of Belshazzar by the old prophet Daniel. As a youth he falls in love with the Hebrew princess Nehushta. Both he and Nehushta are brought to the court of Darius, now ruler of the region after Belshazzar's death; there, through the scheming of Atossa, the wife of Darius who has fallen for Zoroaster but who is scorned by him, he and Nehushta have a falling out and Zoroaster leaves the court. He lives for three years as a hermit, at that time evidently developing his theological principles. He is brought back to the court, gaunt, white-haired, and remote; but Atossa, who still hates him, connives his and Nehushta's death through an attack on the capital while Darius is away. The two, now reconciled, die in each other's arms.

To begin with, let us investigate the historicity of the tale. Zoroaster is traditionally thought to have lived in the sixth century B.C.E. Although some scholars place him as early as the tenth century B.C.E., this traditional date now appears to be generally accepted. Thus far Crawford is on acceptable historical ground; but from this point on he bypasses nearly every fact or legend known about Zoroaster's life. According to tradition, Zoroaster had perhaps three wives and several children, lived to be nearly eighty, and was killed by a priest of the old religion that Zoroastrianism was supplanting. The relation of Zoroaster to Daniel and Belshazzar is entirely imaginary: the Book of Daniel states that Daniel was at the court of Darius and his successor Cyrus, thus making him younger, not older, than Zoroaster. Nehushta is not even a creation of myth and legend. It is true that Zoroaster entered a period of hermitry and religious meditation at age thirty, but this period may have lasted anywhere from ten to twenty years. Darius I (r. 522–486) was indeed converted to Zoroastrianism, but it seems unlikely that he was converted by Zoroaster, who was probably dead by this time. I have no idea what historical evidence Crawford was using for this work; but it seems difficult to doubt that, given the remoteness of the subject, Crawford simply decided to ignore much of the evidence and invent a fictitious narrative around an historically real figure. No doubt Crawford, a devout Roman Catholic, was attracted to Zoroastrianism in general because of its proto-Christian notions of cosmological dualism and a personal saviour. But Crawford does not succeed in giving a sound impression of the development of Zoroaster's religious views. His early beliefs, as inculcated by Daniel, are merely generic mysticism. During his hermitry Zoroaster continues to ponder the nature of the cosmos:

> Gradually . . . as Zoroaster fixed his intuition upon the first main principle of all possible knowledge, he became aware of the chief cause—of the universal principle of vivifying essence, which pervades all things, and in which arises motion as the original generator of transitory being. The great law of division became clear to him—the separation for a time of the universal agent into two parts, by the separation and reuniting of which comes light and heat and the hidden force of life, and the prime rules of attractive action; all things that are accounted material. He saw the division of darkness and light, and how all things that are in the darkness are reflected in the light; and how the light which we call light is in reality darkness made visible, whereas the true light is not visible to the eyes that are darkened by the gross veil of transitory being. And as from the night of earth, his eyes were gradually opened to the astral day, he knew that the forms that move and have being in the night are perishable and utterly unreal; whereas the purer being which is reflected in the real light is true and endures for ever. (13)[1]

This does not help much, either, for the relation of this philosophy to actual Zoroastrianism is tenuous at best. In fact, it is just as well that Crawford did not allow the novel to dwell much on religion or philosophy, since passages like the above slow down what is in reality not a religious novel but a love story.

The great strength of *Zoroaster* is its prose style. It is really a novel-length prose poem, and it is this that raises the otherwise conventionally romantic events of the tale close to the realm of fantasy. Crawford here approaches Oscar Wilde, Lord Dunsany, and Clark Ashton Smith as a wielder of poetic prose:

> There was a terrace that looked eastward from the gardens. Thither Nehushta bent her steps, slowly, as though in deep thought, and when she reached the smooth marble balustrade, she leaned over it and let her dark eyes rest on the quiet landscape. The peace of the evening descended upon her; the birds of the day ceased singing with the growing darkness; and slowly, out of the plain, the yellow moon soared up and touched the river and the meadows with mystic light; while far off, in the rose-thickets of the gardens, the first notes of a single nightingale floated upon the scented breeze, swelling and trilling, quivering and falling again, in a glory of angelic song. The faint air fanned her cheek, the odours of the box and the myrtle and the roses intoxicated her senses, and as the splendid shield of the rising moon cast its broad light into her dreaming eyes, her heart overflowed, and Nehushta the princess lifted up her voice and sang an ancient song of love, in the tongue of her people, to a soft minor melody, that sounded like a sigh from the southern desert. (2)

If *Zoroaster* was in some dim sense intended to underscore Crawford's Catholicism, the same does not appear to be the case for *Khaled: A Tale of Arabia* (1891). In many ways this novel is a pendant to *Zoroaster*, although here there is fortunately not even the pretence of giving the work an historical foundation. We are here concerned with Khaled, "one of the genii converted to the faith on hearing Mohammed read the Koran by night in the valley of Al Nakhlah" (1). Because of some misdeed, Khaled is made a human being and is wedded to the princess Zehowah; and before his mortal death, whenever that shall be, he must persuade his bride to love him so that he can gain an immortal soul. Through a long series of events involving battles and political uprisings in the domain Khaled now rules, he finally wins the love of the cold and indifferent Zehowah.

I have no idea whether this tale is an actual fable, either from the Koran or anywhere else; but it has all the earmarks of a fairy tale similar to the one that La Motte-Fouqué so poignantly transformed into the story of *Undine*. It is amusing that, right at the outset, the truth of Mohammedanism is assumed: the angel Asrael, who comes to Khaled at the beginning of the novel, really has been sent directly from Allah; and, in clothing Khaled in human form, he magically transmutes a handful of leaves into a rich cloak and a locust into a horse. Khaled's human mission has begun. The structural parallels to *Zoroaster* are striking. Aside from the quasi-biblical prose

style, we are once again confronted with a man who is the centre of attention of two women; for Khaled, in trying to inspire Zehowah's love
through jealousy, pretends to extend affection to a slave woman, a Christian named Almasta. She genuinely falls for Khaled and, when repulsed by
him, plots his overthrow. Almasta is simply another Atossa. There is nothing supernatural in this novel, and it too is ultimately a love story. There is
considerable delicacy in the portrayal of Khaled's courtship of Zehowah,
and at one point, when Zehowah urges him languidly to take another wife
(by law he can have four) who will love him better than she can, Khaled
bursts out in anger:

> "I will not take another," he said. "What is the love of any other
> woman to me? It is as dust in the throat of a man thirsting for water. Show
> me a woman who loves me. Her face shall be but a cold mirror in which
> the image of a fire is reflected without warmth, her soft words shall be to
> me as the screaming of a parrot, her touch a thorn and her lips ashes. What
> is it to me if all the women of the world love me? Kindle a fire and burn
> them before me, for I care not. Let them perish all together, for I shall not
> know that they are gone. I love you and not another. Shall it profit a man
> to fill his mouth with dust, though it be the dust of gold mingled with pre-
> cious stones, when he desires water? Or shall he be warmed in winter by
> the reflection of a fire in a mirror? By Allah! I want neither the wealth of
> Hail, nor a wife with red hair. Let them take gold who do not ask for love.
> I want but one thing, and Zehowah alone can give it to me. Wallah! My
> heart burns. But I would give it to be burned for ever in hell if I might get
> your love now. This I ask. This only I desire. For this I will suffer and for
> this I am ready to die before my time." (5)

It has become clear that Khaled seeks Zehowah's love not merely to gain a
soul, but because he has genuinely fallen for her himself.

   The Witch of Prague (1891), written slightly before *Khaled* in the winter of
1889–90, is Crawford's most ambitious work of weird fiction; it is subtitled
"A Fantastic Tale." The plot is considerably convoluted, but its principal
fantastic element is the quest of Unorna, the witch of Prague, and her sardonic partner Keyork Arabian to extend the bounds of human life, perhaps indefinitely, through the power of hypnotism. The two have kept an
aged man under hypnosis for years in the hope that this process, plus the
replacement of his old blood with the blood of a younger man, will rejuve-
nate him. What makes the novel interesting is the ever-unresolved tension
as to whether Unorna's hypnotic powers are natural or supernatural. Crawford was writing just at the time when the science of psychology was making startling advances in charting the functions of the mind; in a footnote
Crawford even cites the leading psychologist prior to Freud, Baron Richard
von Krafft-Ebing (1840–1902). When a young victim, Israel Kafka, is put

under hypnosis for a month and made to transfer some of his blood into the aged man, there is speculation on the phenomenon:

> By a mere exercise of superior will this man, in the very prime of youth and strength, had been deprived of a month of life. Thirty days were gone, as in the flash of a second, and with them was gone also something less easily replaced, or at least more certainly missed. In Kafka's mind the passage of time was accounted for in a way which would have seemed supernatural twenty years ago, but which at the present day is understood in practice if not in theory. (12)

Unorna herself, however, has a different view of the matter:

> Unorna was superstitious, as Keyork Arabian had once told her. She did not thoroughly understand herself and she had very little real comprehension of the method by which she produced such remarkable results. She was gifted with a sensitive and active imagination, which supplied her with semi-mystic formulae of thought and speech in place of reasoned explanations, and she undoubtedly attributed much of her own power to supernatural influences. In this respect, at least, she was no farther advanced than the witches of older days . . . (13)

The mere fact that Unorna has come to be called the "witch of Prague" suggests the uneasiness with which her contemporaries regard her strange power of will. But like *Zoroaster* and *Khaled*, *The Witch of Prague* is not so much a weird tale as a love story. Much of the action again centres on a very complicated love triangle. A mysterious man designated only as the Wanderer is seeking his lost love Beatrice, who is being dragged across Europe by her father because he opposes her marriage to the Wanderer; the father dies, and the Wanderer spots Beatrice in a church in Prague, but loses her again. He approaches Unorna for help in finding Beatrice, but Unorna falls in love with the Wanderer herself. She hypnotises him and strives to make him forget Beatrice; apparently she succeeds, but is no closer to being loved herself by the Wanderer for all that.

The novel proceeds with many intense emotional episodes, until at last Unorna yields and unites the Wanderer with Beatrice. The fundamental metaphor behind the whole hypnotism issue is loss of identity or individuality. It is this phenomenon that links hypnotism to old-time effects of demonic possession (it is no surprise that Asenath Waite, in Lovecraft's "The Thing on the Doorstep," exhibits marked hypnotic abilities). When Unorna first hypnotises the Wanderer, he senses his personality ebbing away:

> He was confused, disturbed, and yet wholly unable to shut out her penetrating glance. His fast ebbing consciousness barely allowed him to wonder whether he was weakened by the strong emotions he had felt in the church, or by the first beginning of some unknown and unexpected malady. He was utterly weak and unstrung. He could neither rise from his

seat, nor lift his hand, nor close the lids of his eyes. It was as though an ir-
resistible force were drawing him into the depths of a fathomless whirl-
pool, down, down, by its endless giddy spirals, robbing him of a portion of
his consciousness at every gyration, so that he left behind him at every instant something of his individuality, something of the central faculty of
self-recognition. (2)

Keyork Arabian, on the other hand, is impervious to Unorna's powers because he is the prototypical individualist and egotist:

> "Autology is my study, autosophy my ambition, autonomy my pride. I
> am the great Panegoist, the would be Conservator of Self, the inspired
> prophet of the Universal I. I—I—I! My creed has but one word, and that
> word but one letter, that letter represents Unity, and Unity is strength. I am
> I, one, indivisible, central!" (3)

And yet, Unorna herself, when lost in love for the Wanderer, "seemed to
have no individuality left" (18). It is in passages like this that Crawford unites
the fantasy and love elements in this novel. Keyork Arabian is as invulner-
able to love as he is to hypnosis; in one remarkable scene toward the beginning he claims to profess his love for Unorna in heart-rending tones but
shatters the pretence with devilish cynicism. Indeed, as the novel progresses
Keyork develops into an increasingly evil figure, as his single-minded quest
to triumph over death becomes more and more ruthless and self-serving:

> And he had cause for satisfaction, as he knew well enough when he
> thought of the decided progress made in the great experiment. The cost at
> which that progress had been obtained was nothing. Had Israel Kafka per-
> ished altogether under the treatment he had received, Keyork Arabian
> would have bestowed no more attention upon the catastrophe than would
> have been barely necessary in order to conceal it and protect himself and
> Unorna from the consequences of the crime. In the duel with death, the life
> of one man was of small consequence, and Keyork would have sacrificed
> thousands to his purposes with equal indifference to their intrinsic value
> and with a proportionately greater interest in the result to be attained. (12)

As a weird tale the novel is, however, only of intermittent interest; for
in spite of the subtitle, it is clear that the romantic entanglement is at the
heart of the novel. The moments of horror are scattered: a prose-poetic
paean to death (7), the display of Keyork Arabian's studio, filled with
specimens from his previous attempts to conquer death (9); and, most
gripping of all, a hallucination by Israel Kafka induced by Unorna, wherein
he is made to experience the torture of Simon Abeles, a seventeenth-
century Jew punished by his father for converting to Christianity (15). This
allows Crawford to indulge not only in loathsome descriptions of physical
torment but some equally repulsive anti-Semitism. An earlier passage,
where Unorna stumbles into Keyork's gallery of specimens, is potent:

This time Unorna saw as well as heard. The groan came, and the wail followed it and rose to a shriek that deafened her. And she saw how the face of the Malayan woman changed; she saw it move in the bright lamplight, she saw the mouth open. Horrified, she looked away. Her eyes fell upon the squatting savages—their heads were all turned towards her, she was sure that she could see their shrunken chests heave as they took breath to utter that terrible cry again and again; even the fallen body of the African stirred on the floor, not five paces from her. Would their shrieking never stop? All of them—every one—even to the white skulls high up in the case; not one skeleton, not one dead body that did not mouth at her and scream and moan and scream again. (9)

Although this is later explained away as hallucination, it may be the most powerful passage in the book. Ultimately, however, *The Witch of Prague* is a disappointment for not delivering upon its fantastic premise: aside from its great length (it was first published, in good Victorian fashion, in three volumes), the hypnotism issue is unsatisfactorily and hastily resolved at the end, as the old man is suddenly resuscitated in health and vigour. Crawford is simply not a profound or subtle enough novelist to keep the reader's interest on the basis of the love element alone, and he would have done better to have written more concentratedly on the distinctively horrific theme of the novel.

But Crawford will hold a worthy niche in weird fiction merely for the seven stories in *Wandering Ghosts*. These stories were written over at least a twenty-year span, "The Upper Berth" dating to as early as 1885 and "The Screaming Skull" to around 1908; the impression is that Crawford wrote these tales whenever mood and opportunity arose. Perhaps he himself did not put much stock in them; it is significant that they were collected only posthumously. There is no especial progression or development of technique in these stories, and accordingly no virtue to studying them chronologically. A thematic approach will be more revealing and illuminating.

"The Dead Smile" (1899)[2] is one of the most grippingly horrifying tales ever written, although Crawford could not have thought that the supposed surprise ending—that Gabriel Ockram and Evelyn Warburton, engaged to be married, turn out to be brother and sister—was really much of a surprise. Crawford fills his story with references to "their strangely-like eyes" and "their faces, that were so strangely alike"; all this is a little too obvious, but fortunately the story's effectiveness, like much of Lovecraft, does not depend on the concealing of the plot's outcome. The very title signals the loathsome perversion of the good that is at the heart of the tale: just as a smile is ordinarily an indication of happiness, so is a "dead smile" not merely suggestive of the grinning of a skeleton but a symbol for the near-incest that is warded off at the story's conclusion. Its disfiguring effect on Evelyn is vividly etched at the beginning:

And as she looked into her uncle's eyes, and could not turn her own away, she knew that the deathly smile was hovering on her own red lips, drawing them tightly across her little teeth, while two bright tears ran down her cheeks to her mouth, and dropped from the upper to the lower lip while she smiled—and the smile was like the shadow of death and the seal of damnation upon her pure, young face.

The atmosphere of horrific gloom hovering over the entire narrative is almost oppressive; and when Gabriel descends into the family crypt ("There was a frightful stench of drying death") to discover the secret of Evelyn's birth, the culmination of horror is reached:

The dead face was blotched with dark stains, and the thin, grey hair was matted about the discoloured forehead. The sunken lids were half open and the candle light gleamed on something foul where the toad eyes had lived.

But yet the dead thing smiled, as it had smiled in life; the ghastly lips were parted and drawn wide and tight upon the wolfish teeth, cursing still, and still defying hell to do its worst—defying, cursing, and always and for ever smiling alone in the dark.

The extravagance of the tone and language throughout this tale is strangely effective; and although Crawford was more restrained in his other works, we miss the luridness of what might be called the "oh-my-God" school of horror embodied in this story.

"For the Blood Is the Life" (1905) was praised by Lovecraft, but is in reality a confused story of vampirism. It is one of several stories in which Crawford uses the framework of two individuals chatting idly over drinks, with one of them eventually supplying a casual narration of a ghost story; this device can be effective in allowing the horrific atmosphere to build gradually, but here it is the logic of the tale itself that is at fault. A young woman in Italy is killed by two robbers as she sees them burying their treasure on a mound, and they hurl her body into the pit along with their ill-gotten prize; but in some inexplicable fashion this woman becomes one of the undead, and repeatedly drains the blood of her still-living lover. How this transition occurred is never clarified. And yet, the tale contains one supremely powerful moment at the beginning where one of the interlocutors, puzzled at the ghostly appearance of the mound, goes up to investigate it:

Then he went on till he reached the mound and stood upon it. I could see the Thing still, but it was no longer lying down; it was on its knees now, winding its white arms around Holger's body and looking up into his face. A cool breeze stirred my hair at that moment, as the night wind began to come down from the hills, but it felt like a breath from another world.

The Thing seemed to be trying to climb to its feet, helping itself up by Holger's body while he stood upright, quite unconscious of it and apparently looking toward the tower, which is very picturesque when the moonlight falls upon it on that side.

"Come along!" I shouted. "Don't stay there all night!"

It seemed to me that he moved reluctantly as he stepped from the mound, or else with difficulty. That was it. The Thing's arms were still round his waist, but its feet could not leave the grave. As he came slowly forward it was drawn and lengthened like a wreath of mist, thin and white, till I saw distinctly that Holger shook himself, as a man does who feels a chill. At the same instant a little wail of pain came to me on the breeze—it might have been the cry of the small owl that lives among the rocks—and the misty presence floated swiftly back from Holger's advancing figure and lay once more at its length upon the mound.

Even here, however, there is confusion; for now this undead girl has been transformed from a vampire into an insubstantial wraith. Crawford evidently forgot in this story that even the supernatural must have a logical rationale.

It might not occur to us to rank Crawford among the great practitioners of the sea-horror tale—in the manner of William Hope Hodgson, Capt. Marryat, or even Oliver Onions, on the strength of his one story "Phantas"—but at least three of his short stories directly or indirectly involve the sea, and do so with great effectiveness. The least interesting, perhaps, is "The Screaming Skull" (1908), where an old sea-captain tells to a friend the story of a strange murder and its supernatural revenge. The tone of the work is surprisingly similar to Lovecraft's "Pickman's Model" (1926), but it appears that Lovecraft read the story after writing his own.[3] In any case, the offhand manner of the narration here results merely in flatness and a failure to realise the atmospheric potential of the situation. In an author's note at the end Crawford informs us that the core of the plot is based on an actual English legend; this is perhaps one more piece of evidence that the best weird tales are ordinarily based on ersatz, not real, myths.

"'Man Overboard!'" (1903), a novelette first published as a booklet, is one of Crawford's subtlest works. Here, in a story that displays nautical erudition rivalling anything in Hodgson, the actual supernatural manifestation—the ghost of one of a pair of twins, Jim and Jack Benton, who either fell overboard during a storm or was deliberately murdered by his brother—is not displayed until the very end: throughout the story we see the ghost only indirectly, and the cumulative power and suspense are overwhelming. We first learn that, although Jim Benton has been lost from the crew, the cook still finds the same number of plates used after every meal; then we see the dead man's brother holding two pipes in his hand, one of them waterlogged; then the cook appears to go mad and stabs at something near the surviving brother, Jack, shouting: "There were two of them! So help me God, there were two of them!" The tale gives the impression of winding down when the ship ends its journey with no further mishaps; but then we learn that the narrator has been asked by Jack Benton to attend his wedding. After the ceremony the narrator sees this:

> I looked after the couple in the distance a last time, meaning to go down to the road, so as not to overtake them; but when I had made a few steps I stopped and looked again, for I knew I had seen something queer, though I had only realised it afterwards. I looked again, and it was plain enough now; and I stood stock-still, staring at what I saw. Mamie was walking between two men. The second man was just the same height as Jack, both being about a half a head taller than she; Jack on her left in his black tail-coat and round hat, and the other man on her right—well, he was a sailor-man in wet oil-skins. I could see the moonlight shining on the water that ran down him, and on the little puddle that had settled where the flap of his sou'wester was turned up behind; and one of his wet shiny arms was round Mamie's waist, just above Jack's.

The quiet narration of this tale renders this climactic moment the more effective, and "'Man Overboard!'" must rank as one of Crawford's great triumphs.

In spite of the merits of some of Crawford's other tales, there is little reason to contradict the standard affirmation that "The Upper Berth" (1886) is his best weird tale. Here again it is the narrative voice that is the secret to the tale's power. We are dealing with a hardy, gruff, no-nonsense figure named Brisbane, one who is not easily rattled:

> Brisbane was a man of five-and-thirty years of age, and remarkable for those gifts which chiefly attract the attention of men. He was a strong man. The external proportions of his figure presented nothing extraordinary to the common eye, though his size was above the average. He was a little over six feet in height, and moderately broad in the shoulder; he did not appear to be stout, but, on the other hand, he was certainly not thin; his small head was supported by a strong and sinewy neck; his broad, muscular hands appeared to possess a peculiar skill in breaking walnuts without the assistance of the ordinary cracker, and, seeing him in profile, one could not help remarking the extraordinary breadth of his sleeves, and the unusual thickness of his chest.

This description inspires confidence in the reliability of Brisbane's story; indeed, at the outset Brisbane displays acerbic wit in describing his cabin:

> Upon the uninviting mattresses were carefully folded together those blankets which a great modern humorist has aptly compared to cold buckwheat cakes. The question of towels was left entirely to the imagination. The glass decanters were filled with a transparent liquid faintly tinged with brown, but from which an odour less faint, but not more pleasing, ascended to the nostrils like a far-off, sea-sick reminiscence of oily machinery.

And yet, the paragraph ends on a suddenly ominous note: "Sad-coloured curtains half closed the upper berth. The hazy June daylight shed a faint illumination upon the desolate little scene. Ugh! how I hate that state-room!"

The gradual accumulation of horrific details—the porthole that refuses to stay closed; the air of musty dampness in the room; the fact that we never get a good look at the doomed occupant of the upper berth, who leaps to his death on the first night out—creates an intensely potent atmosphere, and prepares us for the actual confrontation with the loathsome:

> I remember that the sensation as I put my hands forward was as though I were plunging them into the air of a damp cellar, and from behind the curtains came a gust of wind that smelled horribly of stagnant sea-water. I laid hold of something that had the shape of a man's arm, but was smooth, and wet, and icy cold. But suddenly, as I pulled, the creature sprang violently forward against me, a clammy, oozy mass, as it seemed to me, heavy and wet, yet endowed with a sort of supernatural strength. I reeled across the state-room, and in an instant the door opened and the thing rushed out.

Even here, however, Brisbane immediately discounts the supernatural ("It was absurd, I thought. The Welsh rare-bit I had eaten had disagreed with me"), thereby setting the stage for another encounter with the cold, dead thing in the upper berth. The tale ends in Brisbane's usual clipped manner: "It was a very disagreeable experience, and I was very badly frightened, which is a thing I do not like. That is all. That is how I saw a ghost—if it was a ghost. It was dead, anyway."

The two remaining stories in *Wandering Ghosts*, "By the Waters of Paradise" and "The Doll's Ghost," are very different from the clutching horror of Crawford's other tales. Here Crawford skirts close to a major danger in weird fiction, something that Lovecraft (in reference to Algernon Blackwood) aptly termed "the flatness of benignant supernaturalism." The cheerful or wistfully happy ghost story always runs the risk of seeming blandly innocuous and unreasoningly optimistic; and although "By the Waters of Paradise" (1887), which may not even be supernatural, probably fails for this reason, "The Doll's Ghost" (date of first publication unknown) surmounts the difficulty and becomes a poignant little vignette. The former is nothing but a love story, in which a man sees in his garden a vision of a lovely young woman, finally tracks her down, marries her, and saves her from death by drowning, robbing the "Witch of the Water" of a new victim. It is all elegantly told, and the courtship of the couple is handled with genial wit, but we have heard too many such tales before. "The Doll's Ghost" portrays an aged doll-repairer who falls in love with a doll brought to his shop and lovingly repairs it; in return the doll helps him to

locate his lost daughter, ultimately found in a hospital after being attacked
by young boys. It is a charming work where, for once, the happy ending
does not seem forced or contrived.

John C. Moran has brought to our attention an eighth, uncollected tale
by Crawford, "The King's Messenger" (1907). This story, too, is a masterpiece of narrative subtlety. At an elaborate dinner party the narrator notices
one unoccupied seat, but is informed by the young woman, Miss Lorna, sitting next to him that the final guest shall shortly arrive. The guest is Death.
The whole story becomes a *double entendre*, as everything Lorna says about
the expected guest takes on another meaning under the bland conventionality of her words. Lorna will run away with the guest that night; the narrator
thinks it merely an elopement, but we begin to suspect something more sinister when she confesses her love for "the King's Messenger":

> "Oh, I don't pretend that I fell in love with him at first sight; I went
> through a phase of feeling afraid of him, as almost everyone else does. You
> see, when people first meet him they cannot possibly know how kind and
> gentle he can be, though he is so tremendously strong. I've heard him
> called cruel and ruthless and cold, but it's not true. Indeed it's not! He can
> be as gentle as a woman, and he's the truest friend in all the world."

In fact, the woman will commit suicide. The narrator later finds that he has
been dreaming (thereby accounting for the otherwise anomalous fact that
all the other guests save himself seem to know the missing man's identity),
but he receives a telegram shortly afterward telling of Lorna's death. "The
King's Messenger" is an unrecognised jewel of weird fiction.

In the history of the weird tale F. Marion Crawford occupies roughly the
same place as Robert W. Chambers. Both wrote tales of horror and the supernatural sporadically over their lifetimes, although Chambers did so principally at the beginning of his career and Crawford, if anything, toward the
end; both will be remembered primarily for their scattered weird work rather
than their voluminous mainstream work; and both exercised only a marginal
influence on later writers in the field. The supernatural was, for both writers,
a diversion or a recreation; and both were under the impression that their
lasting work would be their many novels of romance—an impression, to be
sure, apparently justified by the tremendous popular and (for Crawford) critical success they enjoyed during their lifetimes, but one which subsequent
readers and critics have not sustained. Let us not be unfair to Crawford: his
mainstream work is not nearly as ephemeral or insubstantial as Chambers',
and he will occupy a markedy more significant place in American literature
than Chambers ever will; but it is as unlikely that such of his works as *Paul
Patoff* (1887) or *Via Crucis* (1899) will ever be resurrected, even by industrious
doctoral candidates, as it is that Chambers' endless series of frivolous romances will ever again be held in much esteem. The small and restricted
domain of weird fiction is often kinder to its practitioners—even those, like

E. F. Benson, John Buchan, or Ralph Adams Cram, who do not make it their exclusive literary focus—than mainstream fiction tends to be; and in this domain the work of F. Marion Crawford will not go unappreciated.

Notes

1. References to all three of Crawford's novels here discussed will occur by chapter in the text. No special citation will be made of Crawford's short stories from *Wandering Ghosts* (titled *Uncanny Tales* for the British edition).

2. Dates in parentheses refer to date of first publication, not necessarily to date of composition. My suspicion, however, is that the tales were all written within a year of first publication.

3. Lovecraft first reports reading *Wandering Ghosts* (lent to him by Donald Wandrei) in a letter to James F. Morton dated 1 April 1927, when he made "an XIth hour codicil" about Crawford in *Supernatural Horror in Literature;* at this time "Pickman's Model" had already been written. See *Selected Letters II* (Sauk City, WI: Arkham House, 1968), pp. 122–23.

Edward Lucas White: Dream and Reality

Perhaps Edward Lucas White (1866–1934) would be irked if he knew that, amid the mass of his literary productions spanning more than three decades, virtually the only works that are remembered are his tales of supernatural horror, especially those contained in the scarce collection *Lukundoo and Other Stories* (1927). Such a fate has befallen many other writers—from F. Marion Crawford to Robert W. Chambers—renowned in their own day for work of a very different sort. It is perhaps a testament to the timeless quality of so much weird fiction that it can be relished by today's readers far longer than social or political novels whose interest fades so rapidly after the circumstances engendering them have lapsed from public attention. In White's case it must be doubly frustrating, in that his weird tales were in his day received so unenthusiastically that a number of them failed to find lodgment in magazines even after repeated submissions, whereas his historical novels—all ably written and several of them still compellingly readable—achieved near-bestseller status.

White was born on 11 May 1866, in Bergen, New Jersey. George T. Wetzel, for whose invaluable biographical research on White I am deeply indebted,[1] notes that shortly after his birth White's family moved to Brooklyn, where his father, Thomas Hurley White, was ruined in the "Black Friday" panic of 1869. The family was forced to separate, Edward going with his mother, Kate Butler (Lucas) White, to the town of Caxsackie, New York, while his father continued to work in the New York area. An attempt to run a farm in Ovid, New York, in the western part of the state, failed after a few years, and by 1874 Thomas had moved to Baltimore, where his side of the family now resided. The poverty that plagued the family through much of Edward's early years left a lasting impression on him.

For a variety of reasons Edward's mother was unwilling to reunite the family in Baltimore, and for five years she and her husband saw little of each other. Edward was educated largely by his parents, but in 1877 was sent to the Pen Lucy School in Baltimore. His formal schooling was somewhat sporadic, but he made up for it by poring over books at the Peabody Institute Library. It was there that he developed his lifelong fascination for ancient history, specifically the history of Rome.

In 1884 White entered Johns Hopkins University, where he impressed future president Woodrow Wilson (then an instructor in history) with his skills in a debating club. White had been plagued by migraine headaches since the age of ten, and throughout his life they caused serious disruptions in his life and work. However, the headaches that he experienced during his first year at Johns Hopkins were caused not by migraines but by overwork (another recurring problem for White), and a doctor advised him to take a long sea voyage. In June 1885 he did so, sailing on the freight vessel *Cordorus* to Rio de Janeiro. At that time he wrote the first version of his utopian novel, *Plus Ultra*, but on the return journey he found it unsatisfactory and threw it overboard.

White had been writing fiction and poetry since his teenage years, but upon his return to Baltimore he destroyed virtually every scrap of this work—which he estimated as consisting of more than 1200 items. Returning to Johns Hopkins in the fall of 1886, he received his B.A. in Romance Languages in 1888 and immediately began postgraduate studies, hoping to earn a Ph.D. But by June 1890 he was forced to withdraw, as his father no longer had the money to fund his education. It was a bitter blow to White, seemingly dashing his hopes to secure a teaching position in a university. By 1892, however, he was hired to teach freshman Latin at Dartmouth, but he taught poorly and his assignment was not renewed. He subsequently landed a teaching job at Friends High School in Baltimore, thereby beginning a lifelong career as a high school teacher that would make him a legend to generations of boys in the Baltimore area. In 1899 he was hired at the Boys Latin School, where he remained until 1915. In 1900, after a long courtship, he married Agnes Gerry, the sister of one of his school friends.

In the 1890s White resumed writing, and produced a great quantity of poetry. Among the products of this period were two striking poems, "The Ghoula" and "Azrael." The latter, written in 1897, was not published until White included it in his book *Matrimony* (1932). Addressed to his future bride, the poem's chief feature is its suggestion of White's recurrent nightmares. White had been a vivid dreamer since the age of five, and nearly all his weird tales are the product of dreams, in many cases being literal transcripts of them. "The Ghoula" was inspired by a chance remark in Rudyard Kipling's "Her Majesty's Servants," in *The Second Jungle Book* (1895), in which Hindu oxen are said to be instinctively afraid of the English because they know that the English will eat them. This set White to thinking of the reverse phenomenon: what if there were a creature that ate human beings? Hence "The Ghoula," a chilling poem about a female ghoul, and the clear predecessor to White's striking tale "Amina."

White published two stories in a small Baltimore magazine, *Dixie*, but the bulk of his short fiction was written in a remarkable span between 1905 and 1909. Among the first of them was "The House of the Nightmare," which White dated to 1905 when it appeared in *Lukundoo*. Unlike many of his stories, it sold readily, appearing in *Smith's Magazine* for September 1906. "The Flambeau Bracket," written in January 1906, had a less happy fate: it was rejected by 75 magazines over a 51-month period, finally landing in *Young's Magazine* (the date of publication is uncertain; it probably appeared in late 1910 or early 1911). The story is a remarkable testament to Edgar Allan Poe's influence on White. He had been a devotee of Poe since his early teenage years, and late in life he made the confession that "I have had to banish from my home every scrap of [Poe's] printed writings, else I should waste my time and fuddle myself and reread him when I should be doing other things" (quoted in Wetzel [I], p. 98). He also confessed that he destroyed nearly every scrap of his work that was influenced by Poe, but "The Flambeau Bracket" survived: although based upon a dream, White admits that the dream itself was largely triggered by "The Cask of Amontillado." It is White's solitary excursion into non-supernatural horror.

"Amina," written in 1906, appeared in the *Bellman* for 1 June 1907, but several other weird tales—"The Message on the Slate" (written 1906), "The Pig-skin Belt" (written 1907), "The Picture Puzzle" (written 1909), and "The Snout" (written 1909)—did not find periodical publication and appeared for the first time in *Lukundoo*. The title story of that collection— far and away White's finest weird tale—was also written in 1907, but was not published until it appeared in *Weird Tales* for November 1925—one of his few contributions to a pulp magazine. "The Song of the Sirens" appeared in severely truncated form as "The Man Who Had Seen Them" in *Sunset Magazine* (March 1909).

White published a number of other stories around this time, but they are not weird. One, "The Little Faded Flag" (*Atlantic Monthly*, May 1908), is a fine tale of the Civil War.[2] Another, a humorous story entitled "A Transparent Nuisance" (*New York Herald*, 17 June 1906), is marginally weird in being derived from Wells' *Invisible Man*. "The Buzzards" (*Bellman*, 25 July 1908) is a melding of romance and suspense. On the whole, however, White's uncollected stories are not of high quality.

Wetzel describes several unpublished stories found among White's effects. Two in particular seem of interest to devotees of the weird. The first is "Mandola," written as early as 1890, and Wetzel summarises the plot as follows:

> Mountjoy, the narrator, is studying prehistoric man and owns a plaster cast of an ancient skeleton found at Neanderthal, Germany. Later he has a nightmare in which he sees the Neanderthal relic as a living being, stalking in the woods. After waking he remarks, "In dreams the nightmare effect of terror is tenfold that which one feels awake. The agony of dread, the sickness and cold sweat, and the total inability to move is made up of a torture unpaintable." (Here, of course, White is clearly describing his own reactions to nightmares.) Over a period of time the terror of this nightmare affects Mountjoy's memory. One day he decides to see how badly his memory has been affected by trying to recall details from his dreams. He evokes the Neanderthal image, and sees it again as if in his nightmare—but now it strikes down with its club at a shawl near where he is sitting. Later he looks for his fiancée, Mandola, who earlier had wandered off for a walk in the wood. He finds her seated on a stone, dead from fright, at her feet her pet dog a pulp of blood and bones; and on the ground footprints bigger than any human's. His ability to visualize has actually conjured into existence the horror from his nightmare.

Wetzel describes the other story as follows:

> "The Serge Coat" is another story based on White's actual dreams. He described it as "of double location and thought-transference," but it would more accurately be termed a variation on the *doppelgänger* theme. Hume, the narrator, is walking in the autumnal countryside. Becoming overheated, he takes off his jacket and puts it under his arm along with a thin serge topcoat he is already carrying. Later in his walk he discovers that the serge coat is missing. The following spring he is tramping again over the same countryside, and by an accidental series of events enters a barn wherein he finds the lost coat. Several young women in the adjoining house chat with him as he passes. On arriving home, he tosses the coat in a drawer and lies down to nap. When he awakes, he believes he dreams of entering the barn and talking again to the women. And as he stirs, his landlady, who had been nursing him as he lay actually unconscious for ten days, notices the serge coat, which she is sure was not in the house at the onset of his illness. Hume keeps his puzzlement to himself. Not long after he encounters the young women, who say they met him not on the day he believes, but during the time of his unconsciousness. (Wetzel [III], pp. 236–37)

It is evident that White was frustrated by the lack of commercial success of his short fiction. Other aspects of his work met a similar fate. In 1908 he published his first book, a slim volume of poetry entitled *Narrative Lyrics*. Although it appeared under the imprint of the prestigious G. P. Putnam's Sons, it was (as commonly, both then and now) issued at White's own expense, and sold only 78 copies in two years. As a result, White decided to turn to the writing of novels, and here he enjoyed markedly better success.

El Supremo: A Romance of the Great Dictator of Paraguay, which White began as early as 1910, was published in 1916 by E. P. Dutton and was both a popular and a critical success. This historical novel, set in 1815, deals with Dr José Gaspar Rodriguez de Francia, the autocrat who ruled Paraguay from 1813 to 1840. Although more than 700 pages in length, it was reprinted at least ten times, the last in 1943. White followed this up with two superlative historical novels about his beloved Rome, *The Unwilling Vestal: A Tale of Rome under the Caesars* (1918) and *Andivius Hedulio: Adventures of a Roman Nobleman in the Days of the Empire* (1921), both published by Dutton. Both were well received by critics and readers; the former went through twelve printings by 1937, and the latter had been printed fourteen times by 1941. H. P. Lovecraft, also an ardent devotee of Rome, considered *Andivius Hedulio* the finest and most realistic novel about the Roman Empire he had ever read, far surpassing such popular works as Henryk Sienkiewicz's *Quo Vadis* (1896) and William Stearns Davis' *A Friend of Caesar* (1900). White, however, was not able to sustain his popularity. *Helen* (1925) was a lacklustre novel about Helen of Troy, and the nonfiction work *Why Rome Fell* (1927)—which, in a reprise of Gibbon's *Decline and Fall of the Roman Empire*, blamed the fall of Rome on the spread of Christianity—received very mixed reviews, some praising the work but others condemning it for superficiality and factual errors. White's final book, *Matrimony* (1932), is a touching account of his marriage with Agnes, who had died on 30 March 1927.

White's two collections of tales, *The Song of the Sirens* (1919) and *Lukundoo*, were also accorded a mixed reception, and neither sold well. Aside from the title story and "The Flambeau Bracket," *The Song of the Sirens* is largely devoted to tales of ancient Rome. In his afterword to the book White takes pride in maintaining that these stories are "veracious glimpses of the past, without any marring anachronisms," but as stories they are often weighed down with excessive historical baggage. Another story in this volume, "Disvola," is a vivid tale of the Italian Renaissance, based on a dream. As noted, most of the stories in *Lukundoo* date to 1905–09, but he did manage to write the tale "Sorcery Island" in 1922, although it too remained unpublished until its inclusion in the collection. This story is perhaps dimly related to the unpublished "Diminution Island," a work dating to as early as 1896.

For much of his adult life, however, White was at work on a variety of rewrites of his destroyed utopian novel, *Plus Ultra*. He had begun rethinking the work from as early as 1901, and in 1918–19 he produced a short novel, *From Behind the Stars*, but it remained unpublished. Then, beginning in 1928, a year after his wife's death, White devoted the next five years to *Plus Ultra*, incorporating *From Behind the Stars* as the opening "book" of the work. The result is an immense, 500,000-word novel with many science-fictional elements that might well be of interest to present-day readers; but the novel's length caused it to be rejected by several publishers, and it remains unpublished among White's effects.[3]

It is perhaps fortunate that White—who in later years sported a long white beard and came to look rather strikingly like Bernard Shaw—did not attempt to be a full-time writer, for he would have suffered even greater poverty than he experienced as an impecunious schoolteacher, especially prior to his novel-writing period. Wetzel's biography is full of charming recollections by White's students, and he clearly came to love the instruction of young scholars into the mysteries of the ancient languages. From as early as 1911 he had begun teaching at the University School for Boys in Baltimore, and he started working there full-time in 1915, remaining until his retirement in 1930. Edward Lucas White died on 30 March 1934— seven years to the day after his beloved wife.

It is difficult to convey in small compass the distinctive qualities of White's weird tales. Aside from their inspiration from dreams, their most salient feature is perhaps the sheer bizarrerie of their weird manifestations. Rarely do we find the conventional ghost in White's work; instead, we come upon the female ghoul in "Amina," the hideous growth that plagues the protagonist in "Lukundoo," the monster that is Hengist Eversleigh in "The Snout," and so many others. Even when a ghost is present—as perhaps is the case in "The Message on the Slate"—it exhibits itself in a piquant and novel way.

White admitted that he had renounced all religious belief as early as the age of fourteen, and this very lack of belief may have contributed to the effectiveness of his tales. As H. P. Lovecraft noted in *Supernatural Horror in Literature:*

> It may be well to remark here that occult believers are probably less effective than materialists in delineating the spectral and the fantastic, since to them the phantom world is so commonplace a reality that they tend to refer to it with less awe, remoteness, and impressiveness than do those who see in it an absolute and stupendous violation of the natural order. (Lovecraft 58)

It is this sentiment that lends a poignancy to the charlatan clairvoyant's confession, in "The Message on the Slate," that the supernatural phenomenon he has just experienced "has demolished the entire structure of my spiritual existence."

There is perhaps a reason to complain that White's development of his narrative is at times a bit slow and drawn-out. Indeed, it would appear that several of his lengthier tales were rejected largely on the grounds of length; as noted, "The Song of the Sirens" was first published only in a heavily abridged form. But in most instances, White's leisurely narration is designed to build up an insidious atmosphere of horror by the slow accretion of bizarre details, and in the end we find that few of his tales are open to the charge of prolixity. He had learned well from his early idol Poe, and adhered fully to Poe's conceptions of the "unity of effect."

White was able to mingle his love of classical antiquity and his love of the weird only in "The Song of the Sirens"; but his tales feature other interesting bits of autobiography. The ship *Medorus* that is the setting for "The Song of the Sirens" is a clear reflection of the *Cordorus*, on which he sailed in 1885. "Sorcery Island"—a weird and ambiguously supernatural tale that uncannily foreshadows the "Prisoner" television series—may also owe something to White's travels. "The House of the Nightmare" evokes the rural setting of his early years in New York state.

White's most famous story, "Lukundoo," is worth considering in some detail. He makes the interesting comment that, although the story was based on a dream, he would never have had that dream if he had not read H. G. Wells' "Pollock and the Porroh Man," included in *The Plattner Story and Others* (1897). In this story Wells (who, like Kipling, was an occasional correspondent of White's) depicts the fate of an Englishman, Pollock, who, while on an expedition in West Africa, has a violent encounter with a "Porroh man" (witch doctor), wounding him in the hand with a pistol shot. Subsequently

Pollock is harassed by a variety of minor but ever intensifying annoyances— incursions of snakes, darts and arrows that narrowly miss him, an aching in his muscles, and the like. Feeling that the Porroh man is responsible, Pollock hires another African to kill him. The latter does so with alacrity, bringing the Porroh man's decapitated skull back to Pollock. But a Portuguese associate tells Pollock that he has made a grave mistake: the only way to end the "curse" is for Pollock to have killed the Porroh man himself. Pollock is now haunted by the skull, as it keeps returning to him even though he has successively buried it, tossed it into the river, and burned it. Returning to England, Pollock seems to see the skull, dripping with blood, everywhere; as his desperation and fear grow, he finally kills himself.

A supernatural explanation is not required to account for the events in "Pollock and the Porroh Man"; indeed, at the end Wells suggests that the entire scenario is largely a series of hallucinations brought on by Pollock's fear of the Porroh man's supposed powers. In "Lukundoo" White has duplicated only the barest outline of the plot of Wells' tale: the curse inflicted upon a white man by an African sorcerer. "Lukundoo" is, however, manifestly supernatural, and is still more terrifying in that the curse actually invades the explorer Ralph Stone's body. And yet, both tales are fundamentally tales of revenge, and in both tales we find the victims overcome by remorse at their mistreatment of African natives and inexorably losing their very will to live.

It is regrettable that White never wrote a full-length weird novel, for the crisp character development he displays in his historical novels could have been fused with his powerful weird conceptions to produce a stellar work in this field. Perhaps he was too wedded to Poe's restriction of weirdness to the short story (with the notable exception of *Arthur Gordon Pym*); perhaps, too, the tradition of the weird novel was not sufficiently established in his day to render it commercially feasible for White. Whatever the case, Edward Lucas White has left us a small but potent body of weird short fiction that has waited too long to find a new generation of appreciative readers.

Notes

1. Wetzel's account (see Bibliography) proceeds only up to 1909, cut short by his own death in 1983.

2. It is now reprinted in my anthology, *Civil War Memories* (Nashville, TN: Rutledge Hill Press, 2000).

3. For a synopsis and analysis see A. Langley Searles, "'Plus Ultra': An Unknown Science-Fiction Utopia," *Fantasy Commentator* 4, No. 2 (Winter 1979–80): 51–59; 4, No. 3 (Winter 1981): 162–69, 176–77; 4, No. 4 (Winter 1982): 240–42; 5, No. 1 (Winter 1983): 44–49; 5, No. 2 (Winter 1984): 100–105.

II. Some Englishmen of the Golden Age

Sir Arthur Quiller-Couch: Ghosts and Scholars

The weird tales of Sir Arthur Quiller-Couch (1863–1944) are distinguished by their variety of tone and motif, their elegance of diction, their vivid evocation both of the English landscape—especially of the Cornwall that was their author's native region— and of a variety of historical epochs, and perhaps most impressively of all, their quiet professionalism. As we read these stories we are fully aware that they are the product of a noted short story writer, novelist, critic, and scholar—in short, an author thoroughly the master of his trade.

Quiller-Couch was born in Bodmin, in Cornwall, on 21 October 1863, the eldest child of a doctor, Thomas Quiller Couch, and Mary Ford. (He would begin hyphenating his name only in 1889.) Both the Quillers and the Couches—the two sides of his father's family—had long resided in Cornwall, and the Couches made their living chiefly from the sea, either by seafaring or fishing. Quiller-Couch attended a boy's school in Devon, Newton Abbot College, between the ages of ten and seventeen, then went to Clifton College in Bristol. In October 1882 he entered Trinity College, Oxford, where he studied classics. In late 1884 he was almost forced to leave school with the death of his father, but his maternal grandfather came to his rescue by supplying funds. But by the summer of 1886 this grandfather told Quiller-Couch that he could no longer afford to send money for his schooling, and that Quiller-Couch would have to support his mother, two brothers, and two sisters. He immediately left college and decided to become a full-time writer.

The decision was not surprising. As early as his days at Clifton he had written a prize poem, and at Oxford he had written much verse for the *Oxford Magazine*, where he began using the quasi-pseudonym "Q." But Quiller-Couch knew that one could not make a living writing poetry, so he turned to fiction. He quickly produced his first novel, *Dead Man's Rock;* it was published in the summer of 1887. Its relative success convinced Quiller-Couch that he could indeed succeed at writing, and he departed for London.

Quiller-Couch established a connexion with the publishing firm of Cassell's, both as a writer and as an editor. His second novel, *The Splendid Spur* (1889), set the tone for much of his fictional work: it is a plainly but vigorously told adventure novel, with briskly paced action and crisp dialogue. Quiller-Couch also did much writing for a Liberal paper, the *Speaker,* for a ten-year period beginning in 1889; many of his earlier stories appeared here. In fact, he was doing so much work that his health broke down in the winter of 1891–92. Feeling the need for rest, he initially rented quarters at the small town of Fowey (pronounced "Foy") in Cornwall; shortly thereafter he purchased a moss-covered stone house, commanding a magnificent

view of the harbour and open sea, called The Haven. He and his wife
Louise Amelia Hicks (whom he had married in 1889) would remain there
for the rest of their lives.

While continuing to write fiction, Quiller-Couch also gained a reputation
as a literary critic. His frequent train-rides from Cornwall to London were
occupied in reading prodigious amounts of Greek, Latin, and English literature, and the result was his first critical volume, *Adventures in Criticism* (1896).
In 1898 he was given the distinction of completing Robert Louis Stevenson's
unfinished novel, *St Ives*. (More than half a century later, Daphne du Maurier
would perform the same service for him by completing his last, unfinished
novel, *Castle D'Or* [1961].) He was also chosen to edit *The Oxford Book of English Verse* (1900), an enormously influential volume that achieved nearly canonical status in the first several decades of the new century.

Quiller-Couch's most prolific period spanned the years 1901 to 1912,
when he wrote twenty works of fiction (including thirteen novels), as well
as anthologies, essays, poetry, and other work. As a result of his labours, he
was knighted in 1910. He received an additional honour in 1912 by being
appointed the first King Edward VII Professor of English Literature at
Cambridge. The man whose financial difficulties had forced him to leave
the university without a degree was now firmly ensconced as a distinguished British academician.

Quiller-Couch continued to shuttle back and forth between Cornwall
and Cambridge on the train. He became a much renowned and popular
professor, and with the outbreak of World War I he continued his teaching, even though his son Bevil Bryan (born in 1890) was called to the front.
Quiller-Couch did his part in the war effort, however, by raising and
equipping a battalion of the Duke of Cornwall's Light Infantry. But writing
and teaching were his forte: the highly regarded volumes *Shakespeare's
Workmanship* (1918) and *The Art of Reading* (1920)—based upon lectures
given during the war—were among his literary productions of the period.

In early 1919 Quiller-Couch was crushed when he heard that his son
Bevil had died of pneumonia in Germany, but he carried on his literary labours. By now he had virtually ceased the writing of fiction, and he turned
his attention more and more to criticism and editorial work. In the 1920s
the publisher J. M. Dent chose him to edit The King's Treasuries of Literature, a 250-volume series of English texts for use in schools. In 1921 he
teamed up with J. Dover Wilson to produce a landmark edition of Shakespeare (the New Cambridge Edition), although after 1931 Wilson carried
on with the editing alone. Rather surprisingly for an author whose fiction
was so characteristic of the late Victorian and Edwardian age, J. M. Dent
decided in 1928–29 to issue a thirty-volume edition of Quiller-Couch's fiction, the Duchy Edition, for which he slightly revised all his novels and
tales and wrote introductions defending his "plain" adventure and historical novels. Regrettably, he offered no defence or rationale for the super-

natural fiction that is sprinkled throughout his work. Quiller-Couch's last volume of criticism was *The Poet as Citizen and Other Papers* (1934). In 1939 he revised his *Oxford Book of English Verse*, including work up to 1918. He continued to teach at Cambridge during World War II, but was slowed by injuries and illness. He spent the summer of 1940 at Fowey, narrowly escaping being killed in an air raid. A few months after he celebrated his eightieth birthday, at Fowey, he was injured by a fall and never fully recovered. Sir Arthur Quiller-Couch died on 12 May 1944.

Perhaps the reason Quiller-Couch's weird tales have never before been gathered into a single volume is that they are scattered among no fewer than ten of his short-story collections, from his first, *Noughts and Crosses* (1891) to one of his last, *News from the Duchy* (1913). *Wandering Heath* (1895) and *Old Fires and Profitable Ghosts* (1900) perhaps contain the greatest proportion of weird work, but even these volumes are filled with stories of other types, ranging from historical tales to tales of adventure, mystery, and romance. It is clear that, although Quiller-Couch frequently broached the supernatural in his work, he did not consider it a separate and distinct "genre" segregated from other modes of literature.

In reading his stories we are struck by the fact that Quiller-Couch has utilised a great many of the tropes and elements known to weird fiction: the standard ghost of course appears frequently, but so does the witch ("The Lady of the Ship" [OF]), reincarnation ("A Blue Pantomime" [IS]), metempsychosis ("Psyche" [NC], "The Mystery of Joseph Laquedem" [OF]), the "familiar" or "brownie" ("The Laird's Luck" [LL]), and personality exchange ("Mutual Exchange, Limited" [CS]). This last story is of particular interest, in that it points to a recurring motif in Quiller-Couch's work. The anomalous melding of two personalities is also the subject of a story in *Old Fires and Profitable Ghosts*, "The Room of Mirrors": this account of two men who hate each other precisely because they are so much alike in temperament is a gripping suspense tale with only the faintest hint of the supernatural (one man, who has just seen his nemesis kill himself, seems to see his own face on the corpse). However, this topos becomes frankly supernatural not only in "Mutual Exchange, Limited" but in Quiller-Couch's last completed novel, *Foe-Farrell* (1918), where two implacable enemies do in fact exchange personalities.

Quiller-Couch is also a master of tonal variation. Such a tale of brooding horror as "Old Æson" [NC]—inspired by the birth of his son Bevil—can be placed next to the grotesquerie of "Widdershins" [WH], the macabre humour of "My Grandfather, Hendry Watty" [WH], the self-parodic humour of "John and the Ghosts" [WW], and the delicate wistfulness of "The Talking Ships" [WW]. Understandably, Quiller-Couch frequently melded the supernatural into the other modes of fiction in which he habitually worked—the adventure story in "The Haunted Dragoon" [IS],

"The Seventh Man" [OF], and "The Haunted Yacht" [WW], the historical tale in "The Horror on the Stair" [TS] and "The Lady of the Ship," and the military narrative in what is perhaps his most famous and perhaps finest weird tale, "The Roll-Call of the Reef" [WH].

Throughout all his fiction Quiller-Couch eschewed the idea of a "message." His tales and novels were meant to provide entertainment, nothing more. As a result, his weird tales rarely have any overarching philosophy; but now and again some deeper concerns appear. "Oceanus" [OF] is, plainly, a religious allegory, attempting to answer the question that has perplexed countless generations of Christians: Why is there death and suffering in the world, if God is both omnipotent and benevolent? Whether the answer Quiller-Couch provides here is acceptable to all readers is beside the point; what is relevant is the author's intent to probe the question, and to do so by means of the supernatural. Such a story as "The Magic Shadow" [NC]—in which a boy's shadow, in the shape of a girl, is in the end seen to be a metaphor for the poet, with his androgynous soul—seems to me distinctly in advance of its time. Tales of this kind may represent a minority in Quiller-Couch's output, but their mere existence demonstrates that the author saw weird fiction as a viable vehicle for metaphorically treating profound questions of morality and existence.

It is high time that the weird work of Sir Arthur Quiller-Couch be brought to the attention of devotees of supernatural fiction. As the substantial contributions of a distinguished author and critic, these tales retain more than historic interest. Few of them, perhaps, can be classed in the very first rank of weird fiction, but cumulatively they are an impressive achievement. Their influence upon subsequent work is now difficult to gauge, but it is unquestionable that they added their bit to make the period between 1880 and 1940 the Golden Age of the weird tale.

Rudyard Kipling: The Horror of India

Well over a century has passed since Rudyard Kipling (1865–1936) published his earliest books, and he has now comfortably taken his place among the standard English classics. It is, accordingly, somewhat difficult for us to grasp what a revolution he effected in both fiction and poetry. For decades following the widespread dissemination of his work in the 1880s, a furious controversy raged among the guardians of English literature as to whether Kipling really belonged in the "canon." He began publishing just at the time when a disjunction was occurring between what ordinary readers enjoyed and what was deemed "genuine" literature by critics and academicians; and the 1890s in particular was a period when such rarefied figures as Oscar Wilde, Walter Pater, and the Pre-Raphaelites (several of whom, ironically, were close friends of Kipling) were producing work specifically designed for a select coterie of aesthetes rather than for the public at large.

Kipling's plain-spoken, readily comprehensible prose and verse cut through both the stilted ponderosity of the older Victorians (Edward Bulwer-Lytton, George Eliot, Charles Reade) and the arch sophistication of the aesthetes. It was a breath of fresh air in English literature; but his critics were not slow to attack him for the very qualities his devotees considered his strengths. Oscar Wilde in 1890 tartly remarked: "From the point of view of literature Mr. Kipling is a man of talent who drops his aspirates"— a suggestion that Kipling was a kind of literary Cockney invading a domain reserved for his literary and cultural superiors. But Kipling would have none of it, and his own legion of literary disciples made sure that he and his work would carry the day.

Kipling was, although perhaps without consciously intending to do so, combating the widespread "feminization" of literature that had occurred during the Victorian era, when women gradually became both the chief producers and chief consumers of literary work. This was the heyday of such now-forgotten popular writers as Dinah Maria Craik ("Mrs. Mulock"), Marie Corelli, Charlotte Mary Yonge, Mary Louisa Molesworth, and other caterers to sentiment and sentimentality. Kipling's work, rough-hewn and masculine, was clearly intended for a male readership—and specifically the readership of those solitary, hard-working Englishmen who served in the administration of India and other far-flung colonies. Preeminently, Rudyard Kipling was their bard, and as such he also brought the harsh realities of these colonies back home to readers in England.

Kipling's literary revolution even has some bearing upon the weird tales he wrote over much of his career. In contrast to the assertion of Swiss scholar Peter Penzoldt, who in *The Supernatural in Fiction* (1952) asserted that the use of slang and dialect in many of Kipling's ghost stories ruined their effect, it could be said that they actually enhance it: the verisimilitude engendered both by Kipling's first-hand knowledge of the scenes and characters of which he writes and by his rugged, no-frills prose creates a harrowing sense of the palpable *reality* of his supernatural phenomena— especially since, in many cases, the reader is left uncertain whether anything supernatural has even occurred.

Kipling's entire literary output is more intimately connected with his life than that of many other writers; in a real sense, every single work is a fragment of autobiography. Born in Bombay on 30 December 1865, the young Rudyard (named after Lake Rudyard in Stafford, where his father, John Lockwood Kipling, and his mother, Alice Macdonald, first met) grew up as a fringe member of the British ruling class of India. His father had come to the province as a professor of architectural sculpture at a new art college in Bombay, and Kipling grew up in a bungalow on the college grounds. Kipling's first taste of England occurred as early as the age of two and a half, when his parents returned home so that his sister Alice could be born there. By the summer of 1868 the family had gone back to India.

In 1871 Rudyard and Alice were sent to England to commence their education, living with a retired naval officer and his wife at Southsea. The next six years were difficult ones: not only did Rudyard feel the pangs of separation from his beloved parents, but the family with whom he was staying mistreated him. Kipling's only reprieve occurred each December, when he stayed with his Aunt Georgie, the wife of celebrated Pre-Raphaelite painter Edward Burne-Jones. In 1877 his mother rescued him from this purgatory, and the next year he enrolled in the United Services College, a public school set up by army officers who wanted cheap education for their sons. Here Rudyard had a much better time (the pranks in which he and his friends engaged are delightfully recounted in the novel *Stalky & Co.* [1899]), although in the end Kipling did not take the civil service examination. Instead, he returned to India in September 1882.

Rudyard had already shown literary talent by editing the *United Services College Chronicle*. In addition, Kipling's mother had—without his knowledge or permission—paid for the publication of his first "book," *Schoolboy Lyrics* (1881). The Kipling family was now settled in Lahore, in the then Indian province of the Punjab (now a part of Pakistan), and Rudyard became an assistant editor of the *Civil and Military Gazette*. He plunged into this work, gaining a love for the mechanical aspects of printing that would never leave him. The work was onerous, especially as the editor-in-chief of the small staff would frequently absent himself for long periods. By 1884 Kipling was already writing short sketches for the paper; one of the earliest, "The Dream of Duncan Parenness" [LH], is his first tale of the supernatural. This story of a *doppelgänger* could be read as a kind of anticipation of Oscar

Wilde's *The Picture of Dorian Gray* (1890) in its suggestion of a "double" whose features reveal both the years and the sins of the protagonist. Another effective story, though not strictly a weird tale, is the brooding prose poem "'The City of Dreadful Night'" (1885; LH). The title derives from the pessimistic poem of that name by the Victorian poet James Thomson ("B. V.")—a poem that, as Kipling admits in his autobiography, *Something of Myself* (1937), "shook me to my unformed core" when he read it as a teenager. Kipling's haunting account of the thousands of men and women who sleep in the streets of Lahore because of the oppressive heat conveys much of the exoticism he found in the land of his birth. He knew India better than he knew England, and yet he was not himself an Indian: the barrier between Caucasian and "colored," between ruler and ruled, was unbridgeable.

In the winter of 1885 the Kiplings produced a family magazine, *Quartette*, published by the *Civil and Military Gazette*. It contained several more of Kipling's weird tales, including "The Phantom 'Rickshaw" [PR] and "The Strange Ride of Morrowbie Jukes" [PR]. The publication in 1886 of the poetry volume *Departmental Ditties*, and in 1888 of two notable story collections, *Plain Tales from the Hills* (the title derives from the hills around Simla, where the British government would spend the summers to escape the heat) and *The Phantom 'Rickshaw and Other Tales*, sealed Kipling's reputation. Although issued first in India, these volumes were later published in England to great acclaim. By his early twenties, Rudyard Kipling was an established author.

The original preface to *The Phantom 'Rickshaw*—not reprinted in later editions—supplies what few hints we have regarding Kipling's intentions or purposes in writing weird tales:

> This is not exactly a book of downright ghost stories, as the cover makes belief. It is rather a collection of facts that never quite explained themselves. All that the collector is certain of is, that one man insisted upon dying because he believed himself to be haunted ["The Phantom 'Rickshaw"]; another man either made up a wonderful lie, or visited a very strange place ["The Strange Ride of Morrowbie Jukes"]; while the third man was indubitably crucified by some person or persons unknown, and gave an extraordinary account of himself ["The Man Who Would Be King"].
>
> The peculiarity of ghost-stories is that they are very seldom told first-hand. I have managed, with infinite trouble, to secure one exception to this rule ["My Own True Ghost Story"]. The other three stories you must take on trust; as I did.

Brief and reserved as this is, it perhaps tells us more than is evident at first glance. The comment on "The Phantom 'Rickshaw" plainly suggests that a supernatural interpretation is not necessitated by the "facts" of the story. This chilling tale of a man apparently haunted by the ghost of a woman whom he jilted can be accounted for on strictly naturalistic grounds, as hallucinations engendered by the man's consuming guilt. (One wonders, too, whether the scenario is meant in some way to echo an unrequited love affair on Kipling's own part: he had fallen in love with an English girl, Flo Gerrard, just prior to returning to India in 1882, but was prevented by her family from marrying her.) The horror in this tale rests in the fact that the ghost, far from being vengeful, seeks only to ingratiate herself back into her loved one's favor. In this sense it strikingly anticipates Robert Hichens' classic tale, "How Love Came to Professor Guildea" (1900).

"The Strange Ride of Morrowbie Jukes" is similarly a non-supernatural suspense tale; here there is not even a pretense at the supernatural. "My Own True Ghost Story" might be termed pseudo-supernatural, in that the supernatural is suggested throughout but in the end is explained away naturalistically. Are we to believe that the incident actually happened to Kipling? There is no reason to doubt it, and his preface to *The Phantom 'Rickshaw* explicitly asserts that it did.

The fact that the adventure story "The Man Who Would Be King" was included in *The Phantom 'Rickshaw* at all is of significance in a different way. It shows that Kipling himself did not conceive the "ghost story" or weird tale to be a separate genre of literature that must be segregated from mainstream work. Indeed, such a distinction of genre did not occur until well into the twentieth century, perhaps beginning only with the establishment of the pulp magazines in the 1920s. The weird was a mode that any author could utilise to convey a theme or message that could not be conveyed otherwise, and no stigma was attached to the procedure.

In the end, the most prominent feature in Kipling's earlier weird tales is neither character nor language, but place—specifically, India. The fact that the first nine of his horror stories were written when Kipling was in India, and that thirteen of the first fourteen are set either there or in neighboring Afghanistan, points to the consuming fascination that this exotic realm exercised upon Kipling's imagination. In *Something of Myself* he provides hints of how India drew out his penchant for the strange:

> The dead of all times were about us—in the vast forgotten Muslim cemeteries round the Station, where one's horse's hoof of a morning might break through to the corpse below; skulls and bones tumbled out of our mud garden walls, and were turned up among the flowers by the Rains; and at every point were tombs of the dead. Our chief picnic rendezvous and some of our public offices had been memorials to desired dead women; and Fort Lahore, where Runjit Singh's wives lay, was a mausoleum of ghosts.

The prevalence of heat, of death, of disease (chiefly cholera, typhoid, and dysentery), and of the ancient, brooding, mystical civilisation of India—these things are perhaps all we need to account for Kipling's tendency toward the weird. His first-hand knowledge of India is evident on every page of his tales, whose realism is also enhanced by the liberal use of numerous

Indian words that had so thoroughly entered the English vocabulary at this time that Kipling did not bother to define them. At the same time, the loneliness and homesickness that he must have felt, and which were certainly felt by many of the English civil servants in India—poignantly conveyed in "At the End of the Passage" (1890; MP)—are constantly in evidence.

Kipling spent the years 1887–89 in Allahabad, working for the *Pioneer* and its magazine supplement, the *Week's News*. He was particularly prolific in short-story writing in the years 1887 and 1888. In 1889 he spent much of the year traveling across the world, visiting not only the United States (where his vituperative letters on America were not received with favour) but also Japan. Coming to London in 1890, he was lionised as a literary titan, although his pleasure was marred by the rampant pirating of his work by American publishers, whose depredations were entirely legal in the absence of international copyright. It was during this period that Kipling wrote his poignant tale "'The Finest Story in the World'" [MI], inspired in part by a friend, "Ambo" Poynter, a would-be writer who occupied much of Kipling's time telling of stories he would like to write.

In 1891 two substantial story collections, containing several weird items, appeared: *Mine Own People* and *Life's Handicap*. The former contained one of Kipling's grisliest ghost stories, "The Recrudescence of Imray" (whose original title I prefer to the bland later title, "The Return of Imray"), while the latter features what is without question Kipling's most accomplished horror tale, "The Mark of the Beast." Although the "moral" of the story—an Indian magician seeks revenge upon a hapless Englishman who had wronged him—is elementary, many of the details are uncommonly fine. The gradual transformation of the man into a beast is signaled at one point by his grovelling in the dirt and his blunt assertion, "The smell of the earth is delightful"; and upon his complete transformation he is suddenly referred to by the narrator as "it" rather than "he."

Kipling came back to India briefly in late 1891, but left shortly thereafter, nevermore to return. By this time he had met Caroline Balestier, an American woman whom he married on 18 January 1892. They settled in Brattleboro, Vermont, where Kipling wrote his two *Jungle Books* (1894, 1895) as well as *Captains Courageous* (1897). A variety of personal difficulties compelled the couple to leave in 1896 for England, where they settled briefly in a house near Torquay. It was the unwholesome atmosphere of this house that, years later, inspired "The House Surgeon" (1909; AR). Kipling writes of the matter in *Something of Myself*:

> . . . a growing depression . . . enveloped us both—a gathering blackness of mind and sorrow of the heart, that each put down to the new, soft climate and, without telling the other, fought against for long weeks. It was the Feng-shui—the Spirit of the house itself—that darkened the sunshine and fell upon us every time we entered, checking the very words on our lips.

A talk about a doubtful cistern brought another mutual confession. "But I thought *you* liked the place?" "But I made sure *you* did," was the burden of our litanies. Using the cistern for a stalking-horse, we paid forfeit and fled. More than thirty years later on a motor-trip we ventured down the steep little road to that house, and met, almost unchanged, the gardener and his wife in the large, open, sunny stable-yard, and, quite unchanged, the same brooding Spirit of deep, deep Despondency within the open, lit rooms.

The Kiplings resettled in the town of Rottingdean, near Brighton.

Kipling continued to be productive. He became interested in South African affairs, spending every year from January to March there in the years 1900 to 1908. In February 1899 his poem "The White Man's Burden" spanned the globe in a few days, capping his reputation as "the poet laureate of the people" but later engendering accusations that Kipling was an imperialist and a racist. The former charge cannot perhaps be denied, but the matter of Kipling's attitudes toward other races is too complex to be dealt with in small compass. Mercifully, the issue rarely enters his weird work.

In 1902, the year *Just So Stories* was published, the Kiplings settled in their final home—"Bateman's," in Etchingham, Sussex. The bittersweet ghost story "'They'" (1904; TD) was largely inspired by their drives around the English countryside—in a primitive vehicle called a "Locomobile"—while searching for a house. In 1907 Kipling was awarded the Nobel Prize for literature.

The outbreak of World War I saw Kipling write several stories about the war, including his final weird tale, "'Swept and Garnished'" (1915; DC). This moving tale of the ghosts of children killed in the war manages to extend at least a modicum of sympathy toward the lonely German woman at the centre of the narrative, although Kipling's loyalties clearly lay with the Allies. The war became an even grimmer reality to him when his seventeen-year-old son, John, having enlisted shortly after England's entry into the war, was declared "wounded and missing" in September 1915. Two long years passed before the Kiplings finally learned that he had been killed; his body was never recovered.

Kipling's final years were plagued with a variety of illnesses. In early 1936 he suffered a hemorrhage while staying with friends at Hampstead. Kipling died on 18 January 1936, a few days before the death of his good friend, King George V. He was buried in Westminster Abbey.

Rudyard Kipling's horror stories are a small but distinctive facet of his diverse work. He wrote several works of pure fantasy (preeminently the *Jungle Books* and *Just So Stories*, but also *Puck of Pook's Hill* [1906]) and even a few tales that might be considered early excursions into science fiction ("Wireless," "With the Night Mail"); but his horror tales—many of them evocative of the India and England he knew so well—represent a form to which he returned again and again during the first twenty years of his literary career. They vary widely in tone, style, and subject matter—from comic ghost stories ("Haunted Subalterns" [PT]) to grim tales of psychological terror ("The Wandering Jew" [LH]) to chilling stories of revenants ("The Lost Legion" [MI]).

Kipling's influence on subsequent work in weird fiction is difficult to gauge; but certainly, he lent an added legitimacy to the form merely by working in it. If one of the most popular British writers from 1890 to 1930—one who was frequently considered for the honour of poet laureate, and whose opinions on leading issues of the day were constantly being solicited—could find aesthetic value in the supernatural, then perhaps others might be led by his example to try their hands at this difficult art form. And that plain-spoken style that he pioneered may, albeit indirectly, have inspired the similar "common man's prose" of such later practitioners as Richard Matheson, William Peter Blatty, and Stephen King. Kipling rarely descended to their levels of mundanity, and his prose, if lacking the enervated elegance of Oscar Wilde, nonetheless has a music and rhythm of its own. If some of his other work now seems dated, his weird tales remain perennially fresh by their uncannily authentic evocation of the terrain, people, and events that infused his own richly varied life.

E. F. Benson: Spooks and More Spooks

The ghost stories of E. F. Benson (1867–1940) are, in every sense of the term, neglected classics. Benson's four collections of weird tales are among the rarest jewels of the collector of fantasy and horror, and it is precisely their fabulous scarcity that has made them undeservedly neglected when a case could, and should, be made that they ought to take their place next to the stories of M. R. James, Oliver Onions, and Walter de la Mare as a watershed in the British ghost story tradition.

Such a case can now be put to the test by the emergence of Richard Dalby's edition of *The Collected Ghost Stories of E. F. Benson* (1992). The volume, of course, contains an ambiguity found in all titles that utilise the word "collected": it can either be a synonym for "complete," or (somewhat disingenuously) it can simply mean those works that happen to have been collected for this edition. Here it is the latter meaning that applies. All that Dalby has done is to print, unchanged, the contents of Benson's four collections of weird tales—*The Room in the Tower* (1912), *Visible and Invisible* (1923), *Spook Stories* (1928), and *More Spook Stories* (1934)—along with an introduction by himself, a foreword by Joan Aiken, and an early article by Benson on a witchcraft trial. He has not printed the few weird tales found in Benson's otherwise mainstream collection, *The Countess of Lowndes Square* (1920), and (a little uncharitably) does not so much as mention Jack Adrian's admirable volume of Benson's uncollected weird tales, *The Flint Knife* (1988). Adrian's edition of Benson's *Desirable Residences and Other Stories* (1991) also contains a few more weird specimens not in Dalby's volume. Dalby has not even been very helpful in indicating the breakdowns of the four collections he has printed; let me therefore state here that, as printed in this volume, *The Room in the Tower* comprises the first seventeen stories, *Visible and Invisible* the next twelve, *Spook Stories* the next twelve, and *More Spook Stories* the final thirteen.

This range of writing—covering more than two decades in a literary career that spanned almost five—must testify to the persistence of a sense of the weird in Benson. Benson was, of course, in his time better known for his mainstream novels, stories, and nonfiction works; and in some bizarre fashion his "Mapp and Lucia" society novels experienced a resurgence in popularity not long ago. But it would not be unkind to Benson to say that his weird tales will survive—and deserve to survive—long after all this other matter has fallen into merited oblivion.

And yet, Benson does not appear to have had a very exalted or carefully worked-out view of the writing of ghost stories. In his autobiography, *Final Edition* (1940), he writes offhandedly, "Now ghost stories . . . are a branch of literature at which I have often tried my hand"; going on merely to speak of certain fairly obvious points of technique ("The narrator, I think, must succeed in frightening himself before he can hope to frighten his readers" [258–59]). Benson was, at least in his own mind, pretty much of a traditionalist in the ghost story tradition; a fact emphasised by his presence at a celebrated meeting of the Chitchat Society in 1893 at which M. R. James read some of his earliest ghost stories (see Lubbock 37–39). It would be nearly twenty years before Benson's own first weird volume would appear, by which time James had already published the first two of his collections; and yet, I do not believe that Benson can be passed off merely as an imitator of James, or even one who followed very closely in his footsteps.

The curious thing about Benson is that, almost in spite of himself, he modernised or updated the Jamesian ghost story in several ways. James' tales always hark backward, sometimes into the very distant past, as is perhaps fitting for an authority on mediaeval manuscripts; Benson's tales rarely do so, and are sometimes aggressively set in the present. One of his earliest stories, "The Dust-Cloud" (RT), involves the ghost of a motor-car ("Seems almost too up-to-date, doesn't it?" one character remarks). In "The Confession of Charles Linkworth" (RT) the ghost of a man who has been executed for murder communicates by telephone to a chaplain, pleading for absolution; "In the Tube" (VI) takes place in the London underground. Other stories, in order to introduce the weird subtly and covertly, are written in that archly sophisticated manner found in his society novels, but in so doing they create a "modern" atmosphere precisely analogous to contemporary writers' setting weird tales at rock concerts or nightclubs. The opening pages of "The Shootings of Achnaleish" (RT) involve a comic banter and emphasis on the mundane ("Rent only £350!") that suggest anything but the weird, so that the supernatural phenomenon is the more striking and powerful when it finally does emerge.

But there is more to this than merely using the observable tokens of the present in a tale. It must be declared that Benson was a confirmed spiritualist—his brief discussion of ghost stories in *Final Edition* is prefaced by a perfectly serious account of an apparition he and a friend claim to have seen—and many of his tales present elaborate pseudo-scientific justifications of ghosts and other weird phenomena on spiritualistic grounds. This also serves to "modernise" his tales, and in two ways: first, Benson is riding a wave of spiritualism that gathered strength after the first world war; and second, Benson's very need to account for his apparitions by means of philosophy or science (or what for him passes for such) betrays his unconscious absorption of the positivism of his day, whereby spiritualistic phenomena could not be accepted on their own but required a (usually specious) "proof" to overcome the scepticism that had already become ingrained in the majority of intelligent people.

It should be pointed out that Benson is not exactly an occultist, in spite of his passing mention in "The Dust-Cloud" of "occult senses" by which

the supernatural can be perceived. But his tales (as well as some of his otherwise mainstream novels) are full of ouija boards, séances, and other
paraphernalia of the spiritualism popular in his day, and there is no question—in spite of the flippancy of some of his treatments of these matters—that he took the whole subject quite seriously. The canonical
spiritualistic/philosophical "defence" for the weird occurs in "The Other
Bed" (RT):

> "Everything that happens," he said, "whether it is a step we take, or a
> thought that crosses our mind, makes some change in its immediate mate-
> rial world. Now the most violent and concentrated emotion we can imag-
> ine is the emotion that leads a man to take so extreme a step as killing
> himself or somebody else. I can easily imagine such a deed so eating into
> the material scene, the room or the haunted heath, where it happens, that
> its mark lasts an enormous time. The air rings with the cry of the slain and
> still drips with his blood. It is not everybody who will perceive it, but sensi-
> tives will."

This is all very elegant, even though upon analysis it devolves into mere
poetic metaphor instead of science or philosophy. But it neatly accounts
for the "haunting" of a given spot (which in nearly all Benson's stories is
the product of a crime—usually murder or suicide—committed there) and
for why only "sensitives" can perceive it rather than most of us hard-
headed materialists. In effect, what Benson is arguing for is (as he says in
an another story, "Outside the Door" [RT]) "how inextricable is the interweaving between mind, soul, life . . . and the purely material part of the
created world"—an utterance, incidentally, that betrays the flaw in Benson's thinking at this point in its invalid distinction between "mind, soul,
life" and what he fallaciously takes to be "dead" matter. But let that pass;
the mere fact that Benson felt the need for such justifications—rather laboured on occasion—is telling. No longer could the weird be presented
merely as such, without at least the gesture of rationalisation.

It is perhaps not wise to read Benson's weird tales all at once, for they
(like nearly all their kind, including James') become repetitive and monoto-
nous after a time. I do not see much development, either conceptually or
aesthetically, in the corpus of Benson's stories; if anything, his first two
collections represent (again like James) a pinnacle from which he only declined in later years. And all those séances really do become a little tiresome after a while. Benson has great fun with them in some tales,
especially "Mr Tilly's Séance" (VI), in which a real spirit exposes a fraud
medium, but at the very time that this fraud is being exposed, the "reality"
of the spiritual world is confirmed.

The truth of the matter is that some of Benson's most successful tales
are not ghost stories at all (note that he never used that phrase in the titles
of any of his collections, as James did for his first two) but pure "weird

tales" where the phenomena are of a much more unclassifiable sort. Already in "Between the Lights" (RT), an early tale, Benson is declaring, "The paraphernalia of ghosts has become somehow rather hackneyed." His best tale may be "The Man Who Went Too Far" (RT), in which a young man, Darcy, seems to have developed some unnatural sense of communion with the natural world. And yet, phrased this way, it becomes clear that what Darcy has actually done (whether from psychic possession by Pan or not) is to have sloughed off the "unnatural" encumbrances of civilisation and returned to the purity of Nature. But because Darcy has adopted a perhaps one-sided view of Nature as pure benevolence and joy, he is overwhelmed by the revelation of the violent side of creation. "The Man Who Went Too Far" is a tale that wondrously combines ecstasy, awe, and horror into an inextricable union.

Other non-ghost stories are nearly as effective. "Mrs Amworth" (VI) is a classic vampire tale; "Caterpillars" (RT) introduces us to an image—huge writhing slugs—that Benson uses frequently in his tales; "'And the Dead Spake'" (VI) chillingly tells of a scientist who has found some way to "tap" into the brains of the dead; in "The Horror-Horn" (VI) we find a hideous race of dwarfish quasi-human beings said to live in caves in the Alps; elementals are put on stage in "'And No Bird Sings'" (SS); and so on. Later tales utilise seemingly conventional ghost-story scenarios to convey moral or social messages, usually the anguish of marital discord, a theme to which the lifelong bachelor Benson recurs with anomalous frequency. Then there is the delicate "Pirates" (MSS), a poignant story of a lonely elderly man recovering his childhood. An autobiographical reading can scarcely be avoided here.

There is much more one can say about the weird tales of E. F. Benson, and a substantial article on his work has yet to be written. Neither Joan Aiken's foreword (which harps on Benson's possible misogyny, as if literature were designed to promote proper social behaviour) nor Dalby's chatty biographical introduction do much to lay the groundwork for such a piece, but all the evidence one needs is in the actual tales in this volume—along, of course, with the other volumes of Benson's work mentioned earlier. Once such an analysis is made, it may well become evident that Benson was a key transitional figure between the "classic" ghost story of M. R. James and the psychological ghost stories of Walter de la Mare, Oliver Onions, and L. P. Hartley. In the meantime, *The Collected Ghost Stories of E. F. Benson* is a volume no weird library can afford to be without. If nothing else, it will save us all a great deal of time and money hunting for those rare collections that have vanished like all the will-o'-the-wisps Benson saw in every haunted wood or lonely cottage.

L. P. Hartley: The Refined Ghost

L. P. Hartley (1895–1972) occupies a distinctive position in the realm of weird literature. A noted British novelist, author of the "Eustace and Hilda" trilogy (1944–47), *The Go-Between* (1953), and several other acclaimed novels, Hartley also wrote more than sixty short stories scattered through six collections. While by no means a majority of these stories are weird, a representative proportion of them deal with crime, violence, and psychological terror, occasionally crossing over into the genuinely supernatural. However, a few of his best tales are of a form now termed "non-supernatural horror" or "psychological suspense," a form that really came into its own with Robert Bloch's *Psycho* (1959) and gained wide notice in the 1980s with the novels of Thomas Harris. Hartley, then, can be seen as a precursor of this now prominent subgenre, although it does not appear likely that he actually influenced today's leading writers of non-supernatural horror.

Our first task is to ascertain the scope of Hartley's weird work. This is not a simple undertaking, for the publication history of his short stories is very peculiar. Hartley's first published book was a collection, *Night Fears and Other Stories* (1924). So far as I have been able to ascertain, some of the seventeen tales in this volume appeared in magazines prior to book publication, but a good many seem not to have been previously published. After publishing a non-weird novelette, *Simonetta Perkins*, in 1925, Hartley issued another collection, *The Killing Bottle*, in 1932; this volume contained only eight stories. After this point Hartley appeared to turn his attention largely to novels.

When August Derleth and Donald Wandrei founded Arkham House in 1939, Derleth was keen on signing up a number of leading British weird writers to lend prestige to his fledgling company; Hartley was, along with Lord Dunsany, Algernon Blackwood, and Cynthia Asquith, among the first of these. His *The Travelling Grave and Other Stories* appeared in 1948, but its contents consisted of two stories from *Night Fears*, seven from *The Killing Bottle*, and three previously uncollected stories. The selection was judicious, for, in spite of their titles, not nearly all the tales from Hartley's two previous collections were weird, and *The Travelling Grave* does collect nearly all the tales written up to this time that could even remotely be termed weird or horrific. This volume is still a landmark collection, and ought to be in every weird connoisseur's library.

In 1954 *The White Wand and Other Stories* appeared, containing five stories from *Night Fears,* one from *The Killing Bottle,* and eight uncollected stories. No more than three tales in this volume can be considered weird. *Two for the River* (1961) contains fourteen stories, of which five or six are perhaps weird. His last collection, *Mrs. Carteret Receives and Other Stories* (1971), contains ten stories, of which perhaps four are weird.

When Hartley compiled his *Collected Short Stories* in 1968, he left out a full ten stories from the *Night Fears* collection, although none of these is genuinely weird. The omission is somewhat curious; perhaps he felt that these tales were somehow not worth preserving. The posthumously published *Complete Short Stories* (1973) adds the entire contents of *Mrs. Carteret Receives* but fails to rectify the omission of the ten *Night Fears* stories. What is more, at least three further stories published in magazines or anthologies but not gathered in any of Hartley's collections are also omitted from the *Complete Short Stories*. Only one of these is weird—"The Sound of Voices," published posthumously in *The Seventh Ghost Book* (1973), edited by Rosemary Timperley, and very likely Hartley's last short story.

It can be seen, therefore, that weird themes claimed Hartley's interest throughout his short-story writing career. Nearly half of his sixty-three (or more) stories are at least on the borderland of the weird, and some—notably "A Visitor from Down Under" and "The Travelling Grave"—are among the most distinguished and frequently reprinted horror tales of their time. And yet, it may have been from external encouragement that Hartley actually entered the realm of supernatural horror. Although a number of tales in *Night Fears* skirt the weird, it was not until Cynthia Asquith asked him to write an original story for *The Ghost Book* (1926) that Hartley produced an authentically supernatural story. This was "A Visitor from Down Under," later collected in *The Killing Bottle* and *The Travelling Grave*. Other Hartley stories appeared in Asquith's second (1952) and third (1955) *Ghost Books* as well ("W. S." and "Someone in the Lift," respectively); he also wrote "The Cotillon" for Asquith's *When Churchyards Yawn* (1931).

As a noted mainstream novelist, Hartley wrote a number of important essays on the art of the novel, the short story, and the future of fiction. These were collected in *The Novelist's Responsibility* (1967), but, as with his *Complete Short Stories,* the volume does not gather all his critical work. Among the omissions is an interesting early essay (1927) on Saki, who could perhaps be considered a model for the sort of tightly knit, carefully crafted, and subtly nasty or even misanthropic tale that became Hartley's trademark. Another important omission, from a weird perspective, is the brief but very thoughtful introduction to Asquith's *Third Ghost Book* (1955), which contains one especially memorable remark on the weird tale: "If not the highest, it is certainly the most exacting form of literary art, and perhaps the only one in which there is almost no intermediate step between success and failure. Either it comes off or it is a flop" (vii).

This is not of any especial help in elucidating Hartley's own methodology of the weird, but some other comments are more illuminating. Hartley makes the questionable, but all too familiar, assertion that "the taste for it [the ghost story] is slightly abnormal, a survival, perhaps, from adolescence, a disease of deficiency suffered by those whose lives and imaginations do not react satisfactorily to normal experience and require an extra thrill" (vii). He then contrasts the methods of the detective story and the weird tale:

> Detective-story writers give this thrill by exploring the resources of the *possible;* however improbable the happenings in a detective story, they can and must be explained in terms that satisfy the reason. But in a ghost story, where natural laws are dispensed with, the whole point is that the happenings cannot be so explained. A ghost story that is capable of a rational explanation is as much an anomaly as a detective story that isn't. (vii–viii)

But Hartley is careful to add the following caveat: "The ghost-story writer's task is the more difficult, for not only must he create a world in which reason doesn't hold sway, but he must invent laws for it. Chaos is not enough. Even ghosts must have rules and obey them" (viii).

Some years later, in the introduction to *The Second Fontana Book of Great Ghost Stories* (1965), Robert Aickman presented an opposing view: ". . . the ghost story draws upon the unconscious mind, in the manner of poetry; . . . it need offer neither logic nor moral; . . . it is an art form of altogether exceptional delicacy and subtlety . . ."[1] Hartley would have agreed with everything here except the notion that the ghost story "need offer neither logic nor moral": this is exactly what he was warning against when he wrote that "Chaos is not enough." I think Hartley's is the sounder position, for what is required in the weird tale—and what we get from most of Hartley's, as distinguished from many of Aickman's admittedly fine stories—is a sort of *pseudo-logic* that satisfies the reader on a moral or aesthetic level, if not on an intellectual or scientific one. The supernatural "out" must be maintained—a ghost should not be explained away entirely as a phenomenon wholly within the bounds of the known—but there must be some rationale for the ghost's very existence, otherwise a tale will seem random and unmotivated, full of weird incidents that lack even an internal logic.

Hartley's final point in his introduction to *The Third Ghost Book* is that the modern ghost appears in many more forms than his chain-clanking predecessor. He does not appear to have been entirely sympathetic to this extension of the ghost's functions or manifestations, and remarks a little wryly that "Now their liberties have been greatly extended; they can go anywhere, they can manifest themselves in scores of ways. Like women and other depressed classes, they have emancipated themselves from their disabilities" (viii). What this really means is that the ghost is now capable of appearing in a tale in such a way that we scarcely realise it is a ghost until the last moment; indeed, oftentimes the fact that a character *is* a ghost, and not an ordinary human being as we have up to that point assumed him to be, forms the climax of a Hartley tale. As he says in his introduction: "There must come a point, and it must strike the reader with a shock of surprise and horror, a tingling of the spine, at which we realise that he is *not* one of us" (viii–ix).

These basic principles—the manifestation of the weird as governed by some internally consistent set of "laws," and extreme subtlety in the presentation of the supernatural—are all we need to understand the bulk of Hartley's weird tales. Both his supernatural and his non-supernatural tales are much concerned with the analysis of aberrant mental states, and in many instances we are not certain until the very end whether the supernatural actually comes into play; in some tales this uncertainty is not resolved, nor is it intended to be.

Some of Hartley's tales of crime can be dispensed with quickly, for there is nothing either weird or horrific about them. "The Island" involves a man who has been invited to an island resort owned by a Mrs Santander. Rather than meeting his hostess, the narrator meets an odd man whom he first takes to be a mechanic but who eventually turns out to be Mrs Santander's husband. It becomes clear that the narrator is Mrs Santander's lover; after an initial discussion at cross-purposes (one of Hartley's favourite devices, and one that he uses to spectacular effect in several of his horror tales), the two men have a tense dispute in which it is finally revealed that Mr Santander has just killed his wife, who is lying strangled in the library. Hartley somewhat telegraphs the punch in this story, but it remains a gripping tale of crime and suspense.

Somewhat closer to the horrific is "The Killing Bottle," a rather long-winded crime story that contains a hideous description of the death of a butterfly in a killing bottle:

> The butterfly must have been stronger than it looked; the power of the killing bottle had no doubt declined with frequent usage. Up and down, round and round flew the butterfly; its frantic flutterings could be heard through the thick walls of its glass prison. It clung to the cotton-wool, pressed itself into corners, its straining, delicate tongue coiling and uncoiling in the effort to suck in a breath of living air. Now it was weakening. It fell from the cotton-wool and lay with its back on the plaster slab. It jolted itself up and down and, when strength for this movement failed, it clawed the air with its thin legs as though pedalling an imaginary bicycle. Suddenly, with a violent spasm, it gave birth to a thick cluster of yellowish eggs. Its body twitched once or twice and at last lay still. (C 251)

The effectiveness of this passage rests in Hartley's exquisitely polished diction and his drawing out the death-throes of the wretched creature to agonising proportions.

The graveyard humour that Hartley can create when his characters talk at cross-purposes in some particularly hideous context is no better displayed than in his celebrated tale, "The Travelling Grave." This is an entirely non-supernatural tale, but pungent satire raises it to the level of horror. Richard Munt has developed a peculiar penchant for collecting coffins, but his friend Valentine Ostrop, one of the guests invited to spend a weekend with him, is unaware of this predilection, and by misunderstanding the dialogue of the other guests assumes that Munt collects baby perambulators. One can imagine the consequences:

> "Oh, we've been together for *hours,*" said Valentine airily, "and had the most enchanting conversation. Guess what we talked about?"
> "Not about me, I hope?"
> "Well, about something very dear to you."
> "About you, then?"
> "Don't make fun of me. The objects I speak of are both solid and useful."
> "That does rather rule you out," said Munt meditatively. "What are they useful for?"
> "Carrying bodies."
> Munt glanced across at Bettisher, who was staring into the grate.
> "And what are they made of?"
> Valentine tittered, pulled a face, answered, "I've had little experience of them, but I should think chiefly of wood."
> Munt got up and looked hard at Bettisher, who raised his eyebrows and said nothing.
> "They perform at one time or another," said Valentine, enjoying himself enormously, "an essential service for us all." (C 102)

Some of this is a little staged: it is unlikely that anyone, talking of the function of perambulators, would say that they are used for "carrying bodies." Nevertheless, this dialogue continues for a full page, becoming more and more unnerving until we read this:

> [Valentine:] "You keep them empty?"
> Bettisher started up in his chair, but Munt held out a pallid hand and murmured in a stifled voice:
> "Yes, that is, most of them are." (C 103)

I wish to detour here to study "The Cotillon," for although this is a supernatural tale, it contains more of this talking at cross-purposes whose loathsomeness we perceive only when we reach the end of the tale and fully understand the scenario. Marion Lane, who has just jilted Henry Chichester, attends a party by her friend Jane Manning. Throughout the evening there is talk of gate-crashers, and one particularly odd fellow is seen skulking about in a sort of death-mask. Finally Marion meets the man: it is Henry. They have a tense conversation; then Henry pulls a revolver:

> "What am I to do with this?" she asked.
> "You are the best judge of that," he replied. "Only one cartridge has been used."
> . . .
> "I was always an empty-headed fellow," he went on, tapping the waxed covering [of his mask] with his gloved forefinger, so that it gave out a

wooden hollow sound—"there's nothing much behind this. No brains to speak of, I mean. Less than I used to have, in fact." (C 158)

In fact, Henry is a ghost; he had blown his brains out earlier that evening.

A great many of Hartley's weird tales are tales of supernatural revenge. This, I think, is what he meant when he said that the weird writer must "invent laws" for his supernatural phenomena. It is not enough to have a ghostly manifestation that serves no purpose; but if the ghost is on a mission to avenge some wrong, either against himself or against others, then the scenario gains that internal or aesthetic logic that satisfies the reader. It is remarkable how many of Hartley's tales are of this one type; but he has rung enough changes on the theme in scene and atmosphere to produce a handful of weird masterpieces.

"A Visitor from Down Under" once again displays a macabre wit, this time in its punning title: the disheveled man who hunts down Mr Rumbold in his elegant London hotel is indeed from Australia, but is also from some other place "down under." The plot of this story is extremely simple— Rumbold has killed his colleague in Australia, presumably for gain, and the colleague comes back to avenge his murder—but the greatness of the tale rests in the extraordinarily subtle manipulation of details and symbolism. Mr Rumbold is seen lounging contentedly in his hotel, revelling in "his untroubled acceptance of the present and the future" (C 63). As he lapses into a doze, he seems to hear a radio programme in which a children's game is being broadcast. This programme is narrated at anomalous length, and a number of peculiarities in the account finally make us realise that it is in fact a sort of dream or hallucination on Rumbold's part; it is, also, very prophetic, as it tells ingenuously of some horrible revenge about to take place:

> And who will you send to fetch him away,
> Fetch him away, fetch him away;
> Who will you send to fetch him away
> On a cold and frosty morning? (C 66)

When the corpse arrives at the hotel, dripping icicles, he demands to see Rumbold; the latter tries to evade him, but finally throws caution to the winds and has the porter tell him: "'Mr. Rumbold wishes you to Hell, sir, where you belong, and says, "Come up if you dare!"'" (C 73). The outcome is inevitable, and the tale ends on one final hideous detail as seen by the porter in Rumbold's room: "But what sickened him and kept him so long from going down to rouse the others was the sight of an icicle on the window-sill, a thin claw of ice curved like a Chinaman's nail, with a bit of flesh sticking to it" (C 73).

One of Hartley's most powerful tales of supernatural revenge is "Podolo" (TG). Actually, doubt is retained to the end as to whether the supernatural comes into play: all we know is that something horrible has occurred. This exquisitely modulated story tells of an English couple, Angela and Walter, who wish to visit an uninhabited island, Podolo, off the coast of Venice. When they arrive, Angela comes upon a scrawny cat who has evidently been abandoned on the island. She immediately takes pity on the cat ("'It's hungry. Probably it's starving'" [C 75]), feeds it some scraps of chicken, and tries to capture it to take it back with them. But the cat proves surprisingly feisty, refusing all Angela's attempts to catch it. Frustrated, Angela makes a hideous resolve: "'if I can't catch it I'll kill it'" (C 77). Mario, the Italian boatman who took them to the island, remarks wistfully, "'She loves it so much . . . that she wants to kill it'" (C 78). No one can dissuade Angela from her twisted mission, but night falls as she scours the island alone hunting down the cat. Walter and Mario begin to worry about Angela, and then see some dark figure in the distance. Mario remarks: "'There *is* someone on the island . . . but it's not the signora'" (C 80). At this point Hartley reveals an astonishing ability to create terror by means of a simple dialogue:

"It was a man, then?" said I [Walter].
"It looked like a man's head."
"But you're not sure?"
"No, because it did not walk like a man."
"How then?"
Mario bent forward and touched the ground with his free hand. I couldn't imagine why a man should go on all fours, unless he didn't want to be seen. (C 80)

Mario and Walter get out of the boat and explore the island; they find the crushed head of the cat, then one of Angela's slippers. Mario, wandering off alone, finds Angela; more tense conversation ensues:

"When I found her," he whispered, "she wasn't quite dead."
I began to speak but he held up his hand.
"She asked me to kill her."
"But, Mario!"
"'Before it comes back,' she said. And then she said, '*It's* starving, too, and it won't wait . . .'" (C 82)

The tale ends in tantalising inconclusiveness: it is clear that the entity on all fours has avenged the death of the cat by killing Angela, but what is the nature of that entity itself? Is it human (but if so, how did it get to the island?—there is no other boat aside from Mario's)? Is it some hideous Darwinian ape-thing? Hartley wisely refrains from resolving the issue.

An extremely effective and compact revenge tale is "The Waits" (TR). A strange man and a young boy come to the home of the Marriner family at Christmas time. They appear to be choristers, but they refuse to be satisfied when Jeremy, Mr Marriner's young son, offers them a guinea: "'He wouldn't take it,' he said. 'He said it wasn't enough. He said you would know why'" (C 521). Marriner's daughter Anne offers them a Christmas box, but they won't take that either. The encounter becomes more and more tense until Mr Marriner begins to run out the door with a pistol. Once again Hartley achieves tremendously powerful effects through dialogue:

> "But it isn't any good, it isn't any good!" Anne kept repeating.
> "What isn't any good, darling?"
> "The pistol. You see, I've seen through him!"
> "How do you mean, seen through him? Do you mean he's an imposter?"
> "No, no, I've really seen through him." Anne's voice sank to a whisper.
> "I saw the street lamp shining through a hole in his head." (C 522–23)

It is only then that we understand that the man and boy had been blackmailing Marriner, that Marriner had killed them, and that now they are coming back to exact vengeance upon him. We also come to understand the true significance of several enigmatic statements in the opening paragraph:

> Mr. Marriner knew that financially quite a heavy drain was being made on his resources [from the blackmailers]. And later in the evening when he got out his cheque-book to give his customary presents to his family, his relations and the staff, the drain would be heavier. But he could afford it, he could afford it better this Christmas than at any other Christmas in the history of his steadily increasing fortune [because his blackmailers are dead]. And he didn't have to think, he didn't have to choose; he only had to consult a list and add one or two names, and cross off one or two [the man and the boy]. There was quite a big item to cross off, quite a big item [the sum he was paying to the blackmailers], though it didn't figure on the list or on the counterfoil of his cheque-book. (C 518)

The seemingly irrelevant repetition of certain phrases—"he could afford it, he could afford it"; "quite a big item, quite a big item"—tips us off to something peculiar and significant, although we do not grasp the significance until the end.

"W. S." (WW), which appeared in Asquith's *Second Ghost Book* (1952), is a *Doppelgänger* story involving Walter Streeter, a successful author who begins receiving postcards from someone who signs himself only "W. S." This person initially appears to be an enthusiastic but somewhat critical fan of Streeter's: "'I have enjoyed all your books, but do you really get to grips with people?'" (C 382). That latter remark becomes a refrain repeated in nearly every postcard ("'Perhaps we shall come to grips after all'" [C 384]), and then Streeter notices that the postmarks on the cards show that the writer is drawing successively closer to him. All this is handled with Hartley's usual subtlety and sense of dramatic tension, but the solution of the mystery is rather obvious, especially when Streeter recalls that he had once created a character named William Stainsforth:

He had written about him with extreme vindictiveness, just as if he was a real person whom he was trying to show up. He had experienced a curious pleasure in attributing every kind of wickedness to this man. He never gave him the benefit of the doubt. He had never felt a twinge of pity for him, even when he paid the penalty for his misdeeds on the gallows. He had so worked himself up that the idea of this dark creature, creeping about brimful of malevolence, had almost frightened him. (C 385–86)

It is rather remarkable that Streeter could have forgotten about the existence of this character, and the fact that the character bore his own initials, up to this point. W. S. is, of course, Stainsforth, and it is also clear that Streeter, in depicting this evil figure, had transferred all his own evil traits to him, as Stainsforth remarks when he finally encounters Streeter in the flesh: "'You unloaded all your self-dislike on me'" (C 390). Stainsforth kills Streeter in a melodramatic conclusion hardly worthy of Hartley's artistry.

A much better tale of this type is "Fall In at the Double" (MC). Philip Osgood has inhabited a house in the West Country since the end of World War II. He hires a new butler, Alfred, but on his second day of work Alfred confesses that he didn't sleep a wink because he kept hearing a man gruffly shouting, "Fall in at the double!" Could the house be haunted? This seems very likely, especially when Alfred tells him the history of the house as he heard it from the locals: the place had been an Army barracks during the war, and the commander, a very harsh Lieutenant-Colonel named Alexander McCreeth, was eventually found drowned in the river near the house, probably at the hands of the soldiers whom he brutalised. Eerie phenomena continue, until at one point Osgood, wandering in his garden late at night, seems to see a group of soldiers converging upon a colonel:

They were beginning to close in on him, their hands were already round his legs, when he called, "You've done this before. Take him, he's my double!" And he pointed to Philip, shivering behind him on the lawn. (C 666)

It is at this point that we realise that the title of the story is a nasty pun. The fact that Alfred saves Philip at the end does not diminish the power and subtlety of this grim ghost story.

"The Two Vaynes" (WW) is interesting in being a sort of pseudo-*Doppelgänger* tale. Vayne is a sculptor of life-size statues, which he displays in his spacious garden; he has just finished creating a statue of himself in plaster. He invites a number of his friends for the weekend, and they decide to play hide and seek on the grounds (recall the game motif in "The Travelling Grave" and "The Visitor from Down Under"). The tale develops an eerie atmosphere as the guests scatter through the capacious grounds as night falls; then one of the guests sees an odd encounter between Vayne and the statue:

For a moment the two figures stood one behind the other, motionless as cats. Then a scream rang out; there was a whirl of limbs, like the Manxman's wheel revolving; a savage snarl, a headlong fall, a crash. Both fell, both Vaynes. When the thuds of their descent were over, silence reigned. (C 400)

Has the statue taken vengeance upon its creator? It has, but the significance is not what we imagine it to be: the statue was not some double of Vayne but a man, Postgate, whom Vayne had killed three years ago for ruining him in business. The skill of the story's narration makes us overlook the implausibility of Postgate coming back to life just at this moment to exact his revenge.

A number of Hartley's best tales are so unclassifiable that they must be placed in the weird only by default. Here the supernatural may or may not come into play, and yet the stories develop such an atmosphere of the odd that they present an excellent case for the extension of the weird to encompass tales of psychological terror. "Night Fears" (NF, TG) is among the best of these. Here a night watchman encounters a strange derelict who repeatedly torments him about the disadvantages of this type of work: the pay is bad, it is difficult to sleep in the daytime ("'Makes a man ill, mad sometimes. People have done themselves in sooner than stand the torture'" [C 227]), you don't get to see much of your children, you don't know what your wife is doing ("'You leave her pretty much to herself, don't you? Now with these women, you know, that's a *risk*'" [C 228]). The pacing of the story is masterful, and it may be a textbook instance of the *conte cruel*, in which, as Lovecraft noted, "the wrenching of the emotions is accomplished through dramatic tantalisations, frustrations, and gruesome physical horrors."[2] While there is gruesome physical horror here—the derelict ultimately kills the night watchman and leaves him dead at his post—Hartley also manages to leave the subtlest hint that the derelict himself is some otherworldly creature.

Still more curious is the very brief tale "A Summons" (NF, WW), in which a young woman tells her brother as they go to sleep in separate bedrooms: "'Now, if I dream I'm being murdered I shall knock on the wall, and I shall expect you to come'" (C 315). The brother passes this off as merely a morbid jest, but sure enough there is a tapping on the wall—first four times, then three times, then twice ("It was much feebler that time" [C 317]). The brother does nothing as he frantically tries to rationalise that it is all a joke. This is the end of the story:

> Minutes passed, and the knocking was not renewed. I turned over. The bed was comfortable enough, but I felt I should sleep sounder if my sister changed her room. This, after all, could easily be arranged. (C 317)

That is all. Is the sister actually being murdered? Is she simply dreaming of being murdered? We never know, and never will know.

Other Hartley stories are perhaps too nebulous for detailed analysis: "Home, Sweet Home" (MC), a strange, dreamlike tale that tells of a couple who return to their long-deserted home and find the ghosts of disturbed children who had been interred there; "The Shadow on the Wall" (MC), perhaps a conscious nod to the story of a similar title by Mary E. Wilkins-Freeman, in which a woman has a peculiar encounter in her bath with a man who may be a ghost; "Conrad and the Dragon" (KB, TG), a twisted fairy tale; "Feet Foremost" (KB, TG) and "Monkshood Manor" (WW), stories of supernatural curses; "Three, or Four, for Dinner" (TG), a somewhat obvious tale of a man who returns from the dead; and several others. All these tales, some more effective than others, testify to Hartley's pervasive interest in the weird, an interest that must be regarded as central to his entire literary work.

The virtues of Hartley's weird writing, as of his writing as a whole, speak for themselves: a polished, fluid, exquisitely restrained style; an attention to fine nuances of character portrayal; a penetrating awareness of the psychological impact of the weird upon human consciousness; and an elegant nastiness that only the British seem capable of getting away with. Hartley's actual weird scenarios are on the whole very simple, but are narrated with such oblique subtlety, and with such attention to atmospheric tensity, that many can stand as models of weird writing.

Hartley's place in weird fiction is a little harder to specify. The bulk of his "ghost stories" were written after those of M. R. James, whose final collection, *A Warning to the Curious*, appeared in 1925; along with Walter de la Mare and Oliver Onions, Hartley led the way in transforming the pure ghost story into the psychological ghost story, where the weird is manifested as much in the analysis of a disturbed mentality as in the actual supernatural phenomenon. As such, Hartley led the way for such later writers as Shirley Jackson and Robert Aickman, although it would be difficult to establish whether either writer was directly influenced by his work. Hartley wisely eschewed the attempt to extend the supernatural to novel length—his one futuristic novel, *Facial Justice* (1960), is painfully clumsy and superficial—and his work forms one more testimonial to the superiority of the short story over the novel as a vehicle for the weird. A volume gathering all Hartley's weird tales would be very welcome, for modern practitioners could learn much from him on both the mechanics and the aesthetics of the weird. Whether they could ever match his deftness and understated power is another question.

Notes

1. Robert Aickman, "Introduction" to *The Second Fontana Book of Great Ghost Stories* (London: Fontana, 1965), p. 7.
2. H. P. Lovecraft, *The Annotated Supernatural Horror in Literature*, ed. S. T. Joshi (New York: Hippocampus Press, 2000), p. 41.

III. H. P. Lovecraft and His Influence

H. P. Lovecraft: The Fiction of Materialism

> Now all my tales are based on the fundamental premise that common human laws and interests and emotions have no validity or significance in the vast cosmos-at-large. To me there is nothing but puerility in a tale in which the human form—and the local human passions and conditions and standards—are depicted as native to other worlds or other universes. To achieve the essence of real externality, whether of time or space or dimension, one must forget that such things as organic life, good and evil, love and hate, and all such local attributes of a negligible and temporary race called mankind, have any existence at all. Only the human scenes and characters must have human qualities. *These* must be handled with unsparing *realism*, (*not* catchpenny *romanticism*) but when we cross the line to the boundless and hideous unknown—the shadow-haunted *Outside*—we must remember to leave our humanity and terrestrialism at the threshold. (SL 2.150)

This landmark statement, made in a letter by H. P. Lovecraft upon the resubmittal of his seminal tale, "The Call of Cthulhu," to *Weird Tales* in 1927 (the story had been rejected a few months earlier), can stand as one of the central documents of Lovecraft's aesthetic of the weird, and it also justifies a philosophical approach to his work as a whole. Lovecraft is remarkable in having articulated a highly complex, detailed, and carefully considered world view that structured his entire work. This world view, which underwent significant modifications in various particulars over the course of his life, is embodied not so much in his relatively few and insignificant philosophical essays as in tens of thousands of letters, published and unpublished, in which he tirelessly debated points of philosophy and conduct with colleagues of both like and dissimilar temperament. It will repay us, therefore, to consider briefly the fundamentals of Lovecraft's philosophical thought before we attempt to see how that thought provides the underpinning for his weird fiction.[1]

I. Materialism

Lovecraft's early readings in the *Arabian Nights*, Grimm's fairy tales, and the tales of Poe (all of which he encountered before the age of eight) impelled a lifelong love of the strange and the bizarre; but almost coincident with this absorption of the weird were two other influences of equal importance: the discovery of classical antiquity—literature, philosophy, and art—and fascination with the sciences, particularly chemistry and astronomy. Lovecraft speaks of the significance of these two interests in a charming essay, "A Confession of Unfaith" (1922):

The most poignant sensations of my existence are those of 1896, when I discovered the Hellenic world, and of 1902, when I discovered the myriad suns and worlds of infinite space. Sometimes I think the latter event the greater, for the grandeur of that growing conception of the universe still excites a thrill hardly to be duplicated. . . . By my thirteenth birthday I was thoroughly impressed with man's impermanence and insignificance, and by my seventeenth, . . . I had formed in all essential particulars my present pessimistic cosmic views. (MW 536)

I shall return to that final sentence presently; what is important to emphasise here is how early Lovecraft's "cosmic" point of view—an awareness of the vast size of the known universe and a consequent appreciation of the relative insignificance of all human life when measured on the scale of cosmic infinity—was imbued in him.

In some ways Lovecraft's classical and scientific interests worked in tandem, for among his classical readings was the philosophy of materialism as embodied in Leucippus and Democritus and its ethical corollary in the philosophy of Epicurus. If nothing else, ancient materialism and modern science—the nebular hypothesis of Laplace; Dalton's analysis of the atom; the evolutionary theory of Darwin and Huxley; the anthropological work of Edward Burnett Tylor (*Primitive Culture*, 1871), John Fiske (*Myths and Myth-Makers*, 1872), and Sir James George Frazer (*The Golden Bough*, 1890) —allowed Lovecraft to slough off whatever remnants of religious belief his early upbringing may have instilled in him. In "A Confession of Unfaith" he speaks wryly of his pestiferous questioning of a Sunday school teacher and his eventual removal from the class: "No doubt I was regarded as a corrupter of the simple faith of the other 'infants'" (MW 534). Much later in life Lovecraft codified his religious views:

I certainly can't see any sensible position to assume aside from that of *complete scepticism tempered by a leaning toward that which existing evidence makes most probable*. All I say is that I think it is *damned unlikely* that anything like a central cosmic will, a spirit world, or an eternal survival of personality exist. They are the most preposterous and unjustified of all the guesses which can be made about the universe, and I am not enough of a hair-splitter to pretend that I don't regard them as arrant and negligible moonshine. In theory I am an *agnostic*, but pending the appearance of rational evidence I must be classed, practically and provisionally, as an *atheist*. The chances of theism's truth being to my mind so microscopically small, I would be a pedant and a hypocrite to call myself anything else. (SL 4.57)

Lovecraft defended his atheism in a spirited series of articles in 1921 (now titled *In Defence of Dagon*), whose scintillating rhetoric and logical force must be read to be appreciated.

Around this time Lovecraft began solidifying his entire metaphysics, reading such works as Ernst Haeckel's *The Riddle of the Universe* (1899) and

Hugh Elliot's *Modern Science and Materialism* (1919). Elliot enunciates three main principles of materialism, all of which Lovecraft accepted:

1. The uniformity of law.
2. The denial of teleology.
3. The denial of any form of existence other than those envisaged by physics and chemistry, that is to say, other existences that have some kind of palpable material characteristics and qualities. (Elliot 138–41)

The uniformity of law means that the sequence of cause and effect is constant throughout the universe, from the smallest sub-atomic particle to the largest quasar or nebula. This principle is important to Lovecraft's aesthetic of the weird because the sense of imaginative liberation he sought depends upon it:

I choose weird stories because they suit my inclinations best—one of my strongest and most persistent wishes being to achieve, momentarily, the illusion of some strange suspension or violation of the galling limitations of time, space, and natural law which for ever imprison us and frustrate our curiosity about the infinite cosmic spaces beyond the radius of our sight and analysis. ("Notes on Writing Weird Fiction" [MW 113])

It is important not to be led astray here: Lovecraft is not somehow renouncing his materialism—his belief in the uniformity of law—by seeking an imaginative escape from it; indeed, it is precisely *because* he believes that "time, space, and natural law" *are* uniform, and that the human mind cannot defeat or confound them, that an imaginative escape is sought. Lovecraft emphasises this point in a letter:

The real *raison d'être* of [weird] art is to give one a temporary illusion of emancipation from the galling and intolerable tyranny of time, space, change, and natural law. If we can give ourselves even for rather a brief moment the illusory sense that some law of the ruthless cosmos has been—or could be—invalidated or defeated, we acquire a certain flush of triumphant emancipation comparable in its comforting power to the opiate dreams of religion. Indeed, religion itself is merely a pompous formalisation of fantastic art. Its disadvantage is that it demands an *intellectual* belief in the impossible, whereas fantastic art does not. (SL 4.417–18)

The contrast with religion is to be noted. If Lovecraft actually believed in the defiance of natural law—if, for example, he actually believed in the literal reality of his entity Cthulhu (as, regrettably, some occultist enthusiasts appear to do)—he would simply feel like a fool, since he knew that Cthulhu does not and cannot exist in the real world; it is, instead, a metaphor for that defiance of natural law which Lovecraft required as an aesthetic escape.

The point about teleology—the belief that either the human race or the cosmos as a whole is progressing toward some goal, usually under the direction of some deity—need not be discussed in detail: Lovecraft whole-heartedly rejected this notion, once accusing an adversary of misusing the theory of evolution to bolster a teleological view of the universe:

> He sees a process of evolution in operation at one particular cosmic moment in one particular point in space; and at once assumes gratuitously that *all the cosmos* is evolving steadily *in one direction* toward a fixed goal. . . . So when it is shewn that life on our world will (relatively) soon be extinct through the cooling of the sun; that space is full of such worlds which have died; that human life and the solar system itself are the merest *novelties* in an eternal cosmos; and that all indications point to a gradual breaking down of both matter and energy which will eventually nullify the results of evolution in any particular corner of space; when these things are shewn Mr. Wickenden recoils, and . . . cries out that it's all nonsense—it just *can't* be so!! (MW 153)

In Lovecraft's fiction we shall see this denial of teleology appear in some rather dismal predictions as to the humiliating petering-out of the human race and the eventual entropic decline of the universe as a whole. As early as 1915 he painted a vivid portrait of such a universe in an astronomy column:

> A vast, sepulchral universe of unbroken midnight gloom and perpetual arctic frigidity, through which will roll dark, cold suns with their hordes of dead, frozen planets, on which will lie the dust of those unhappy mortals who will have perished as their dominant stars faded from their skies. Such is the depressing picture of a future too remote for calculation.[2]

For Lovecraft, both philosophically and aesthetically, the most important aspect of materialism was the denial of "any form of existence other than those envisaged by physics and chemistry." Specifically, this refers to the existence of an immaterial soul, and Lovecraft has great fun demolishing theistic views of the immaterial and immortal soul:

> How may we . . . assume in one wild guess the existence of a whole world of entity, distinct from any provable substance, giving no evidence of itself, and independent of the known laws of matter? If it was hard to conceive of life as the product of lifeless matter, is it indeed easier to conceive of the existence of an airy nothing which can have no source at all, but which is claimed without proof or probability to hover around certain substances for certain periods, and subsequently to retain the personality of the substance around which it last hovers? (MW 159)

But for Lovecraft the whole notion is broader, and he wishes to deny the existence of *any* substance or entity not encompassed by current science. This point gains importance when, as we shall see presently, he is compelled to defend his materialism against the potentially threatening discoveries of modern astrophysics.

II. The Ethics of Materialism

Some of the ethical ramifications of Lovecraft's materialism are worth investigating here, as they shall have some bearing on our analysis of his fiction. I now wish to return to that curious phrase in "A Confession of Unfaith," wherein Lovecraft states that his awareness of the vastness of the cosmos and the insignificance of human beings led to his "pessimistic cosmic views." The fact is that there are several fallacies in his thinking at this point. Dale J. Nelson has recently remarked astutely: "Sometimes Lovecraft makes a category error: given the perhaps infinitely greater physical dimensions of the universe than those of mankind and the earth (quantitative), mankind and the earth are insignificant (qualitative)" (Nelson 4n). Even if mankind's insignificance is accepted as a valid inference from the vastness of the universe, why should this lead to pessimism or misanthropy, as it seems to have done in the early Lovecraft? In fact, Lovecraft was at this time strongly under the influence of Schopenhauer, whose *Studies in Pessimism* he quotes frequently and with clear approval in his essay, "Nietzscheism and Realism" (1922).[3] Even later in life, when he had become more of an "indifferentist" and less of a pessimist, he was still adhering to certain of Schopenhauer's beliefs:

> Ol' Art Schopenhauer had the straight goods—however you look at it, there's so goddam much *more* pain than pleasure in any average human life, that it's a losing game unless a guy can pep it up with pure moonshine—either the literal 95-proof pink-snake-evoker, or the churchly hootch of belief in immortality and a benign old gentleman with long whiskers . . . and a cosmick purpose . . . or else the Dunsanian conjuration of an illusion of *fantastick and indefinite possibility* as shadow'd forth in certain aesthetic interpretations of selected objective phenomena, time-sequences, and cosmical and dimensional speculations. (SL 3.139–40)

This is all very neat, and again shows the *unity* of Lovecraft's thought: given that life has so much more pain than pleasure, the option for someone like Lovecraft, who does not drink and cannot accept the opiate of religion, is to write weird fiction. This sort of cynical cosmicism made for an interesting aesthetic argument, as he wrote to Edwin Baird in 1923: "Only a cynic can create horror—for behind every masterpiece of the sort must reside a driving daemonic force that despises the human race and its illusions, and longs to pull them to pieces and mock them" (MW 509). Although Lovecraft toned this down later, he never wholly repudiated it, and we shall see instances in his fiction where this sort of misanthropy exhibits itself very powerfully. I have no wish, incidentally, to condemn Lovecraft for any misanthropic tendencies he may have had, since there is every reason to believe that the misanthropy of such writers as Swift, Bierce, Lovecraft, and Shirley Jackson has much philosophical justification. If nothing else, Lovecraft could express his misanthropy very piquantly: "Honestly, my hatred of the human animal mounts by leaps and bounds the more I see of the miserable vermin" (SL 1.211).

But, as I said, Lovecraft came to amend this view. A lifelong believer in Epicurean *ataraxia* ("freedom from cares and trivial thoughts" [SL 1.87]), he came to realise that misanthropy may be both a limiting and a philosophically invalid position if taken too far:

> Anti-humanism, in its extreme phases, becomes exceedingly ridiculous; since it assumes as many values of purely arbitrary unreality as does pro-humanism. Both attitudes are essentially silly and unscientific, since mankind is merely one type of matter among many, and no more to be loved and respected, or hated and repudiated, than any other type of matter. (SL 2.165)

This leads the way to Lovecraft's mature ethical stance:

> Contrary to what you may assume, I am *not a pessimist* but an *indifferentist*—that is, I don't make the mistake of thinking that the resultant of the natural forces surrounding and governing organic life will have any connexion with the wishes or tastes of any part of that organic life-process. Pessimists are just as illogical as optimists; insomuch as both envisage the aims of mankind as unified, and as having a direct relationship (either of frustration or of fulfilment) to the inevitable flow of terrestrial motivation and events. That is—both schools retain in a vestigial way the primitive concept of a conscious teleology—of a cosmos which gives a damn one way or the other about the especial wants and ultimate welfare of mosquitoes, rats, lice, dogs, men, horses, pterodactyls, trees, fungi, dodos, or other forms of biological energy. (SL 3.39)

This is a brilliant encapsulation of Lovecraft's entire metaphysical and ethical philosophy: cosmicism makes both pessimism and optimism irrelevant because human beings are simply too *insignificant* to be worth bothering about.

I do not wish to suggest that Lovecraft wholly scorned all human concerns in his ethical thought; indeed, his later views—once he had sloughed off the extreme Schopenhauerianism and Nietzscheism of his early period—are in every sense broad-minded (except in the one issue of race), humane, and civilised. His urgent pleas for social and economic reform in the wake of the depression of the 1930s testifies to his anxiety for the fate of Western culture; and his evolved ethical stance, while still placing humanity on a very humble plane in cosmic entity, brings the humanism of Bertrand Russell to mind:

> Now since man means nothing in the cosmos, it is plain that his only logical goal (a goal whose sole reference is to *himself*) is simply the achievement of a reasonable equilibrium which shall enhance his likelihood of experiencing the sort of reactions he wishes, and which shall help along his natural impulse to increase his differentiation from unorganised force and

matter. This goal can be reached only through teaching individual men how best to keep out of each other's way, and how best to reconcile the various conflicting instincts which a haphazard cosmic drift has placed within the breast of the same person. Here, then, is a practical and imperative system of ethics, resting upon the firmest possible foundation and being essentially that taught by Epicurus and Lucretius. (SL 5.241)

III. The Defence of Materialism

The year 1923 was a critical one for Lovecraft—not so much because it marked his entry into *Weird Tales*, the magazine that published the bulk of his mature fiction, but because it was then that he was no longer able to shield himself from the effects of certain advances in astrophysics, so that he was forced to modify his materialism significantly. First on the scene, as far as his awareness is concerned, was Einstein's relativity theory, one of the first blows against the somewhat cocksure materialism of Hugh Elliot and other late nineteenth-century thinkers. Lovecraft must have known something about relativity before 1923: Elliot himself mentions it with some perplexity in *Modern Science and Materialism* (38), and there is a very curious allusion to Einstein in the story "Hypnos" (1922) ("One man with Oriental eyes has said that all time and space are relative, and men have laughed" [D 165]); but observations made during a solar eclipse in 1923 appeared to confirm the relativity beyond reasonable doubt. Lovecraft's response is perhaps typical of that of many intellectuals of the time:

> My cynicism and scepticism are increasing, and from an entirely new cause—the Einstein theory. The latest eclipse observations seem to place this system among the facts which cannot be dismissed, and assumedly it removes the last hold which reality or the universe can have on the independent mind. All is chance, accident, and ephemeral illusion—a fly may be greater than Arcturus, and Durfee Hill may surpass Mount Everest—assuming them to be removed from the present planet and differently environed in the continuum of space-time. There are no values in all infinity—the least idea that there are is the supreme mockery of all. All the cosmos is a jest, and one thing is as true as another. I believe everything and nothing—for all is chaos, always has been, and always will be. (SL 1.231)

Particularly interesting (and fallacious) is the ethical corollary Lovecraft draws from Einstein ("There are no values in all infinity . . ."). In a few years, however, he had snapped out of this nihilistic attitude and harmonised Einstein into a philosophy that was still broadly materialistic, but modified in certain important respects. Throughout all this Lovecraft is keen on preserving at least two of the fundamental tenets of materialism as enunciated by Hugh Elliot: the denial of teleology and the denial of spirit. As for the first:

> The actual cosmos of pattern'd energy, including what we know as matter, is of a contour and nature absolutely impossible of realisation by the human brain; and the more we learn of it the more we perceive this circumstance. All we can say of it, is that it contains no visible central principle so like the physical brains of terrestrial mammals that we may reasonably attribute to it the purely terrestrial and biological phenomenon call'd *conscious purpose;* and that we form, even allowing for the most radical conceptions of the relativist, so insignificant and temporary a part of it (whether all space be infinite or curved, and transgalactic distances constant or variable, we know that within the bounds of our stellar system no relativistic circumstance can banish the approximate dimensions we recognise. The relative place of our solar system among the stars is as much a proximate reality as the relative positions of Providence, N.Y., and Chicago) that all notions of special relationships and names and destinies expressed in human conduct must necessarily be vestigial myths. (SL 2.261)

It can be seen here that Lovecraft's denial of teleology is tied to his belief in the cosmic insignificance of the human race: if the cosmos were in fact evolving in some definite direction under the guidance of a deity, then there might be cause for thinking that a "special relationship" exists between human beings and that deity, something Lovecraft emphatically denies. As for the second point:

> The truth is, that the discovery of matter's identity with energy—and of its consequent lack of vital intrinsic difference from empty space—is *an absolute coup de grace to the primitive and irresponsible myth of "spirit". For matter, it appears, really is exactly what "spirit" was always supposed to be.* Thus it is proved *that wandering energy always has a detectable form*—that if it doesn't take the form of waves or electron-streams, *it becomes matter itself;* and that the absence of matter or any other detectable energy-form indicates *not the presence of spirit, but the absence of anything whatever.* (SL 2.266–67)

This is really rather clever, and it may even be reasonably similar to the modified materialism adopted by Lovecraft's later philosophical mentors, Bertrand Russell and George Santayana.

Lovecraft had a little more difficulty with quantum theory, which was hailed initially (as it occasionally still is) as spelling the downfall of determinism and even of the basic laws of cause and effect. Lovecraft does not discuss it at all frequently, and he never seems to have understood it fully:

> What most physicists take the quantum theory, at present, to mean, is *not that any cosmic uncertainty exists* as to which of several courses a given reaction will take; but that in certain instances *no conceivable channel of informa-*

tion shall ever tell human beings which courses will be taken, or by what exact
course a certain observed result came about. (SL 3.228)

Lovecraft wants to render the "uncertainty" of quantum theory epistemo-
logical, not ontological: he wants to believe that it is our inability to predict
the behaviour of sub-atomic particles that results in uncertainty. This is in
fact incorrect, as Bertrand Russell has pointed out ("There are reasons for
believing that th[e] absence of complete determinism is not due to any in-
completeness in the theory, but is a genuine characteristic of small-scale
occurrences"); but Russell himself went on to say that "Phenomena involving large numbers of atoms remain deterministic" (Russell 23–24), something Lovecraft would have noted with relief. In terms of any ethical
consequences—specifically as regards free will—Lovecraft would also have
taken heart in J. L. Mackie's statement:

> . . . the crucial but so far unanswered question is whether there are pro-
> cesses by which random sub-atomic occurrences trigger larger scale neural
> processes and so introduce some randomness into them. There could be a
> forceful case for indeterminism about actions along these lines. But what it
> would give us instead of causal regularity is literally randomness, and this is
> not the kind of contra-causal freedom for which the moralists who dislike
> determinism are looking. (Mackie 220)

In the end Lovecraft managed to take relativity, quantum theory, and
even Heisenberg's indeterminacy principle in stride, maintaining the core
of his materialist thought at a time when many others were lapsing into
confused mysticism or wholesale scepticism. Recall that as late as 1933 he
is still referring to "the galling limitations of time, space, and natural law"
—by which he means the galling limitations of our consciousness to sur-
pass or confound the laws of entity, laws that present such an obstacle to
the imagination precisely because they are seen to be inflexible.

IV. The Fiction of Materialism

The relevance of Lovecraft's metaphysical and ethical thought to his
fiction may not be immediately obvious to the casual reader, for his tales
simply seem filled with outlandish monsters with unpronounceable names.
And yet, the manifesto of 1927 quoted at the beginning of this essay suggests that his entire fictional work is an outgrowth of his philosophy, and
that work can be seen to undergo significant changes of conception and
purpose as his philosophy itself evolved in the 1920s and 1930s. Moreover,
it was because Lovecraft was a materialist that he effected one of the bold-
est changes in the entire course of modern weird fiction, shifting the locus
of horror from the terrestrial to the cosmic. It is this that led Fritz Leiber
to call Lovecraft a "literary Copernicus."

Let us first notice that there is in Lovecraft's work a near-complete absence of the standard monsters of horror fiction—the ghost, the vampire, the werewolf. A ghost, with its suggestions of duality and spiritualism, would have been completely incomprehensible for Lovecraft—it is something to which he could not even extend aesthetic belief, let alone intellectual credence. The only vampire we find in Lovecraft may perhaps be the peculiar entity in "The Shunned House" (1924), and that story is worth examining for some highly provocative statements that already exhibit his coming to terms with advanced astrophysics. The critical passage is as follows:

> We were not . . . in any sense childishly superstitious, but scientific study and reflection had taught us that the known universe of three dimensions embraces the merest fraction of the whole cosmos of substance and energy. . . . To say that we actually believed in vampires or werewolves would be a carelessly inclusive statement. Rather must it be said that we were not prepared to deny the possibility of certain unfamiliar and unclassified modifications of vital force and attenuated matter; existing very infrequently in three-dimensional space because of its more intimate connexion with other spatial units, yet close enough to the boundary of our own to furnish us occasional manifestations which we, for lack of a proper vantage-point, may never hope to understand. . . .
>
> Such a thing was surely not a physical or biochemical impossibility in the light of a newer science which includes the theories of relativity and intra-atomic action. (MM 251–52)

Indeed, it is the very *materiality* of his monsters that is the trump card for the assertion of a unity between Lovecraft's philosophy and his fiction. The nature of their materiality is, to be sure, peculiar: Cthulhu, in "The Call of Cthulhu" (1926), is capable of reintegrating parts of itself that have been separated, and the fungi from Yuggoth in "The Whisperer in Darkness" (1930) may be able to travel faster than the speed of light (something Lovecraft knew to be impossible given the relativity theory). But there is nothing in his tales that stretches the limits of materialism beyond recognition. Indeed, the "vampire" in "The Shunned House" is completely dispatched by the use of hydrochloric acid, not by a cross and stake. Of course, in order for Lovecraft to receive the imaginative liberation he sought from weird fiction, his entities or phenomena *did* have to defy "natural law" in some fashion; if they didn't, the tale would not be *weird* but merely mundane. As Lovecraft stated in a discussion of Faulkner's tale of necrophilia, "A Rose for Emily":

> Manifestly, this is a dark and horrible thing which *could* happen, whereas the crux of a *weird* tale is something which *could not possibly happen*. If any unexpected advance of physics, chemistry, or biology were to indicate the *possibility* of any phenomena related by the weird tale, that particular set of phenomena would cease to be *weird* in the ultimate sense because

it would become surrounded by a different set of emotions. It would no longer represent imaginative liberation, because it would no longer indicate a suspension or violation of the natural laws against whose universal dominance our fancies rebel. (SL 3.434)

This is why, from his earliest to his latest fiction, Lovecraft observed the laws of materialism except in one particular direction where a "violation" seems to occur, as in Cthulhu's reintegration of himself. This became a conscious principle in his later years:

> The time has come when the normal revolt against time, space, and matter must assume a form not overtly incompatible with what is known of reality—when it must be gratified by images forming *supplements* rather than *contradictions* of the visible and mensurable universe. And what, if not a form of *non-supernatural cosmic art,* is to pacify this sense of revolt—as well as gratify the cognate sense of curiosity? (SL 3.295–96)

Lovecraft employed such "supplements" by creating entities that emerge from the depths of cosmic space (where natural laws may be very different from those governing our planet) or by setting his tales in geographically remote areas, where disproof is difficult. The very first tale of Lovecraft's mature period, "Dagon" (1917), is of the latter sort. The strange fishlike entity encountered by the narrator after the anomalous upheaval of a land mass in the middle of the Pacific clearly anticipates the emergence of Cthulhu from the depths of his sunken city R'lyeh in "The Call of Cthulhu"; but the palpable materialism of the creature is stressed at every turn. Later tales are set in the wilds of rural Massachusetts ("The Colour out of Space" [1927], "The Dunwich Horror" [1928]) or Vermont ("The Whisperer in Darkness"), in the Antarctic (*At the Mountains of Madness*), or in the Australian desert ("The Shadow out of Time" [1934–35]). But with exploration continuing unabated during Lovecraft's maturity (he speaks ominously of what the "Starkweather-Moore Expedition" [MM 5] may unearth in the Antarctic, and the whole of *At the Mountains of Madness* is a warning against such unwholesome curiosity), the hitherto unknown corners of this planet were slowly disappearing; so that Lovecraft had no option but to transfer the origin of his entities to the boundless depths of space. In so doing, he perhaps accidentally but very powerfully effected a union between the horror tale and the emerging genre of science fiction.

Cosmicism is certainly the hallmark of Lovecraft's fiction, but this feature manifests itself in many different ways in tales both early and late. Recall his statement of 1923 that "only a cynic can create horror"; this sort of cynicism, shading at times into actual misanthropy, may be the source of a celebrated utterance of 1921, when Lovecraft defended himself against charges that he did not write about "ordinary people" in his stories:

I could not write about "ordinary people" because I am not in the least interested in them. Man's relations to man do not captivate my fancy. It is man's relation to the cosmos—to the unknown—which alone arouses in me the spark of creative imagination. The humanocentric pose is impossible to me, for I cannot acquire the primitive myopia which magnifies the earth and ignores the background. (MW 155)

This is a position that, with some modifications, remained fixed throughout his literary career, and in itself it constitutes a defence against the accusations of many critics that Lovecraft is incapable of drawing "real" characters. In the first place, he had no interest in such people ("Individuals are all momentary trifles bound from a common nothingness toward another common nothingness" [SL 5.19]); in the second place, characters who become too "real" or distinctive will actually militate against the perception of the vastness of the cosmos that was his aim. All Lovecraft seeks from his characters is that they be *representative:* that they allow the reader to see events through their eyes, so as to create a genuine and powerful sensation of the "violation of natural law." We cannot be concerned about their individual fates, for in the later stories it is the fate of the entire human race, the entire planet, or even the entire cosmos that is in question. It is also critical for Lovecraft's narrators to be, on the whole, intelligent and rational men (and they are all men): if these people can be convinced that something bizarre has happened, then how can the reader refrain from being convinced? It is for this reason that the narrator of "The Call of Cthulhu" notes toward the end of the tale: "My attitude was still one of absolute materialism, *as I wish it still were*" (DH 144). Here again one should not assume that it is Lovecraft who is renouncing his materialism: rather, the fact that the narrator cannot encompass Cthulhu within his materialistic scheme must mean that some awful suspension of what we know of the laws of nature has taken place.

Some of Lovecraft's misanthropy remained to the end of his life, and it emerges pungently in some of his tales. He is endlessly fond of postulating an ignominious origin of the human race: in *At the Mountains of Madness* the Old Ones—huge barrel-shaped entities from the depths of space who colonized our planet eons ago—appear to have created all earth life (including human beings) "as jest or mistake" (MM 22). When the narrators explore the millennia-abandoned city of the Old Ones in the Antarctic, they find bas-reliefs supplying a detailed history of the alien race on this planet; at one point they remark: "It interested us to see in some of the very last and most decadent sculptures a shambling primitive mammal, used sometimes for food and sometimes as an amusing buffoon by the land dwellers, whose vaguely simian and human foreshadowings were unmistakable" (MM 65). This is probably one of the most fiercely cynical and misanthropic utterances ever made: the degradation of humanity can go no further. In "The Shadow over Innsmouth" (1931) it is suggested that we are ultimately related to the loathsome fish-frogs that populate that sinister New England backwater; as Zadok Allen tells the narrator: "'Seems that human folks has got a kind o' relation to sech water-beasts—that everything alive came aout o' the water onct, an' only needs a little change to go back agin'" (DH 331). Here again the guiding principle is the utter decimation of human self-importance by the attribution of a grotesque or contemptible origin of our species.

Lovecraft rarely passes up an opportunity to diminish human achievements. In many tales it is suggested that all the accomplishments of human civilisation are as nothing when gauged against the incalculably greater works of the alien civilisations that have occupied—and will in the future, after humanity's demise, occupy—the planet. In "The Shadow out of Time" there is a hint that all the great geniuses of human history were really the result of a process of mind-exchange with a "Great Race" inconceivably superior to us in intellect. When the narrator of this tale stumbles upon the archives of the Great Race, where repose the histories of all the varied entities throughout the universe, the narrator's account lies in the "lowest or vertebrate level" (DH 396). Here not only humanity but nearly all earthly life is seen to occupy a derisively inferior status in the realm of cosmic entity.

Those of Lovecraft's alien races who still inhabit the dark corners of our planet are not cowering in fear of humanity; indeed, they are allowing *us* to dwell on this planet by *their* sufferance. Of the fungi from Yuggoth in "The Whisperer in Darkness" it is said: "They could easily conquer the earth, but have not tried to so far because they have not needed to. They would rather leave things as they are to save bother" (DH 218). It is not even worth their while to destroy us. The hybrid entities of "The Shadow over Innsmouth" feel superiority to human beings: "They seemed sullenly banded together in some sort of fellowship and understanding—despising the world as if they had access to other and preferable spheres of entity" (DH 321). And Zadok Allen lets us know of their power: "'They cud wipe aout the hull brood o' humans ef they was willin' to bother'" (DH 331).

Even when Lovecraft modified his misanthropy into "indifferentism," a certain anti-humanist bias remained: his canonical statement of 1927 still refers to "a negligible and temporary race called mankind." We can finally address that statement and its manifold implications. On the surface, Lovecraft is simply noting that alien entities, if they are said to have emerged from the cosmic void, should not have human attributes. This seems to us unexceptionable, but we must recall that Lovecraft was battling against a tidal wave of naive science fiction of the "space opera" type that was achieving widespread publication in the pulp magazines. As he remarked in "Some Notes on Interplanetary Fiction" (1935): "The human-like aspect, psychology, and proper names commonly attributed to other-planetarians by the bulk of cheap authors is at once hilarious and pathetic" (MW 121). The absurdity of naming an entity "Cthulhu" vanishes when placed in this perspective; it is a name that, as Lovecraft frequented noted

in letters, "was invented by beings whose vocal organs were not like man's
. . . *hence could never be uttered perfectly by human throats"* (SL 5.10–11). Why
should such an extraterrestrial entity have a humanoid name? Such names
as Yog-Sothoth, Azathoth, and Nyarlathotep are less exotic, and their
roots in Arabic, Egyptian, and other languages has been traced; but this
does not mean that these entities are Arabic or Egyptian, but rather that
their names were set down in this approximate fashion by ancient Arabic
and Egyptian scholars such as Abdul Alhazred, author of the *Necronomicon.*
Lovecraft takes extraordinary care in nomenclature, a care he learnt from
his mentor Lord Dunsany.

But what Lovecraft is really claiming in his statement of 1927 is a sort of
moral independence of his alien entities from any sort of human psychology
or motivation. They cannot—or at least need not be—motivated by "good
and evil, love and hate, and all such local attributes" of the human race. This
is why it is stated, in reference to the entity in "The Shunned House": "It
might be actively hostile, or it might be dictated merely by blind motives of
self-preservation" (MM 252). It is, however, not a contradiction for Lovecraft's character to add: "In any case such a monster must of necessity be in
our scheme of things an anomaly and an intruder, whose extirpation forms a
primary duty with every man not an enemy to the world's life, health, and
sanity" (MM 252). This is the human perspective on the matter: of course, in
"our scheme of things," we must destroy this entity, lest it destroy us; but
nothing is said about the moral superiority or inferiority of the entity in relation to human beings.

Similarly, what is it that Cthulhu actually wants when it emerges from
the waves? To be sure, his human followers foresee an overthrow of mankind upon Cthulhu's release:

> . . . then mankind would have become as the Great Old Ones; free and
> wild and beyond good and evil, with laws and morals thrown aside and all
> men shouting and killing and revelling in joy. Then the liberated Old Ones
> would teach them new ways to shout and kill and revel and enjoy them-
> selves, and all the earth would flame with a holocaust of ecstasy and free-
> dom. (DH 141)

But can these emotions be attributed to Cthulhu? This is doubtful, even
though the narrator, paraphrasing the account of an encounter with
Cthulhu by a hapless Norwegian sailor, states: "After vigintillions of years
great Cthulhu was loose again, and ravening for delight" (DH 152). But
there is no reason to believe that either the narrator or the sailor is correct
in attributing such motives to Cthulhu. Indeed, it should be remarked that
all the cult-followers of the alien entities in Lovecraft's fiction appear to be
on the whole misguided as to the nature and purpose of the creatures they
worship. In particular, they assume that such creatures are gods, when by
and large they appear to be simply extraterrestrials who have come into

contact with the earth and its denizens by accident. An entity like Azathoth, "that last amorphous blight of nethermost confusion which blasphemes and bubbles at the centre of all infinity" (MM 308), seems nothing more than a symbol for the unknowability of a boundless cosmos.

Lovecraft's most successful portrayal of an amoral entity—or, rather, an entity whose motivations human beings are wholly at a loss to fathom—is in his masterpiece of subtlety and atmosphere, "The Colour out of Space" (1927). This landmark tale of a creature—or perhaps a group of creatures—that comes to the earth when a meteorite lands in the property of a rustic Massachusetts farmer and slowly corrupts everything it encounters, is horrifying precisely because the entity exhibits none of the traits attributable to any sentient being on this planet or perhaps in the known universe. Consider the poignant dying utterance of Nahum Gardner, the farmer whose land and family is inexorably destroyed by this alien force:

> "'. . . the colour . . . it burns . . . cold an' wet, but it burns . . . it lived in the well . . . I seen it . . . a kind o' smoke . . . suckin' the life out of every-thing . . . it must a' come in that stone . . . pizened the whole place . . . dun't know what it wants . . . it beats down your mind an' then gits ye . . . burns ye up . . . can't git away . . . draws ye . . . ye know summ'at's comin', but 'tain't no use . . . it come from some place whar things ain't as they is here . . .'" (DH 71–72)

In the midst of frank admissions of the incomprehensibility of the entity's motives ("'dun't know what it wants'"), its paradoxical nature ("'cold an' wet, but it burns'"), and an awareness of its utterly non-mundane origin ("'it come from some place whar things ain't as they is here'"), Gardner can still not help pitiably anthropomorphising the creature, as does a character later on: "'it come from beyond, whar things ain't like they be here . . . now it's goin' home . . .'" (DH 77). The expression of these sentiments in the crude patois of rustics only augments the horror and the tragedy.

Alien entities in Lovecraft's later tales, curiously, seem more motivated by comprehensible—and reprehensible—human motives than these. There can hardly be a doubt that the monster in "The Dunwich Horror" is impelled by blind rage against the human race, and when Professor Henry Armitage dispatches the creature by implausibly muttering some sort or counter-incantation, he delivers a naive and bombastic moral lecture:

> "It was—well, it was mostly a kind of force that doesn't belong in our part of space; a kind of force that acts and grows and shapes itself by other laws than those of our sort of Nature. We have no business calling in such things from outside, and only very wicked people and very wicked cults ever try to." (DH 197)

The purport of this passage is perhaps subject to debate. I would very much like to see it, as Donald R. Burleson has, as a parody, but I have my doubts about the matter. Armitage is very similar in function to Dr. Willett of *The Case of Charles Dexter Ward* (1927), who utters a similar sort of moral catechism to Joseph Curwen. Curwen, who has devoted his life to the resurrection of the dead in order to drain whatever knowledge their "essential salts" may contain, remarks in defence of his actions: "'There is no evil to any in what I do, so long as I do it rightly'" (MM 181), an amusing appeal to moral relativism; but we are clearly meant to side with Willett on the matter, who notes harshly: "'Curwen, a man can't tamper with Nature beyond certain limits, and every horror you have woven will rise up to wipe you out'" (MM 233). This attribution of pure evil to Curwen may be plausible, in that Curwen is indeed a human being even if he has by sorcery far exceeded his rightful tenure on this planet; but the similar attribution to the "very wicked people and very wicked cults" who "called in" the Dunwich horror strains credulity. "The Dunwich Horror" is, indeed, in spite of its evident popularity with readers, one of Lovecraft's great failures in its clumsy moral didacticism and ludicrous use of white magic versus black magic; it is exactly the sort of pulpish tripe Lovecraft so despised in the pages of *Weird Tales.*

"The Whisperer in Darkness" is similarly troubled by a peculiar ambivalence in the portrayal of its alien entities. These creatures, the fungi from Yuggoth, have clearly come from the depths of space—indeed, Yuggoth (Pluto) is not even their place of origin but only their "main *immediate* abode" (DH 240). And yet, they seem strangely motivated by such conventional moral failings as violence and treachery. They engage in a furious—and somewhat comical—battle, involving guns and dogs, with Henry Wentworth Akeley, an isolated Vermont rustic who resists their attempts to remove his brain from his body and take it with them on vast cosmic voyagings. Then at one point Albert Wilmarth, who has been trying to assist Akeley through correspondence, receives a letter from Akeley stating that the hostilities are over and that he has become reconciled to his erstwhile foes.

> All that the Outer Ones wish of man is peace and non-molestation and an increasing intellectual rapport. This latter is absolutely necessary now that our inventions and devices are expanding our knowledge and motions, and making it more and more impossible for the Outer Ones' necessary outposts to exist *secretly* on this planet. The alien beings desire to know mankind more fully and to have a few of mankind's philosophic and scientific leaders know more about them. With such an exchange of knowledge all perils will pass, and a satisfactory *modus vivendi* be established. The very idea of any attempt to *enslave* or *degrade* mankind is ridiculous. (DH 239)

On the face of it this idea sounds perfectly rational; but, since this letter is not in fact written by Akeley but forged by one of the aliens, it is in reality a sort of slick attempt to pull the wool over Wilmarth's eyes to prevent him from disseminating information about the entities. The aliens, even though "their brain-capacity exceeds that of any other surviving life-form"

(DH 240), do not even seem very adept at forgery, as earlier they had sent a telegram to Wilmarth but misspelled Akeley's name (DH 232). "The Whisperer in Darkness" is still one of Lovecraft's great tales, full of a densely textured atmosphere derived from realistic but poetic descriptions of the dark woods of Vermont; but he does not appear to have been entirely clear on the motivations of his alien entities.

But with *At the Mountains of Madness* and "The Shadow out of Time" all such problems have passed. In both instances the extraterrestrial entities are *initially* presented as horrifying—although only from a human perspective, and only because of their extreme *difference* in appearance from human beings—but gradually they become, as it were, the "heroes" of the tale as opposed to entities still more alien than they. Who can forget that paean to the Old Ones delivered by the narrator after he has seen what a rich, flourishing civilisation they once had on the Antarctic, and understood that their prime motivation was a pure and disinterested pursuit of knowledge?

> Scientists to the last—what had they done that we would not have done in their place? God, what intelligence and persistence! What a facing of the incredible, just as those carven kinsmen and forbears had faced things only a little less incredible! Radiates, vegetables, monstrosities, starspawn—whatever they had been, they were men! (MM 96)

It certainly does not appear as if "men" are a "negligible and temporary race" here. In "The Shadow out of Time" the pattern is completed. The Great Race "had learned all things that ever were known or ever would be known on the earth" (DH 385); they are the supreme entities in the universe. It is true that, early in the tale, the narrator is filled with horror and loathing as he sees them in his dreams: "Their actions, though harmless, horrified me even more than their appearance—for it is not wholesome to watch monstrous objects doing what one had known only human beings to do" (DH 392). But this fear dissipates once the narrator learns that the Great Race does the things that only human beings are supposed to do—reading, writing, speaking, learning—far better than we.

Lovecraft's belittling of the human race might be called the negative side of his cosmicism; on the positive side he is capable of suggesting the vast gulfs of space and time as powerfully as any writer in the history of literature. Again *At the Mountains of Madness* and "The Shadow out of Time" are the two masterworks here, and the fact that both appeared in *Astounding Stories* shows what an exquisite union of horror and science fiction Lovecraft has accomplished in these lengthy tales. Indeed, length is one of their important features; for Lovecraft was among the first to realise the value of the novelette or short novel form for the expression of complex weird scenarios. Incredibly, his first draft of "The Shadow out of Time" was a mere sixteen pages (SL 5.71), and he rightly discarded this version in lieu of one approximately four times as long. What this length allows a writer like Lovecraft—who, let us recall, does not rely upon character but atmosphere to sustain a tale—is to develop the plot with enormous richness but without destroying that unity of effect which he, like Poe, felt essential to the short story. In both tales we have extensive discourses on the biology, history, and even politics of his alien species, as well as a compact history of the entire cosmos, beginning millions of years before humanity's emergence on this planet and continuing long after the human race shall have ceased to exist. Indeed, at one point the narrator of "The Shadow out of Time" writes harriedly: "What was hinted . . . of the fate of mankind produced such an effect on me that I will not set it down here" (DH 396). This single sentence casts such a cloud of doom upon the future of humanity that all our achievements seem trivial and futile.

V. Style

In conclusion I wish to address an issue that is not directly connected to the philosophy of Lovecraft's fiction, but one that has evidently led many critics to condemn his work out of hand. Edmund Wilson was among the first to dismiss Lovecraft's stories as "bad taste and bad art" (Wilson 47), largely because of his style. This criticism has, with little variation, been made on many occasions, and Jacques Barzun has referred to the "frequently portentous but unintelligible H. P. Lovecraft" (Barzun xxvi), a remark that unwittingly testifies to nothing more than Barzun's inability to understand Lovecraft.

There is no denying that Lovecraft evolved a very idiosyncratic style to express his horrific conceptions—a style that is a union of the stateliness of the eighteenth century ("I suppose I picked up my peculiar style from Addison, Steele, Johnson, and Gibbon" [SL 1.11]), the atmospheric floridity of Poe and Wilde (the latter a much ignored but very significant influence on Lovecraft's style as well as on his entire aesthetic theory), and the precision of nineteenth- and twentieth-century philosophic writing. But what is forgotten in all this is, firstly, that Lovecraft's style actually *works*—it is as appropriate to his subject-matter as any style can be—and, secondly, that his style *evolved* over the course of his life, so that it progressively became less archaic and less florid. Let us examine both these points in greater detail.

Lovecraft is frequently not given credit for being master, not slave, of his style. As Steven J. Mariconda has pointed out in two brilliant papers on Lovecraft's style,[4] such a coldly repertorial story as "Beyond the Wall of Sleep" (1919) actually preceded by three years the wildly—and intentionally—overwritten tale "The Hound" (1922), the latter so obviously a self-parody that it is remarkable how few critics have picked up on the fact. It is nevertheless true that in his writing up to 1926 Lovecraft did not always seem entirely in control, and his early work suffers not so much from shoddiness of style but the immaturity of his own temperament, brought on by reclusiveness, bookishness, and a general ignorance of the world. Such tales as "The Tomb" (1917) and "The Outsider" (1921) could indeed have been written by Poe—not only because of their archaic diction, but because they show almost no awareness that the twentieth century actually exists.

But, as in so many other ways, "The Call of Cthulhu" (1926) changes all this. The opening paragraph must be quoted not only for its restraint but for its subtle modulation of prose rhythm and its powerful manipulation of symbol and metaphor:

> The most merciful thing in the world, I think, is the inability of the human mind to correlate all its contents. We live on a placid island of ignorance in the midst of black seas of infinity, and it was not meant that we should voyage far. The sciences, each straining in its own direction, have hitherto harmed us little; but some day the piecing together of dissociated knowledge will open up such terrifying vistas of reality, and of our frightful position therein, that we shall either go mad from the revelation or flee from the deadly light into the peace and safety of a new dark age. (DH 125)

Several factors united in giving Lovecraft a new lease on his life and his work around this time. First, there was his ecstatic return to his native Providence, Rhode Island, in the spring of 1926 after two hellish years spent in New York, where he saw his brief marriage collapse and found himself unable to secure regular work. Perhaps more important, in late 1925 he had been asked by his friend W. Paul Cook to write a treatise on the horror tale for Cook's amateur magazine, *The Recluse;* Lovecraft immediately plunged into work, and the result is the masterful essay *Supernatural Horror in Literature* (1927). The virtues of this treatise speak for themselves: its unfailingly pithy and sympathetic analyses of the weird work of Poe, Hawthorne, Bierce, Machen, Dunsany, Blackwood, M. R. James, and a host of other writers; its important statements on the nature and function of the weird tale; and its clear delineation of the historical progression of this branch of literature. But the reading of all these weird classics gave a forceful impetus to Lovecraft's own work—not in the manner of transparent imitation, as he had done in the early 1920s in a group of generally undistinguished tales modelled after Lord Dunsany, but in terms of a finely honed awareness of the metaphysical and psychological bases for the weird tale and of its most skillful and artistic examples.

From "The Call of Cthulhu" onward, Lovecraft becomes an increasingly assured stylist, aside from curious lapses such as "The Dunwich Horror," "The Dreams in the Witch House" (1932), and "The Thing on the Doorstep" (1933), the latter two being among his most disappointing late stories. By this time, moreover, Lovecraft had evolved a clear theory of weird writing:

> In writing a weird story I always try very carefully to achieve the right mood and atmosphere, and place the emphasis where it belongs. One can-

not, except in immature pulp charlatan-fiction, present an account of impossible, improbable, or inconceivable phenomena as a commonplace narrative of objective acts and conventional emotions. Inconceivable events
and conditions have a special handicap to overcome, and this can be accomplished only through the maintenance of a careful realism in every
phase of the story *except* that touching on the one given marvel. This marvel must be treated very impressively and deliberately—with a careful emotional "build-up"—else it will seem flat and unconvincing. Being the
principal thing in the story, its mere existence should overshadow the characters and events. ("Notes on Writing Weird Fiction" [MW 115–16])

It may seem surprising that Lovecraft is promoting "realism," but in fact
realism—realism of landscape, realism in scientific detail, realism in terms
of human emotions toward the bizarre—is the foundation for his fiction.
But among his great gifts was an extremely sure sense of narrative pacing,
and it is this that leads to a passage toward the end of "The Call of
Cthulhu" that may appear overwritten but which in fact has been prepared
for by thirty pages of "careful emotional 'build-up'":

> The Thing cannot be described—there is no language for such abysms
> of shrieking and immemorial lunacy, such eldritch contradictions of all
> matter, force, and cosmic order. A mountain walked or stumbled. God!
> What wonder that across the earth a great architect went mad, and poor
> Wilcox raved with fever in that telepathic instant? The Thing of the idols,
> the green, sticky spawn of the stars, had awaked to claim his own. The
> stars were right again, and what an age-old cult had failed to do by design,
> a band of innocent sailors had done by accident. After vigintillions of years
> great Cthulhu was loose again, and ravening for delight. (DH 152)

One is at liberty to dislike things like this, but one cannot in fairness condemn them without an awareness of Lovecraft's purpose and of the context in which they are placed.

The study of H. P. Lovecraft—his life, his work, and his thought—has of
late been burgeoning; but it has largely taken place away from the academic
arena. The best work on Lovecraft continues to be written by independent
scholars or enthusiasts, most of whom have emerged from the realm of science fiction and fantasy fandom. Work of this sort has its limitations—many
such scholars do not appear as thoroughly versed in critical method as one
would like—but for the time being Lovecraft's fate rests in their hands.[5]
One of the great difficulties in understanding Lovecraft is the sheer
quantity of ancillary material that has built up around him—letters, essays,
poetry, memoirs and criticism from as early as 1915 to the present day—
much of which has been published in relatively obscure sources and by spe-
cialty publishers largely outside the academic community. Even if we ac-
knowledge that Lovecraft's fiction is, in the short term, the primary basis

for his reputation (I think, however, that a case could be made for his letters as his greatest achievement), much valuable insight can be gained from access to this ancillary material, in particular his letters. It is largely the ignorance of his letters, and the complex intellect they reveal, that has led to many academics' hasty dismissal of Lovecraft as a pulp hack. Even a casual reading of the letters will show that Lovecraft had a carefully evolved philosophy, a scorn of the pulp magazines in which he was forced to publish, and a very clear idea of his motives in writing weird fiction. Lovecraft is, indeed, one of the most articulate spokesmen for the weird tale as a distinctive art form, and few have written more poignantly on the subject than he:

> The imaginative writer devotes himself to art in its most essential sense. . . . He is a painter of moods and mind-pictures—a capturer and amplifier of elusive dreams and fancies—a voyager into those unheard-of lands which are glimpsed through the veil of actuality but rarely, and only by the most sensitive. . . . Pleasure to me is wonder—the unexplored, the unexpected, the thing that is hidden and the changeless thing that lurks behind superficial mutability. To trace the remote in the immediate; the eternal in the ephemeral; the past in the present; the infinite in the finite; these are to me the springs of delight and beauty. (MW 148–155)

Notes

1. In this article I have intentionally avoided any discussion of Lovecraft's political philosophy, not only because it is extremely complex—it underwent more radical changes over the course of his life than any other aspect of his thought—but because it is not intimately related to his metaphysics and ethics, which are what I wish to focus on here. A political analysis, in particular dealing with the racialist element in Lovecraft's fiction, would be very welcome. For some guidance, see my chapter on Lovecraft in *The Weird Tale* (Austin: University of Texas Press, 1990), pp. 214–28, and my lengthier philosophical study, *H. P. Lovecraft: The Decline of the West* (Mercer Island, WA: Starmont House, 1990; rpt. Berkeley Heights, NJ: Wildside Press, 2001).

2. "Clusters and Nebulae: Part II," *Asheville Gazette-News*, 6 April 1915.

3. Actually, this is a series of letter excerpts to his future wife, Sonia H. Greene.

4. "H. P. Lovecraft: Consummate Prose Stylist" and "Notes on the Prose Realism of H. P. Lovecraft," both included in Mariconda's *On the Emergence of "Cthulhu" and Other Observations* (West Warwick, RI: Necronomicon Press, 1995).

5. Some of this material is at last becoming available to an academic audience; see Donald R. Burleson's *Lovecraft: Disturbing the Universe* (Lexington: The University Press of Kentucky, 1990) and *An Epicure in the Terrible: A Centennial Anthology of Essays in Honor of H. P. Lovecraft*, ed. David E. Schultz and S. T. Joshi (Rutherford, NJ: Fairleigh Dickinson University Press, 1991).

Frank Belknap Long: Things from the Sea

The precocious weird fiction of Frank Belknap Long (his first mature story was published just prior to his nineteenth birthday, and his first professionally published tale appeared when he was twenty-three) merits study from a variety of perspectives. Long (1901–1994) has laboured far too long under the shadow of his friend H. P. Lovecraft, but it becomes evident when reading his early work that Lovecraft himself would never have been so taken with Long had the latter not independently exhibited abundant talent as a fiction writer and poet, as well as a provocative thinker who could hold his own in philosophical debate. The bulk of Long's work in the first two decades of his career (1920–39), which will be studied here, is by no means influenced by Lovecraft, and in a few cases may itself have influenced Lovecraft's own tales.

From the beginning Long wished to tackle "big" issues in his work. Not content merely to write a stirring tale of adventure or of the supernatural, he infused his tales with a *moral* vision that commands attention. Even so relatively crude a work as "Dr. Whitlock's Price" (*United Amateur*, March 1920) transcends the hackneyed "mad scientist" trope by its display of the amoralism to which a fanatical pursuit of scientific enquiry can descend. Dr Whitlock, relentlessly seeking a formula to effect the regeneration of dead cells, kills many dogs in the course of his work, but remarks blandly to his assistant's objections: "What have we here? Just an ugly mass of protoplasm which I have managed to keep alive. A thousand such creatures sacrificed would be nothing" (EM 13). As Perry M. Grayson suggests (EM 11), this brief tale is quite likely to have been the immediate inspiration for Lovecraft's "Herbert West—Reanimator" (1921–22).

"The Eye Above the Mantel" (*United Amateur*, March 1921) already shows a significant advance in quality; and it too, in cadenced and stately prose, addresses a "big" issue—nothing less than the extinction of the human race:

> I know that we interested ourselves in evolution, and speculated upon the creature which would some day take man's place upon this tiny planet of ours. That such a creature would come, we had not the slightest doubt, and we merely discussed the *way* of his coming. (EM 16)

The powerful atmosphere of brooding cosmicism in this tale must be read to be appreciated; it is scarcely to be wondered that Lovecraft felt he had found a kindred spirit.

Other early tales of Long's take us to Egypt or, more generally, the Middle East. Long attributes this interest to his having read Flaubert's great historical novel about Carthage, *Salammbô*, three times before the age of fifteen (HT 108). In any event, this tendency is expressed in another sonorous prose-poem, "In the Tomb of Semenses" (*United Amateur*, November 1921), as well as in several early *Weird Tales* stories. "The Desert Lich" (*Weird Tales*, November 1924) has an Arabic setting, but is a non-supernatural *conte cruel* in which a man who had sold an unfaithful wife is forced to lie in a sarcophagus with her corpse. "The Dog-Eared God" (*Weird Tales*, November 1926) perhaps betrays the influence of Lovecraft's "Under the Pyramids" (the story ghostwritten for Harry Houdini, appearing in *Weird Tales* for May–June–July 1924 as "Imprisoned with the Pharaohs") in its rumination on the possible existence of actual entities corresponding to the hybrid gods of Egypt. The setting of "The Were-Snake" (*Weird Tales*, November 1925) is not specified, but its account of a "were-snake" in a temple of Ishtar suggests the Middle East. It is narrated with that arch flippancy which Lovecraft labelled "jauntiness" and condemned in the work of such writers as Robert Louis Stevenson and Oscar Wilde.

The celebrated "A Visitor from Egypt" (*Weird Tales*, September 1930) cannot exactly be considered one of Long's better tales: the notion that a man who visits a New England museum, purporting to be a famous archaeologist, is actually Osiris in disguise is unintentionally ludicrous. And yet, Dashiell Hammett chose the story for his landmark anthology, *Creeps by Night* (1931), so perhaps others have seen virtues in it that I do not.

As it is, a significant proportion of Long's early weird work focuses on the sea. Might his childhood reading of Jules Verne—he specifically cites *Twenty Thousand Leagues Under the Sea* (HT 13)—have had something to do with this? Given that Long was a lifelong New Yorker, the sea was never far from his horizon, and the frequent outings his family took to such beach resorts as Perth Amboy, New Jersey, and Cape Cod could only have strengthened his fascination with the briny deep.

"Death Waters" (*Weird Tales*, December 1924) is a landmark for Long in being a radical improvement in style and polish from his earlier work. The story takes place on a boat heading toward Central America, and one man tells the harrowing tale of how he and his companion once found themselves surrounded by thousands of seemingly harmless water-snakes, toads, and lizards. The companion died, but the other survived—"but my soul is dead!" (HT 48). "The Ocean Leech" (*Weird Tales*, January 1925) is still more powerful with its account of an amorphous monster that crawls aboard a ship:

> The thing upon the deck spread out and became broader at its base. It reared into the air a livid appendage encircled with monstrous pink suckers. We could see the suckers loathsomely at work in the moonlight, opening and closing and opening again. We were affected by a queer aromatic stench and we felt an overpowering sense of physical nausea. (HT 50)

As for "The Sea Thing" (*Weird Tales*, December 1925), this vampire tale—told in diary form—may now seem hackneyed, since we are today inundated with a veritable tidal wave of vampire fiction; but it remains a powerful piece of work. A crew that finds itself half starving on a long boat picks up a man, Francis de la Vega, whom they nickname de Vegie. The name turns out to be an unwitting pun, for he is hardly vegetarian in his tastes. The gradualness with which de Vegie is revealed to be a "sea-vampire"—one crewman is found "white as a squid's belly" (754), while another dies after de Vegie places the man's injured arm to his chest and drains him of blood—makes "The Sea Thing" an effective tale of cumulative horror.

"The Man with a Thousand Legs" (*Weird Tales*, August 1927) uses the documentary style—a succession of diary entries, "statements" to the police, and even a "Curious Manuscript Found in a Bottle" (RU 67)—to convey its effects. The science fictional premise of the story—a scientist's discovery that "etheric vibrations" (RU 68) can cause bodily change, such as the growth of new legs—is merely the occasion for some spectacularly powerful scenes of sea horror, as a man turns into an unthinkably bizarre monster:

> For a moment the thing simply towered and vibrated between the two boats and then it made for the cutter. It had at least a thousand legs and they waved loathsomely in the sunlight. It had a hooked beak and a great mouth that opened and closed and gulped, and it was larger than a whale. It was horribly, hideously large. It towered above the cutter, and in its swaying immensity it dwarfed the two boats and all the tangled shipping in the harbor. (RU 71)

Two stories from the early 1930s prove to be non-supernatural, but in ingenious ways. "The Red Fetish" (*Weird Tales*, January 1930) tells of two men, stranded on a desert island, who feel they have no choice but to swim to a neighbouring island, even though it is infested with cannibals. En route, one man is attacked and killed by sharks. The other, reaching the shore, is cornered by the cannibals and thinks his doom is sealed; but in fact the cannibals have come to honour him for bringing a trophy—the other man's head. "The Horror in the Hold" (*Weird Tales*, February 1932) is—like the earlier "Men Who Walk upon the Air" (*Weird Tales*, May 1925), an engagingly comic narrative about the poet François Villon—an historical tale set, apparently, in the Renaissance, when England and Spain were struggling for naval supremacy. Here the supernatural is suggested but then cleverly explained away: a Spaniard who has sneaked aboard an English ship, with plans to blow it up, is killed and eaten by some nameless monster with "great jaws," a "long, scaly body," and "webbed limbs" (264)—in other words, a crocodile.

All these tales seem merely anticipations or preparations for what may well be Long's greatest tale, "Second Night Out" (published in the October 1933 *Weird Tales* under the charmingly lurid title "The Black, Dead Thing"). In this account of a nameless, monkey-faced creature that haunts a ship sailing to Havana, we are treated to a feat of verbal witchery Long has rarely matched elsewhere, as a man on deck comes under the spell of the creature and suffers a wild hallucination:

> The *base* of the sane, familiar world vanished, was swallowed up. I sank down. Limitless gulfs seemed to open beneath me, and I was immersed, lost in a gray void. . . . I had the illusion of falling, of sinking helplessly through an eternity of space. It was as though the deck chair which supported me had passed into another dimension without ceasing to leave the familiar world—as though it floated simultaneously both in our three-dimensional world and in another world of alien, unknown dimensions. . . . I gazed through illimitable dark gulfs at continents and islands, lagoons, atolls, vast grey waterspouts. I sank down into the great deep. (HT 123–24)

The whole tale must be read to appreciate the finely modulated prose that carries the reader along from first sentence to last. Perhaps the only drawback is the utter lack of explanation as to the nature of the monkey-faced monster or the reason why it is haunting the hapless ship.

As the 1930s advanced, Long realised that he must broaden his fictional palette beyond the purely weird and venture into the realms of science fiction or science fantasy if he were to have a viable career as a pulp writer. And yet, although Long did indeed sell many stories to *Astounding* and other science fiction magazines, such a tendency had long been latent in his work. He had, he admits, read H. G. Wells in his youth (HT 14), so the shift to "scientifiction" was a natural one for him. Several tales of the later 1920s anticipate the powerful weird/science fiction amalgams of the next decade.

First on the agenda, of course, is "The Space-Eaters" (*Weird Tales*, July 1928). This story has perhaps gained unwelcome fame as the first "addition" to the "Cthulhu Mythos" by a writer other than Lovecraft. It bears (although not in its *Weird Tales* appearance and in several other reprints) an epigraph from John Dee's translation of the *Necronomicon*, and of course it features a character clearly based upon Lovecraft. And yet, it has passed relatively unnoticed that John Dee was first mentioned in "The Were-Snake," a tale that also cites Abdul Alhazred; so that Long's "addition" has a nebulous antecedent in his own work. To be honest, however, "The Space-Eaters" is a wild, histrionic, and rather ridiculous story. In its attempt to hint at Lovecraftian cosmicism—to "suggest a horror that is utterly unearthly; that makes itself felt in terms that have no counterparts on earth" (HT 62)—the story lapses into bathos in its idea of monsters eating their way through space. (A later story basically on the same idea—"The Brain-Eaters" [*Weird Tales*, July 1932]—is not much better.)

But then we come to "The Hounds of Tindalos" (*Weird Tales*, March 1929), which may perhaps betray the influence of Lovecraft's "Hypnos" and "The Call of Cthulhu" in various particulars, but which nonetheless remains a breathtakingly cosmic narrative. Halpin Chalmers, repudiating

Einstein and other modern astrophysicists, declares that it is possible to go back through time; and he does just that, seeing a vast panorama of history:

"I watch the migrations from Atlantis. I watch the migrations from Lemuria. I see the elder races—a strange horde of black dwarfs overwhelming Asia, and the Neanderthalers with lowered heads and bent knees ranging obscenely across Europe. I watch the Achaeans streaming into the Greek islands, and the crude beginnings of Hellenistic culture. I am in Athens and Pericles is young." (HT 98)

The tale in its latter sections becomes acutely chilling when Chalmers unwittingly arouses the Hounds of Tindalos ("They are hungry and athirst!" [HT 101]) who move through the angles of space to pursue him:

"All the evil in the universe was concentrated in their lean, hungry bodies. Or had they bodies? I saw them only for a moment; I cannot be certain. *But I heard them breathe.* Indescribably for a moment I felt their breath upon my face. They turned toward me and I fled screaming. In a single moment I fled screaming through time. I fled down quintillions of years." (HT 102)

(Parenthetically, it should be noted that Lovecraft's remark in "The Whisperer in Darkness"—"Do you know that Einstein is wrong, and that certain objects and forces *can* move with a velocity greater than that of light? With proper aid I expect to go backward and forward and time, and actually *see* and *feel* the earth of remote past and future epochs"—is clearly derived from Long's story.)

The Horror from the Hills (*Weird Tales,* January–February and March 1931) has similarly been neglected as a work in its own right because of its genesis: Long has incorporated Lovecraft's account of his great "Roman dream" of Halloween 1927 bodily into the text and has clearly written the novel around this vivid passage. And yet, it would be unfair to Long to say that he has merely padded Lovecraft's dream-account, for *The Horror from the Hills*—especially in its opening portions—is a stirring and engaging work. It picks up from "The Hounds of Tindalos" in introducing us to Algernon Harris, who succeeded "the late Halpin Chalmers" (HH 8) as curator of the Manhattan Museum of Fine Arts. The tale opens with anthropologist Clark Ulman returning from an expedition having discovered a strange entity—Chaugnar Faugn, the elephant god of Tsang. This detail—as well as a later mention of "the desert plateau of Tsang" (HH 15)—also betrays a Lovecraft influence, as Lovecraft notes that Long's original title for the work was *The Elephant God of Leng.*[1]

Early in the novel Long engages in a fascinating moral discourse, as a priest of Chaugnar Faugn proclaims to Ulman:

"Don't imagine for a moment that Chaugnar is a beneficent god. In the West you have evolved certain amiabilities of intercourse, to which you presumptuously attach cosmic significance, such as truth, kindliness, generosity, forbearance and honor, and you quaintly imagine that a god who is beyond good and evil and hence unamenable to your 'ethics' can not be omnipotent. "But how do you know that there *are* any beneficent laws in the universe, that the cosmos is friendly to man? Even in the mundane sphere of planetary life there is nothing to sustain such an hypothesis." (HH 22)

This is really a powerful argument that shatters the idea of an objectively "true" ethical system: if the universe cannot be seen as the product of a beneficent god, then the various moral stances we deem good—"truth, generosity," etc.—have no *ultimate* foundation in the nature of the cosmos.

The rest of the novel remains compelling as a weird/adventure story up to the time Harris and his colleagues, Dr Imbert and Roger Little, rather absurdly pursue Chaugnar Faugn with an "entropy machine" that will presumably send it back into the dimension from which it came. Actually, the machine does not destroy Chaugnar, but sends it back in time, and there is always the possibility that it will return. That return (like that of Cthulhu) "will be presaged in dreams" (HH 99), but for the time being humanity is safe.

The Horror from the Hills is an able venture. As a "Cthulhu Mythos" novel (if in fact it is that) it is fully equal to Donald Wandrei's *The Web of Easter Island* (written in 1932, a few years after Long's) and surpassed only by Colin Wilson's *The Mind Parasites* (1967). And it shows how Long can use "scientifiction" for the purposes of moral rumination, something we shall see dominating his later tales to an increasing degree.

Two stories—"The Malignant Invader" (*Weird Tales*, January 1932) and "In the Lair of the Space Monsters" (*Strange Tales*, October 1932)—are entertaining science fiction adventure tales, but nothing more. Long hits his stride, however, with "The Body Masters" (*Weird Tales*, February 1935), the first of several clearly science fictional tales that were nevertheless published in *Weird Tales*. This account of female "Mechanical Companions" that are designed to satisfy "tired and despondent husbands" (8) boldly probes issues that we are grappling with today. The story takes place in the far future, when divorce and, consequently, jealousy are theoretically abolished. A modern reader would be excused for believing that Long is an unthinking chauvinist for seeming to condone the existence of such Mechanical Companions only for men; and predictably enough, one man falls in love with his companion and prefers her to his wife. But Long has a twist in store: the man is outraged when he finds that his wife has taken up a male Mechanical Companion for herself. A dialogue toward the end perfectly encapsulates the core of the story:

> V67 cursed his wife's lack of erudition. "The new male Companions are exactly like the abominable gigolos of the ancient world," he muttered fiercely. "A more despicable type of parasite never existed."
>
> "But the Dictator of Emotion has announced that Mechanical Companions are perfectly respectable," pleaded his wife, in desperation.

V67 looked at her. His eyes were destitute of compassion. "He was speaking of the female Companions," he said. "That sort of thing is all right for a man."

"It's a strange rule that doesn't work both ways," said the wife, in a despairing tone. (11–12)

And yet, the true thrust of the story is not so much equality of the sexes as freedom of thought and behaviour. The bland narrative voice claims to contrast the enlightened present with the primitivism of the twentieth century, but the mention of such things as a "Dictator of Emotional Arts" (5) and a "Gland Surgeon" (3) who can manipulate one's emotions make it clear that the people of the future have relinquished their emotional independence for very dubious rewards.

"Giants in the Sky" (*Weird Tales*, August 1939) is not quite as powerful, but is an affecting tale. Here two meteorologists, a man and a woman, who are skiing in Switzerland are appalled to find that the sun has changed to an anomalous triangular shape. It turns out that cosmically vast giants from the planet Icurus have snared the entire solar system, removed the sun, and substituted a "metatom" in its place. They capture the female meteorologist for the purpose of studying her, but are then astounded when her companion launches a spacecraft to rescue her. The thrust of the story is a contrast between the excessively cerebral behaviour of the giants with the fully developed emotional capacity of human beings.

This point is made in a different way in another story, "Escape from Tomorrow" (*Weird Tales*, December 1939). Here a strange entity called a "thought-plasm" offers a tart criticism of the society of the future, specifically the role of science at a time when "Controllers" have harnessed the entire human race and suppressed all genuine emotion and ecstasy. The thought-plasm denies that he hates science:

"On the contrary. . . . I believe that Science is the hope of your world. It's just that you've let it get into the hands of the wrong people. The dull, stupid, beauty-hating people. The dry-as-dust people and not—well, poets, artists, dancers, lovers." (ET 19)

Later the entity declares pungently:

"But the controllers enslaved you. They made you ashamed of beauty, ashamed of yourself. Being dull, stern, pleasure-hating men and women, they conditioned your reflexes until you were made to feel that Science was an end in itself. You were made to feel that stern renunciation was more desirable than the enrichment of human life through avenues of shared ecstasy and creative leisure." (ET 19)

This paragraph could stand as the leitmotif of Long's entire science fiction work, and perhaps his work as a whole. He himself went through a succession of enthusiasms in his youth—nineteenth-century French poetry, the

Italian Renaissance, Anglo-Catholicism, even Bolshevism—but in each of them his zeal for knowledge was matched with a passion for emotional ecstasy. Even during his Bolshevist phase of the 1930s, he clearly cast a dubious eye on totalitarianism or any attempt by the state to suppress natural human emotions; and he found in the imaginative freedom of science fiction a potent weapon to express his vision of life and society.

Of course, Long did not abandon the purely supernatural tale in the 1930s. "The Dark Beasts" (*Marvel Tales*, July–August 1934) is a seemingly simple tale of a man who kills the frogs that infest his farm but is later avenged by them; but it gains interest in being told from the point of view of the man's somewhat retarded son Peter. Lovecraft's comment on the story is of some interest:

> I thought it excellent—one of his best *recent* efforts—because of the restrained, brooding atmosphere of menace, & because of the absence of the pseudo-sophisticated snickering irony with which Belknap spoils so many of his tales. The one great fault was the excessive amount of soliloquy attributed to the idiot boy. It was a clumsy, amateurish device to have so much of the explanation of precedent events concentrated in this soliloquy. All this explanatory preparation ought to have been introduced imperceptibly in other places—for no soliloquiser—idiot or not—would ever recapitulate a whole chain of events like that. Also—the *poetic* reflections toward the end of the idiot's soliloquy are wholly out of keeping with the character of a rural nitwit.[2]

Actually, it is possible to be more charitable to Long. The boy Peter's reflections do seem to emerge naturally from his pondering of the situation in which he finds himself, and even his supposedly "poetic" remarks toward the end are still narrated in an artlessly simple manner ("If I got a chance to live forever I wouldn't come back. I'd go walkin' on forever, just happy in the thought that I could see the green grass and smell the wet earth and have someone lovin' me all the time" [HT 137–38]) fully in keeping with his character. Long may well have been influenced by Faulkner's *The Sound and the Fury* (1929), in which a central episode is narrated in a mesmerising stream-of-consciousness manner by the "idiot" Benjy Compson.

Long was one of the few writers to make the transition from *Weird Tales* to John W. Campbell's *Unknown*. His first story for Campbell, "Dark Vision" (*Unknown*, March 1939), is an indisputable masterwork. This is a chilling tale of a man who suffers an accident in an electrical power plant and subsequently gains the unwanted power to probe other people's subconscious thoughts. Those thoughts are not pleasant ones:

> It seemed to him that the people about him were all thinking abnormally. He could sense their thoughts beating in upon him. Thoughts of anger, greed and hate, thoughts of primal malice, of passion that was as unregenerate as a basilisk, as coldly merciless as the dark night of space.

> Thoughts of murderous egotism and revenge, and little, vagrant thoughts repulsive in their childishness, pettiness and spite. The little thoughts were perhaps the worst. Little irrelevant vagaries that insulted the dignity of man. (HT 159)

It is later explained, in a Freudian manner, that these thoughts are so repulsive because the subconscious is the haven of our darkest thoughts, normally suppressed by the "censor" of our conscious minds.

Other stories of the period—"The Creeper in Darkness" (*Strange Stories,* April 1939), about a man plagued by a hideous familiar that attaches itself to him; "The Elemental" (*Unknown,* July 1939), about a man possessed by an elemental—are perhaps slighter, but they set the stage for "Johnny on the Spot" (*Unknown,* December 1939), which in well under a thousand words carries as much of a punch as tales ten times as long. If in many stories Long has fused the weird with science fiction, here he has effected an amalgam of the hard-boiled detective tale with the supernatural. The first-person narrator seems merely some sort of criminal who, in typical tough-guy language, appears to speak off the cuff of his varied nefarious activities; but gradually, with an access of horror, the reader realises that this individual is none other than Death. The story must be read for its impact to be properly felt; and its final paragraph can only be quoted:

> Maybe you'll meet me sometime in a crowd. But you won't recognize me because I take color from my surroundings. I am always fleeing from what I have to do. I am a Johnny on the spot. But in the end—in the end I meet up with practically everyone. (225)

It is somewhat arbitrary to end our study of Frank Long's weird fiction at 1939, for he continued publishing in *Unknown* and other weird and science fiction magazines, and he himself maintained that such late stories as "Cottage Tenant" (*Fantastic,* April 1975) and "Dark Awakening" (in *New Tales of the Cthulhu Mythos* [1980]) were far superior to his earlier tales. Certainly, these later tales have their virtues, but the above remarks should be sufficient to suggest the depth, richness, and variety of Long's work in the realm of the weird, and to hope that both his short stories and his novels continue to come under further scrutiny so that his legacy to the field can be properly assessed. Long, both as man and writer, has been obscured under Lovecraft's shadow, and even if his emergence into the light occurs posthumously, it will not have occurred too late.

Notes

1. H. P. Lovecraft to August Derleth, [c. February 1930] (ms., State Historical Society of Wisconsin).

2. H. P. Lovecraft to Duane W. Rimel, 10 August 1934 (ms., John Hay Library).

A Literary Tutelage: Robert Bloch and H. P. Lovecraft

R obert Bloch (1917–1994) has never made any secret of his literary and personal debt to H. P. Lovecraft. Bloch corresponded with Lovecraft for the last four years of the latter's life, and received invaluable assistance and advice from the elder writer in the craft of weird fiction. Only now, however, are we able to probe the details of this literary tutelage, with the nearly simultaneous publication of Lovecraft's *Letters to Robert Bloch* (1993) and an augmented edition of Bloch's collection of Lovecraftian pastiches, *Mysteries of the Worm* (1993). These documents make two things very evident: first, that Bloch—who first wrote to Lovecraft when he was sixteen, had his first story professionally published when he was seventeen, and died at the age of seventy-seven a revered figure in the field, just as Lovecraft had been—quickly evolved into a skilful writer in the Lovecraftian tradition; and second, that this apprentice work is both intrinsically valuable and of consuming interest for its foreshadowing of Bloch's later and more distinguished work in the realm of psychological suspense.

Bloch first came in touch with Lovecraft in April 1933, and his first object was to read as much of Lovecraft's work as he had not previously found in magazines. To this end he asked his correspondent to lend him many tales; Lovecraft did so, supplying a list of all the tales he had written up to that time, several of which were still unpublished. In his very first letter to Bloch, however, Lovecraft himself asked his young correspondent whether he had written any weird work (L 7) and, if so, whether he might see samples of it. Bloch took up Lovecraft's offer in late April, sending him two short items, "The Gallows" and another work whose title is unknown.

Lovecraft's response to these pieces of juvenilia (which, along with a good many others Bloch sent to the Providence writer, do not survive) is typical: while praising them, he also gave helpful advice derived from his many years as both a critic and a practitioner of the weird tale:

> It was with the keenest interest & pleasure that I read your two brief horror-sketches; whose rhythm & atmospheric colouring convey a very genuine air of unholy immanence & nameless menace, & which strike me as promising in the very highest degree. I think you have managed to create a dark tension & apprehension of a sort all too seldom encountered in weird fiction, & believe that your gift for this atmosphere-weaving will serve you in good stead when you attempt longer & more intricately plotted pieces. . . . Of course, these productions are not free from the earmarks of youth. A critic might complain that the colouring is laid on too thickly—too much overt inculcation of horror as opposed to the *subtle, gradual suggestion of concealed horror* which actually raises fear to its highest

pitch. In later work you will probably be less disposed to pile on great numbers of horrific words (an early & scarcely-conquered habit of my own), but will seek rather to select a *few* words—whose precise position in the text, & whose deep associative power, will make them in effect more terrible than any barrage of monstrous adjectives, malign nouns, & unhallowed verbs. (L 10)

This is a litany that Lovecraft would repeat for at least another year; and although it took Bloch a little while to realise the wisdom of this caveat, he finally did so. Indeed, by the 1940s Bloch had already evolved that tight-lipped, blandly cynical style which would serve him well in his later crime fiction—fiction that, in its relentless emphasis on the psychology of aberrant individuals, is in many ways more potently horrifying than the adjective-choked supernaturalism of his early work.

And yet, Bloch was clearly fond of this thickly laid-on horror at this stage in his career, as indeed Lovecraft was at a corresponding age and for many years later. One gauge of this tendency was Bloch's relative fondness for the tales of Lovecraft's he was reading at this time. It is understandable that he would express enthusiasm for "The Outsider," "The Hound," and "The Lurking Fear," but remain relatively cool toward *At the Mountains of Madness* and "The Shadow over Innsmouth" (L 20), where Lovecraft was attempting to rein in his adjectives and write with more scientific precision and restrained suggestiveness. Although many of Bloch's own early tales do not survive, "The Laughter of a Ghoul"—read by Lovecraft in June 1933 (L 20) and published in the *Fantasy Fan* for December 1934—seems very representative of them: "Slithering secrets dwelt within the archaic avenues of the vast and sombre forest near my manor in the hills—secrets black and hideous, haunting and unspeakable, such as demonian presences mumble nightly in the aeon-dead abysses beyond the light of stars." What Lovecraft probably liked about work of this kind—even though he also recognised that an overuse of fevered prose resulted in unintended humour—was precisely its "atmosphere-weaving," a quality he (correctly) believed sadly lacking in most of the weird fiction published in the pulps. He continually excoriated the brisk, "cheerful" style of the average pulp product, in which spectacular defiances of natural law were regarded both by the characters and by the author with a bland casualness that is fatal to convincingness. Overcoloured as Bloch's early tales may have been, they at least were attempting to achieve an *emotional preparation* for the supernatural.

A few months later Lovecraft read a story of Bloch's entitled "The Grave." Here Lovecraft's advice was the need for clarity in *motivation*. Why would a grave-robber seek his booty in an ancient graveyard, since the skeletons would all have crumbled to dust? Also, how can a skeleton remain articulated after the flesh has fallen off? How were the tunnels leading from the grave dug? Lovecraft also criticises some psychological implausibilities in one character's behaviour. Bloch manifestly took all these recommendations to heart in the course of time.

Lovecraft read something entitled "The Feast" in late June 1933, remarking that it "forms a very clever union of the macabre & the comic" (L 21). It is not clear whether this is an early version of "The Feast in the Abbey," but Lovecraft in any case read that story in September; indeed, he supplied the title, since Bloch had evidently sent it to Lovecraft without one (L 35). This is, of course, Bloch's first published story in *Weird Tales* (it appeared in the January 1935 issue), although "The Secret in the Tomb" (*Weird Tales*, May 1935) had been accepted earlier, in July 1934 (L 50). Lovecraft read the latter tale as well, although apparently not before its acceptance. He did, however, recommend some minor corrections (L 52), which Bloch seems to have made.

Both these stories evince that fascination with the mythical books of the "Cthulhu Mythos" which would remain constant throughout Bloch's early work. It was in these tales, of course, that Bloch devised Ludvig Prinn's *Mysteries of the Worm*, and Lovecraft mentions other titles that were cited in an earlier draft of "The Secret in the Tomb" but later excised (Mazonides' *Black Spell of Saboth*, Petrus Averonius' *Compendium Daemonum*). In "The Suicide in the Study" (*Weird Tales*, June 1935) we find other such titles as "the Black Rites of mad Luveh-Keraph, priest of Bast, or Comte d'Erlette's ghastly *Cultes des Goules*" (M 19). Luveh-Keraph scarcely requires elucidation, save to note that this coinage appears to be Bloch's invention, not Lovecraft's. Some have thought that Bloch merely abstracted this from one of Lovecraft's letters, which frequently include whimsical signatures of this sort; but in fact Lovecraft uses the "Luveh-Keraph" signature for the first time only in April 1935 (L 65), a month after having read "The Suicide in the Study" (L 61). In other words, he picked up the usage from Bloch's story, as a sort of wry acknowledgement.

There is not much to say about these early tales, save that they may be marginally better than most of the other material appearing in *Weird Tales*. If nothing else, the verve of their adjective-laden prose and lurid incidents is engaging. "The Secret in the Tomb" is a preposterous story about a man who battles a skeleton in his ancestral tomb. "The Feast in the Abbey" (not included in *Mysteries of the Worm*) tells of cannibalism in a mediaeval monastery. "The Suicide in the Study" is perhaps the most interesting of the lot: a reprise of the Jekyll/Hyde theme, it tells of a man who believes that the good and evil sides of every individual are *"co-existent"* (M 20) and seeks to bring up his evil side from the depths of his personality. The story is hampered by a conventional conception of what constitutes good and evil; but the evil side, when it finally emerges, presents a loathsome sight:

> Out of the darkness nightmare came; stark, staring nightmare—a monstrous, hairy figure; huge, grotesque, simian—a hideous travesty of all

things human. It was black madness; slavering, mocking madness with little
red eyes of wisdom old and evil; leering snout and yellow fangs of grimac-
ing death. It was like a rotting, living skull upon the body of a black ape. It
was grisly and wicked, troglodytic and wise. (M 22)

Here evil is pictured as simultaneously subhuman (the Darwinian beast)
and somehow superhuman—"wise" and incapable of being controlled by
our "good" side.

The early story of Bloch's that has brought him the greatest celebrity for
its connexions with Lovecraft is "The Shambler from the Stars" (*Weird
Tales*, September 1935). Lovecraft mentions something called "The Shambler in the Night" in a letter of November 1934 (L 55); this may be an early
version of the story, although if so it is odd that Lovecraft makes no mention in his letter of its central feature—the fact that Lovecraft himself is a
character in the story. We all know the story of how "The Shambler from
the Stars" was provisionally accepted by Farnsworth Wright of *Weird Tales*,
who felt that Bloch needed to get Lovecraft's permission to kill him off (although Wright had evidently not felt a similar need when, years before,
Frank Belknap Long had done the same to Lovecraft in "The Space--
Eaters"), so that Lovecraft wrote his whimsical letter to Bloch in late April
1935 authorising him "to portray, murder, annihilate, disintegrate, transfig-
ure, metamorphose, or otherwise manhandle the undersigned in the tale entitled THE SHAMBLER FROM THE STARS" (L 67).

The critical issue about the story is not that it is a "contribution" to the
"Cthulhu Mythos" but that, like Long's tale, it makes Lovecraft a character,
and accordingly assists in the fostering of the Lovecraft legend—the legend of the gaunt, reclusive delver into occult mysteries. Of course, he is
never named, merely identified as a "mystic in New England" who was "a
writer of notable brilliance and wide reputation among the discriminating
few" (M 26–27). But even more interesting, perhaps, is how *Bloch himself*
has become a character in his own story. In its early parts Bloch presents a
sort of objective assessment of his own career as a writer up to that point,
finding much dissatisfaction in it:

> I wanted to write a real story, not the stereotyped, ephemeral sort of
> tale I turned out for the magazines, but a real work of art. The creation of
> such a masterpiece became my ideal. I was not a good writer, but that was
> not entirely due to my errors in mechanical style. It was, I felt, the fault of
> my subject matter. Vampires, werewolves, ghouls, mythological mon-
> sters—these things constituted material of little merit. Commonplace im-
> agery, ordinary adjectival treatment, and a prosaically anthropocentric point
> of view were the chief detriments to the production of a really good weird
> tale. (M 26)

This paragraph could have come directly out of Lovecraft's writings on the
subject, such as "Notes on Writing Weird Fiction" (1933). That last com-

ment about point of view seems to derive from a letter by Lovecraft to Bloch in June 1933, in which he remarks how he had once (in the "Eyrie" for March 1924) advised "having a story told from an unconventional & non-human angle," specifically a story "from the ghoul's or werewolf's point of view" (L 21); he goes on to remark that H. Warner Munn had attempted to embody this conception in "The Werewolf of Ponkert," but had botched the job because Munn's "sympathies were still with mankind—whereas I called for sympathies wholly dissociated from mankind & perhaps violently hostile to it" (L 21). This notion is not in fact present in "The Shambler from the Stars," but does find its way into "The Dark Demon."

Lovecraft's avowed sequel to Bloch's story—"The Haunter of the Dark," written in November 1935 and published in *Weird Tales* for December 1936—continues the fusion of the real and the imaginary in its portrayal of character. Here the protagonist, Robert Blake, is said to come (like Bloch) from Milwaukee (the address given in the story—620 East Knapp Street—was in fact Bloch's address), but the apartment he occupies on a visit to Providence is transparently Lovecraft's own dwelling at 66 College Street. Then again, the titles of the stories Blake is said to have written at this time—"The Burrower Beneath," "The Stairs in the Crypt," "Shaggai," "In the Vale of Pnath," and "The Feaster from the Stars" (DH 94)—form an exquisite union of elements found in both Bloch's and Lovecraft's stories. In early March 1935 Lovecraft had wryly remarked on Bloch's success in landing tales with titles like "The ——— in the ———" (LS 11); he echoes them in the above list, although his own tales very frequently have titles of this sort as well. At the end of "The Haunter of the Dark" Robert Blake is left a glassy-eyed corpse staring through a window—a somewhat more tasteful demise than that of the victim of "The Shambler from the Stars," who ends up torn to pieces by a nameless entity.

For "The Shambler from the Stars" Lovecraft devised the Latin title of *Mysteries of the Worm—De Vermis Mysteriis*—and claimed to have modified the narrator's statement of his ignorance of Latin, "since knowledge of elementary Latin is so universal" (L 65). And yet, the narrator's lack of knowledge of Latin is critical to the development of the plot, since it is precisely because he finds a Latin copy of *De Vermis Mysteriis*, which he is unable to read, that he feels the need to seek out his New England correspondent and show him the work. (Bloch's deficiencies in Latin make themselves all too evident in another title he devised, the nonsensical *Daemonolorum*, cited in "The Brood of Bubastis" [M 95] and elsewhere.)

"The Dark Demon" (*Weird Tales*, November 1936) is interesting in this context because it again displays Lovecraft as a character and, more important, becomes a parable for his early assistance to Bloch's literary development. Here the narrator testifies that he had come into contact with the writer Edgar Gordon, a "reclusive dreamer" (M 62) living in the same town.

They develop a warm correspondence and also meet in person: "What Edgar Gordon did for me in the next three years can never adequately be told. His able assistance, friendly criticism and kind encouragement finally succeeded in making a writer of sorts out of me, and after that our mutual interest formed an added bond between us" (M 62). Lovecraft does not seem to have read this tale prior to publication (L 84), but he warmly commends it; he makes no mention of the above tribute, but no doubt he saw clearly its import and was heartened by it. Although Lovecraft himself is mentioned by name elsewhere in the story (M 62), Gordon becomes a transparent Lovecraft figure in his bizarre dreams and the very strange work he begins writing as a result of it: the "stories [were] in first-person, but the narrator was not a *human being*" (M 64). Gordon, when pressed by the narrator as to where he is getting his ideas, makes cloudy references to a "Dark One," remarking: "He isn't a destroyer—merely a superior intelligence who wishes to gain mental rapport with human minds, so as to enable certain—ah—exchanges between humanity and Those beyond" (M 66). This idea is unquestionably derived from Lovecraft's "The Whisperer in Darkness," in which aliens from the depths of space wish to take the brains of selected human beings on fantastic cosmic voyagings.

The mention of dreams is interesting, since in August 1933 Lovecraft, commenting with amazement on Bloch's claim that he dreamed only twice a year, related a hideous dream in which some mediaeval soldiers attempt to hunt down a monstrous entity but to their horror see it meld insidiously with the body of their leader. Bloch claimed to be working on a story based upon this dream (see L 33), but apparently never completed it; it does not survive. He does, however, in "The Dark Demon" echo Lovecraft's scorn of conventional Freudian interpretations of dreams. Bloch's narrator remarks, "Gordon's fantasies were far from the ordinary Freudian sublimation or repression types" (M 63); Lovecraft in his letter had written: "I may add that all I know of dreams seems to contradict flatly the 'symbolism' theories of Freud. It may be that others, with less sheer phantasy filling their minds, have dreams of the Freudian sort; but it is very certain that I don't" (L 31).

For all Lovecraft's advice to Bloch, he does not seem to have done much actual revision of Bloch's work, as he did—many times unasked—with other young colleagues. In June 1933 Lovecraft remarks that "I added corrections here & there" to a story entitled "The Madness of Lucian Grey," which was accepted for publication by *Marvel Tales* but was never published and is now non-extant. A blurb in *Marvel Tales* described it as "a weird-fantasy story of an artist who was forced to paint a picture . . . and the frightful thing that came from it" (L 13n), which makes one immediately think of Lovecraft's "Pickman's Model." Lovecraft seems to have done much more extensive work in November 1933 on a story called "The Merman":

I have read "The Merman" with the keenest interest & pleasure, & am returning it with a few annotations & emendations. . . . My changes—the congested script of which I hope you can read—are of two sorts; simplifications of diffuse language in the interest of more direct & powerful expression, & attempts to make the emotional modulations more vivid, lifelike, & convincing at certain points where the narrative takes definite turns. (L 41)

But unfortunately this tale also does not survive.

If any extant work of Bloch's can be called a Lovecraft revision, it is "Satan's Servants," written in February 1935. Bloch comments that the story came back from Lovecraft "copiously annotated and corrected, together with a lengthy and exhaustive list of suggestions for revision" (S 117), and goes on to say that many of Lovecraft's additions are now undetectable, since they fused so well with his own style:

From the purely personal standpoint, I was often fascinated during the process of revision by the way in which certain interpolated sentences or phrases of Lovecraft's seemed to dovetail with my own work—for in 1935 I was quite consciously a disciple of what has since come to be known as the "Lovecraft school" of weird fiction. I doubt greatly if even the self-professed "Lovecraft scholar" can pick out his actual verbal contributions to the finished tale; most of the passages which would be identified as "pure Lovecraft" are my work; all of the sentences and bridges he added are of an incidental nature and merely supplement the text. (S 118)

And yet, it is not surprising that the original version of the story was rejected by Farnsworth Wright of *Weird Tales;* his comment as noted by Bloch—"that the plot-structure was too flimsy for the extended length of the narrative" (S 117)—is an accurate assessment of this overly long and unconvincing story.

"Satan's Servants" had initially been dedicated to Lovecraft, and after its rejection Bloch urged Lovecraft to collaborate on its revision; but, aside from whatever additions and corrections he made, Lovecraft bowed out of full-fledged collaboration. He did, however, have much to say on the need for historical accuracy in this tale of seventeenth-century New England, and he had other suggestions as to the pacing of the story. Bloch apparently did some revisions in 1949 for its publication in *Something about Cats,* but the story still labours under its excess verbiage and its rather comical ending: a pious Puritan, facing a mob of hundreds of devil-worshippers in a small Maine town, defeats them all by literally pounding them with a Bible! It is just as well that "Satan's Servants" lay in Bloch's files until resurrected as a literary curiosity.

It is with "The Faceless God" (*Weird Tales,* May 1936) that Bloch begins his twofold fascination with Egypt and with the Lovecraftian "god" Nyarlathotep. One of Bloch's earliest enquiries to Lovecraft was an explanation of some of the invented names and terms that appear in some of his tales. In regard to one such query Lovecraft responds in May 1933: "'Nyar-lathotep' is a horrible messenger of the evil gods to earth, who usually appears in human form" (L 11–12). Bloch, who in his early days was attempting pictorial art, actually drew a picture of Nyarlathotep, which Lovecraft charitably says "just fits my conception" (L 21).

The figure of Nyarlathotep is one of the most intriguing in Lovecraft—perhaps because it was never fully developed or coherently conceived. Nyarlathotep is commonly believed to be a shape-shifter—a view evidently derived from some random passages in *The Dream-Quest of Unknown Kadath*, especially where Nyarlathotep himself refers to "my thousand other forms" (MM 403). One gains the feeling, however, that this was a sort of makeshift excuse for Lovecraft to present Nyarlathotep in so many diverse guises in his work. Bloch could not have read the *Dream-Quest* (it was not typed or circulated in Lovecraft's lifetime), but he uses Nyarlathotep in very much the same way as Lovecraft; indeed, it could be said that Bloch has elaborated the conception more exhaustively than Lovecraft himself did.

It would be of interest to know which of Lovecraft's stories mentioning Nyarlathotep Bloch did in fact read. I see no evidence that he had at this time read the early prose-poem "Nyarlathotep" (1920), which had appeared only in amateur magazines; it is here that the connexion between Nyarlathotep and Egypt is explicitly made, and it is this connexion that Bloch develops. The prose-poem is in fact listed in the list of stories Lovecraft sent to Bloch in April 1933, but it is crossed off; and the subsequent letters do not suggest that Lovecraft ever lent Bloch the story. If Lovecraft had in fact sent the item, one imagines that he would not have had to "define" Nyarlathotep as he did in the letter in May. Nyarlathotep is otherwise very glancingly mentioned in "The Rats in the Walls" (1923), extensively cited in *The Dream-Quest of Unknown Kadath* (1926–27) (which Bloch did not read), and glancingly cited in "The Whisperer in Darkness" (1930) and "The Dreams in the Witch House" (1932).

In fact, Bloch probably derived most of his information on Nyarlathotep from "The Haunter of the Dark," the story Lovecraft wrote in November 1935 and dedicated to Bloch. Toward the end of the tale the character Robert Blake writes in his diary: "What am I afraid of? Is it not an avatar of Nyarlathotep, who in antique and shadowy Khem even took the form of man?" (DH 114). Here is the Egyptian connexion that Bloch picked up on. "The Faceless God" tells the story of the attempts of an evil Dr Stugatche[1] to unearth a statue of Nyarlathotep buried in the sands of Egypt, only to meet a fittingly horrible end. I am not clear why Bloch conceived of Nyarlathotep as faceless—a detail that perhaps inadvertently recalls Lovecraft's night-gaunts.

Bloch notes that his Egyptological ("or Egyptillogical") tales were "conscious attempts to move away from Lovecraft's literary turf" (M 255). How successful Bloch was, in this early period, in these attempts is debatable. He perhaps had not read—or did not know of Lovecraft's hand in—"Under the Pyramids" (the story published in *Weird Tales* as "Imprisoned with the Pharaohs" and attributed to Harry Houdini), and of course Nyarlathotep's Egyptian connexion had indeed been established by Lovecraft. But such a story as "The Opener of the Way" (*Weird Tales*, October 1936), while still perhaps somewhat Lovecraftian in style, does not employ Lovecraft's pantheon of invented deities but seeks to invest horror in the real gods of Egypt (in this case Anubis). "The Brood of Bubastis" (*Weird Tales*, March 1937) is very similar: aside from insignificant references to *De Vermis Mysteriis*, this tale is nothing but a story of the cat-goddess Bubastis, and involves the ingenious idea of an ancient Egyptian colony in England. Lovecraft read the story about two months before his death, noting: "Your Bubastis story is excellent, despite the dubious light in which it presents my beloved felidae" (L 87).

"The Secret of Sebek" (*Weird Tales*, November 1937)—a story probably written just after Lovecraft's death—is an interesting case. The story is set in New Orleans, and concerns the god Sebek, who has the head of a crocodile and the body of a man. A character sees such a figure in a costume ball and, thinking the man in disguise, attempts to pull off his crocodile mask—only to find that "I felt beneath my fingers, not a mask, but living flesh!" (M 129). The dominant influence on this story appears to be "Through the Gates of the Silver Key," which is likewise set in New Orleans and likewise concludes apocalyptically with a character who pulls off an actual mask from another character (Randolph Carter in the body of the extraterrestrial wizard Zkauba), finding a horribly alien countenance underneath. Again, only some random mentions of invented books make this a "Cthulhu Mythos" story.

"Fane of the Black Pharaoh" (*Weird Tales*, December 1937) is perhaps the most interesting of Bloch's Egyptian tales, both for its intrinsic effectiveness and for its connexions with Lovecraft. This is an entire story about the pharaoh Nephren-Ka. The name had been invented by Lovecraft, and is first cited in the early story "The Outsider" (one of Bloch's favourites): "Now I . . . play by day amongst the catacombs of Nephren-Ka in the sealed and unknown valley of Hadoth by the Nile" (DH 52). Lovecraft resurrects him in a single tantalising sentence in "The Haunter of the Dark": "The Pharaoh Nephren-Ka built around it [the Shining Trapezohedron] a temple with a windowless crypt, and did that which caused his name to be stricken from all monuments and records" (DH 106). Bloch elaborates upon this sentence, although departing somewhat from it. In "Fane of the Black Pharaoh" Nephren-Ka is rumoured to have been a worshipper of Nyarlathotep, and his "atrocious sacrifices" (M 134) caused him to be deposed. Then, hiding in a secret temple, Nephren-Ka is granted the gift of prophecy by Nyarlathotep and paints an enormous series of pic-

tures of the years and centuries to come. A modern explorer learns just
how much truth there is in this old fable.

"The Shadow from the Steeple" (*Weird Tales*, September 1950) simultaneously concludes the trilogy begun with "The Shambler from the Stars" and
"The Haunter of the Dark" and is Bloch's final word about Nyarlathotep. As
early as December 1936 Lovecraft wrote, ". . . I hope to see 'The Shadow in
the Steeple' when you get it written" (L 84); this is an early version of the
story, as Bloch notes (S 118–19), but for some reason he put it aside for
many years before resuming it. The story as we have it was either written or
revised around 1950, for it makes mention of Edmund Fiske's "fifteen-year
quest" (M 183) to discover the truth about the death of Robert Blake.

As in "The Dark Demon," both Bloch and Lovecraft become charac-
ters in the story—the latter explicitly and by name. The narrator notes:
"Blake had been a precocious adolescent interested in fantasy-writing, and
as such became a member of the 'Lovecraft circle'—a group of writers
maintaining correspondence with one another and with the late Howard
Phillips Lovecraft, of Providence" (M 180). Later it is said that "another
Milwaukee author" (M 181) had written a story about Nephren-Ka entitled
"Fane of the Black Pharaoh"! With somewhat questionable taste, Bloch
even incorporates Lovecraft's death into the fabric of the plot, noting that
Fiske had intended in early 1937 to visit Lovecraft and query him about
Blake's death, but that Lovecraft's own passing foiled these plans. Bloch
has written on many occasions of the shock he felt at hearing of Lovecraft's death, and the narrator of "The Shadow from the Steeple" remarks
that Lovecraft's "unexpected passing plunged Fiske into a period of mental
despondency from which he was slow to recover" (M 185); but I still wonder whether it was proper for Bloch to make fictional use of both Lovecraft's life and his demise in this fashion. In any event, it transpires that Dr
Dexter—the "superstitious" (DH 114) physician who had hurled the Shining Trapezohedron into the river after Blake's death—is Nyarlathotep
himself, a clever twist on Lovecraft's premise. The story also effectively
incorporates features from the sonnet "Nyarlathotep" from Lovecraft's
Fungi from Yuggoth (1929–30), which says that ". . . at last from inner Egypt
came / The strange dark one to whom the fellahs bowed" and that "wild
beasts followed him and licked his hands."

Bloch's Egyptian tales may have been an attempt to escape partially
from Lovecraft's influence, but we have seen that they were only indiffer-
ently successful in that objective, although many of them are quite successful as stories. Bloch was so steeped in Lovecraft's work at this time that
many borrowings may well have been unconscious. Hence something so
slight as one character's observation in "The Grinning Ghoul" (*Weird Tales*,
June 1936) that there is no dust on the stairs of a crypt (M 57) may be an
echo of the similarly dust-free corridors of the ancient city in *At the Mountains of Madness*, swept clean by the passing of a shoggoth. "The Creeper in

the Crypt" (*Weird Tales*, July 1937) is set in Arkham and makes clear allusion to Lovecraft's "The Dreams in the Witch House"; but it may also betray the influence of "The Shadow over Innsmouth" (the narrator, after his experiences, seeks aid from the federal government to suppress the horror), and also perhaps of "The Terrible Old Man," as the tale involves a Polish and an Italian criminal who kidnap a man only to undergo a loathsome fate in the cellar of an old house, just as in Lovecraft's story a Pole, a Portuguese, and an Italian seek to rob the Terrible Old Man but meet death at his hands instead.

"The Sorcerer's Jewel" (*Strange Stories*, February 1939) is clearly a variation on "The Haunter of the Dark" and its Shining Trapezohedron. A character refers to a "Star of Sechmet":

> "Very ancient, but not costly. Stolen from the crown of the Lioness-headed Goddess during a Roman invasion of Egypt. It was carried to Rome and placed in the vestal girdle of the High-Priestess of Diana. The barbarians took it, cut the jewel into a round stone. The black centuries swallowed it." (M 155)

This is precisely analogous to the "history" of the Trapezohedron, from remote antiquity to the present, provided by Lovecraft in "The Haunter of the Dark"—and it is in this passage that Lovecraft mentions Nephren-Ka. And, just as Blake, when looking into the Shining Trapezohedron, "saw processions of robed, hooded figures whose outlines were not human, and looked on endless leagues of desert lined with carved, sky-reaching monoliths" (DH 104), so a similar experience befalls a character in "The Sorcerer's Jewel":

> A swirling as of parted mists. A dancing light. The fog was dispersing, and it seemed to be opening up—opening to a view that receded far into the distance. . . . At first only angles and angles, weaving and shifting in light that was of no color, yet phosphorescent. And out of the angles, a flat black plain that stretched upward, endlessly without horizon. . . . (M 156–57)

But Bloch's early Lovecraftian tales may be of the greatest interest, at least as far as Bloch's own subsequent career is concerned, for the hints they provide of how he metamphosed his writing from the florid supernaturalism of his youth to the psychological suspense of his maturity. At first glance, these two modes could not be more different; but in several tales of the late 1930s through the 1950s, Bloch shows how elements from both can be fused to produce a new amalgam.

The first thing Bloch had to do was to gain control of his style. Already by late 1934 Lovecraft is noting that "The tendency toward overcolouring so marked last year is waning rapidly, & your command of effective diction . . . is becoming more & more dependable" (L 55). One of the stories that elicited this comment was "The Grinning Ghoul," and indeed it is one of the first of Bloch's stories that plays on the distinction between psychological and ontological horror. The protagonist is a "moderately successful practising psychiatrist" (M 51), one of whose patients is a professor who admits to having bizarre dreams. Naturally, the psychiatrist initially dispenses with the dreams as mere vagaries, but later learns that they have an all too real source.

Still more remarkable, and one of the finest stories of Bloch's early period, is the uncollected tale "Black Bargain" (*Weird Tales*, May 1942).[2] Here both the Lovecraftian idiom and the customary Lovecraftian setting have been abandoned totally, and the subtle incursion of horror in a very mundane environment produces potently chilling effects. A cynical and world-weary pharmacist supplies some odd drugs—aconite, belladonna, and the like—to a down-and-outer who comes into his store clutching a large black book in German black-letter. A few days later the customer returns, but he has been transformed: he is spruced up with new clothes and claims that he has been hired by a local chemical supply house. As the man, Fritz Gulther, and the pharmacist celebrate the former's good fortune at a bar, the pharmacist notices something anomalous about the man's shadow: its movements do not seem to coincide with Gulther's. Thinking himself merely drunk, the pharmacist attempts to put the incident out of his mind.

Gulther then offers the pharmacist a job at the chemical company as his assistant. Going there, the pharmacist finds in Gulther's office the book he had been carrying—it is, of course, *De Vermis Mysteriis*. Eventually he worms the truth out of Gulther: Gulther had uttered an incantation, made a sacrifice, and called up the Devil, who had offered him success on one condition: "'He told me that I'd have only one rival, and that this rival would be a part of myself. It would grow with my success'" (74). Sure enough, Gulther's shadow seems both to be growing and to be subsuming Gulther's own life-force. As Gulther begins to panic, the pharmacist suggests that they prepare a counter-incantation to reverse the effect; but when he returns to Gulther's office with chemicals he has brought from his pharmacy, he finds Gulther transformed:

> I sat. Gulther rested on the desk nonchalantly swinging his legs.
> "All that nervousness, that strain, has disappeared. But before I forget it, I'd like to apologize for telling you that crazy story about sorcery and my obsession. Matter of fact, I'd feel better about the whole thing in the future if you just forget that all this ever happened." (76)

The pharmacist, dazed, agrees, but he knows that something has gone wrong. In fact, the shadow has now totally usurped Gulther.

It is not the use of *De Vermis Mysteriis* that represents the Lovecraftian connexion in this fine, understated tale; instead, it is Gulther's concluding transformation. In effect, the shadow has taken possession of Gulther's body and ousted his own personality—in exactly the same way that, in

"The Thing on the Doorstep" (1933), Asenath Waite ousts the personality of her husband Edward Derby from his body and casts it into her own body. The concluding scene in "Black Bargain" is very similar to a scene in Lovecraft's story where Derby's personality is evicted while he is being driven back to Arkham from Maine by the narrator, Daniel Upton. Asenath (in Derby's body) remarks: "'I hope you'll forget my attack back there, Upton. You know what my nerves are, and I guess you can excuse such things'" (DH 291).

Several years later Bloch wrote another powerful tale, "The Unspeakable Betrothal" (*Avon Fantasy Reader*, 1949)—whose title, Bloch has repeatedly insisted, is not his. Here too we encounter a prose style radically different from the adjective-riddled hyperbole of "The Feast in the Abbey," and Bloch effectively experiments with stream-of-consciousness in capturing the visions that plague a young girl both at night and by day:

> But everything kept going round and round, and when Aunt May walked past the bed she seemed to flatten out like a shadow, or one of the things, only she made a loud noise which was really the thunder outside and now she was sleeping really and truly even though she heard the thunder but the thunder wasn't real nothing was real except the things, that was it nothing was real any more but the things. (M 168)

These visions—which convince the girl's family and friends that she is psychologically aberrant—again prove to be based upon reality, and at the end she is transported into space by the entities have infiltrated her mind. Two years prior to the publication of this story, Bloch had written his first non-supernatural novel of psychological horror, *The Scarf* (1947); and the rest of his career would see an alteration between supernaturalism and psychological suspense, with intermittent fusions of the two. "The Unspeakable Betrothal" is such a fusion in its sensitive delineation of a psyche that has been rendered subtly non-human by outside sources. And yet, even here the influence of Lovecraft can be felt. "The Whisperer in Darkness" is very much in evidence in the "deep, buzzing voice" (M 166) that the girl hears, and also at the conclusion when nothing but the girl's face is left, as her body has been spirited away. Lovecraft himself, however, is not given enough credit for mingling supernatural and psychological horror: he did just that in "The Shadow over Innsmouth" and perhaps also in "The Shadow out of Time," and Bloch may well have found suggestive hints in both.

"Notebook Found in a Deserted House" (*Weird Tales*, May 1951) uses somewhat the same stylistic device as "The Unspeakable Betrothal" in its narration by an ill-educated boy rather than a learned omniscient narrator. This story does not feature much psychological analysis, and in its rather grotesque misconstrual of Lovecraft's shoggoth (here interpreted as some sort of tree spirit) it led the way to Ramsey Campbell's similar error in his juvenile story, "The Hollow in the Woods" (in *Ghostly Tales* [1957/58]). But, if nothing else, it shows how a tale of basically Lovecraftian conception can be adapted to a very different idiom. Here, again, however, perhaps Bloch was simply adapting Lovecraft's own extensive use of New England dialect in such tales as "The Picture in the House," "The Dunwich Horror," and "The Shadow over Innsmouth."

"Terror in Cut-Throat Cave" (*Fantastic*, June 1958) is of interest in combining the crime or adventure story with supernaturalism. The basic plot of the tale may have been conceived as early as 1933, for Lovecraft makes mention of one of Bloch's story plots as the "idea of finding a *Thing* in the hold of a long-sunken treasure-ship" (L 26). This is, indeed, exactly the core of "Terror in Cut-Throat Cave," although by the time Bloch wrote it he had mastered the tough-guy style he would use to such powerful effect in *The Dead Beat* (1960), and his powers of characterisation render the three main figures crisply—Howard Lane, the jaded writer who seeks a thrill from searching for underwater treasure; Don Hanson, a lumbering giant who has eyes for nothing but money; Dena Drake, Don's mistreated companion, who stays with her brutal lover for lack of any other meaningful goal in her life. I am not certain why this story is in *Mysteries of the Worm:* there is no "Mythos" allusion of any kind in it, and Robert M. Price's suggestion that Hanson is "something of a modern Obed Marsh" (M 218) is unconvincing. And yet, there is one fascinating Lovecraftian connexion. Toward the end Lane's mind is taken over by the nameless submerged entity, and he writes: "For already I was a part of it and it was a part of me" (M 249). No reader can fail to recall Robert Blake's poignant reflection of the fusion of his own mind with that of Nyarlathotep in "The Haunter of the Dark": "I am it and it is I . . ." (DH 115). That one sentence in Bloch's story is enough to reveal his borrowing of a central feature of Lovecraft's tale for his own work.

It would be twenty years before Bloch would write another tale that might conceivably be considered Lovecraftian; but when he did so, he did it with a vengeance. *Strange Eons* (1978) is Bloch's most extended tribute to Lovecraft. No one is likely to think it a masterwork of literature, but it may be among Bloch's more successful later novels and is certainly a delight to the Lovecraftian.

The premise of *Strange Eons* is simple: Lovecraft was writing truth, not fiction. This is, of course, the premise under which many occultist groups function; some asserting, with added implausibility, that Lovecraft himself was unaware of the literal truth of his work. This view was already prevalent among a few in Lovecraft's own lifetime; note his amused comment on the beliefs of the mystical William Lumley: "We [the Lovecraft circle] may *think* we're writing fiction, and may even (absurd thought!) disbelieve what we write, but at bottom we are telling the truth in spite of ourselves—serving unwittingly as mouthpieces of Tsathoggua, Crom, Cthulhu, and other pleasant Outside gentry" (SL 4.271).

Bloch actually renders the idea half-believable by the gradualness of his exposition and by his suggestion that Lovecraft was in fact aware of what he was writing and was trying to utter a warning of some kind. The novel opens with an individual discovering a painting that seems strikingly similar to one ascribed to Richard Upton Pickman in "Pickman's Model"; later it is discovered that the painting is in fact by one Richard Upton, who was in touch with Lovecraft and had shown him some spectacular canvases in Boston. As *Strange Eons* progresses, various events seem uncannily to mimic those found in Lovecraft's stories—"The Lurking Fear," "The Statement of Randolph Carter" (*"You fool—Beckman is dead!"* [SE 25]), "The Whisperer in Darkness," and so on.

The focus of the novel is, as might be expected, Nyarlathotep—here embodied in the person of Reverend Nye, a black man who leads the Starry Wisdom sect, seemingly just another of the harmless cults found so bountifully in southern California. But very quickly it becomes clear that Nye and his cult are far from harmless, as character after character dies off after learning too much. Drawing upon the prose-poem "Nyarlathotep," Bloch sees in the figure of Nyarlathotep nothing less than a symbol for—and, indeed, the actual engenderer of—a cataclysmic chaos that could destroy the world and perhaps the universe.

Strange Eons is a grand synthesis of Lovecraftian tales and themes. Bloch fuses elements from the "Cthulhu Mythos" into a convincing unity: Nyarlathotep prepares for the emergence of Cthulhu from the depths of the Pacific; the mind-exchange that Asenath Waite practised in "The Thing on the Doorstep" allows a Starry Wisdom member to deceive an opponent at a critical juncture, just as the mimicry that tricked Wilmarth at the conclusion of "The Whisperer in Darkness" does so at an earlier point in the novel; and the female protagonist serves, like Lavinia Whateley in "The Dunwich Horror," as the unwilling mate in a sexual union with one of the Great Old Ones. Throughout *Strange Eons,* all the characters attempting to thwart Nyarlathotep—including a powerful secret branch of the U.S. government—are themselves thwarted by Nyarlathotep and his minions; and the conclusion offers no reassurance.

The final section of *Strange Eons,* a harrowing account of a severe earthquake that causes the submersion of a large part of California sometime in the near future, is narrated in a hypnotic, quasi-stream-of-consciousness manner that is as potently effective as the most incantatory Lovecraftian prose. Here the resemblance to the prose-poem "Nyarlathotep" is very marked, as all civilisation seems to be cracking at the foundations. It is quite possible that Bloch was thinking not only of the prose-poem but of the passage (which he had already quoted in "The Shadow from the Steeple") in the sonnet "Nyarlathotep" in *Fungi from Yuggoth:*

Soon from the sea a noxious birth began;
Forgotten lands with weedy spires of gold;
The ground was cleft, and mad auroras rolled
Down on the quaking citadels of man.
Then, crushing what he chanced to mould in play,
The idiot Chaos blew Earth's dust away.

That "noxious birth" is, in Bloch's conception, nothing less than the emergence of Cthulhu, and the novel ends grimly and apocalyptically:

> That is not dead which can eternal lie, and the time of strange eons had arrived. The stars were right, the gates were open, the seas swarmed with immortal multitudes and the earth gave up its undead.
> Soon the winged ones from Yuggoth would swoop down from the void and now the Old Ones would return—Azazoth [*sic*] and Yog-Sothoth, whose priest he [Nyarlathotep] was, would come to lightless Leng and old Kadath in the risen continents which were transformed as he was transformed. . . .
> He rose, and mountains trembled, sinking into the sea.
> Time stopped.
> Death died.
> And Great Cthulhu went forth into the world to begin his eternal reign.
> (SE 194)

Such a cheerless ending would be unthinkable to many modern weird writers, who feel obligated to restore bourgeois normality at the end regardless of the havoc their monsters have caused; but Bloch is true to Lovecraft's vision here, for he knew that that vision was a bleak one that saw little place for mankind in a boundless universe in which it was an infinitesimal atom. This is what makes *Strange Eons* the true homage that it is.

Bloch learned much from Lovecraft about the craft of writing weird fiction, and he put that knowledge to good use. But while his early "Cthulhu Mythos" stories entertain, while *Strange Eons* is an affectionate tribute, Bloch's real stature as a writer resides in his short stories of the 1940s onward and in such gripping novels—which combine psychological penetration with hard-boiled cynicism—as *Psycho* (1959) and *The Dead Beat* (1960). Just as Lovecraft's later work straddles the always nebulous borderline between horror and science fiction, so Bloch's most representative writing effects a union between the horror tale and the mystery or detective story. This is his true contribution to literature, and it will be for that that he will be remembered. But his Lovecraftian works will also occupy a place of honour in his canon, if only because they exemplify the ties of friendship that a respected master established with his enthusiastic pupil. Along with Fritz Leiber, Henry Kuttner, C. L. Moore, and a few others, Robert Bloch more than justified Lovecraft's predictions of his future greatness, and in turn Bloch more than repaid the debt he owed to the twentieth century's leading weird writer.

Notes

1. This is the name of the character as given in the *Weird Tales* appearance of the story. Subsequent appearances (beginning with *The Opener of the Way* [1945]) give the name as Carnoti. Stugatche is clearly Bloch's original name for this character, and it is mentioned in several letters by Lovecraft. Bloch remarks of it: "The name comes from a group of imaginary characters who—believe it or not—were invented to serve as players on teams in a card-game called 'Baseball'—the invention of my friends Herb Williams and Harold Gauer. . . . I later used the name for a central character in my story, 'The Faceless God'" (L 70n.205). Perhaps August Derleth advised Bloch to change the name for the book appearance.

2. I am grateful to Robert M. Price for providing me with the text of this story.

Passing the Torch: H. P. Lovecraft and Fritz Leiber

Fritz Leiber's apparently startling remark that H. P. Lovecraft was "the chiefest influence on my literary development after Shakespeare" (cited in Byfield 11) may perhaps be less puzzling if we interpret the statement absolutely literally; for Leiber's emphasis here may be on the word *development*, and if this is the case, then it suggests that Lovecraft's own work—as well as his brief but intense correspondence with Leiber in 1936–37—provided Leiber with suggestions as to the improvement of the style, plotting, motivation, and conception of his early tales, and that these suggestions held Leiber in good stead throughout the subsequent course of his long and fruitful career. It is a truism that Leiber, perhaps alone of Lovecraft's literary associates, did not imitate Lovecraft either stylistically or thematically—except in the late work, "The Terror from the Depths" (1976), commissioned for a volume of pastiches of Lovecraft's "Cthulhu Mythos"—but instead struck out on his own right from the beginning of his career. This aesthetic independence has been a major reason for the survival of Leiber's work while that of other, more derivative writers has achieved merited oblivion; but that Lovecraft taught Leiber much about the craft of writing is evident both in Leiber's several insightful critical essays on Lovecraft and in his early tales, especially those gathered in his first collection, *Night's Black Agents* (1947).

Leiber (1910–1992) wrote four important essays on Lovecraft, all of which are handily gathered in the collection *Fafhrd & Me* (1990). They are: "A Literary Copernicus" (1949); "My Correspondence with Lovecraft" (1958); "The 'Whisperer' Re-examined" (1964); and "Through Hyperspace with Brown Jenkin" (1966). There are some lesser articles—among them "Lovecraft in My Life" (1976) and his contributions to *H. P. Lovecraft: A Symposium* (1963)—but the above four embody Leiber's most significant thought on Lovecraft. Aside from the light they shed on Leiber's own work, they are among the most perspicacious pieces ever written on Lovecraft; many believe that "A Literary Copernicus" may still be the finest single article on Lovecraft to date. All these essays reveal how carefully Leiber had absorbed the essence of Lovecraft's work at a relatively early stage in his career.

"A Literary Copernicus," written for *Something about Cats and Other Pieces* (1949), is a radical expansion of two earlier articles, "The Works of H. P. Lovecraft: Suggestions for a Critical Appraisal" (1944) and "Some Random Thoughts about Lovecraft's Writings" (1945), both published in the Lovecraftian fanzine, *The Acolyte*. The very core of the article—that Lovecraft was a "literary Copernicus" for reinventing the Gothic tale for modern times—is not only one of the most important utterances made about Lovecraft but is what Leiber himself chiefly derived from Lovecraft's stories and applied to his own work, albeit in a somewhat different way. Consider the opening paragraph of the article:

> Howard Phillips Lovecraft was the Copernicus of the horror story. He shifted the focus of supernatural dread from man and his little world and his gods, to the stars and the black and unplumbed gulfs of intergalactic space. To do this effectively, he created a new kind of horror story and new methods for telling it. (FM 65)

When Leiber goes on to say that Lovecraft "firmly attached the emotion of spectral dread to such concepts as outer space, the rim of the cosmos, alien beings, unsuspected dimensions, and the conceivable universes lying outside our own space-time continuum" (FM 66), he is not only stressing that Lovecraft presented a fusion of the traditional horror tale with the nascent science fiction story, but still more significantly presented a *secular* supernatural tale whereby fear is instilled not by conventional appeals to the devil but to the petrifying notion of the vastness of the cosmos and the insignificance of humanity within it. Leiber delivers a scarcely veiled rebuke to August Derleth, who attempted for decades to maintain that Lovecraft's "Cthulhu Mythos" can somehow be reconciled with standard Christian doctrine: "I believe it is a mistake to regard the beings of the Cthulhu Mythos as sophisticated equivalents of the entities of Christian demonology, or to attempt to divide them into balancing Zoroastrian hierarchies of good and evil" (FM 68). It would take twenty years for this remarkably prescient analysis to be elaborated by such modern Lovecraft scholars as Richard L. Tierney ("The Derleth Mythos," 1972) and Dirk W. Mosig ("H. P. Lovecraft: Myth-Maker," 1976).

Leiber's other articles on Lovecraft are less significant for the study of his own work, but are nonetheless perspicacious. "Through Hyperspace with Brown Jenkin" is perhaps the most impressive, being a trenchant exploration of the notion of time-travel in Lovecraft's fiction. It shows how carefully Leiber read such of Lovecraft's tales as "The Dreams in the Witch House" and "The Shadow out of Time"; and it is no accident that these tales are among those that influenced Leiber the most. "The 'Whisperer' Re-examined" is a sharp criticism of "The Whisperer in Darkness" from the point of view of its deficient characterisation: the protagonist, Albert N. Wilmarth, is too easily "hoodwinked" (FM 82) by the alien entities of the tale. This leads to a more general criticism of Lovecraft:

> In "Notes on the Writing of Weird Fiction" Lovecraft summed up [his] limitation: "All that a wonder story can ever be is *a vivid picture of a certain type of human mood.*" This aesthetic dictum, while having some technical validity, breathes loneliness and can be very stultifying to the writer's urge to say things about the real world, set down insights into real people, speculate imaginatively, and get closer to his reader than merely sharing "a vague illusion of the strange reality of the unreal." (FM 83)

This criticism is not entirely fair to Lovecraft—who was not interested in the "real world" or in setting down insights into "real people," and whose cosmic perspective was opposed to the vaunting of human beings against the awesome backdrop of the cosmos—but it points to Leiber's own belief that fantasy, horror, and even cosmicism are not incompatible with the portrayal of vital human characters with whom the reader can identify.

In "My Correspondence with Lovecraft" Leiber tells the story of his brief personal involvement with the Providence writer. He had been profoundly moved by reading "The Colour out of Space" in *Amazing Stories* (September 1927) and *At the Mountains of Madness* and "The Shadow out of Time" in 1936 issues of *Astounding Stories*. No doubt he read Lovecraft's other stories in *Weird Tales* as well, but the citation of the above three tales—Lovecraft's most "science-fictional" works—points to their focal influence upon Leiber's early work. Too shy to write to the great master of weird fiction, however, Leiber nonetheless came into contact with Lovecraft when his wife Jonquil wrote to him through *Weird Tales*. For a time Lovecraft was writing separate letters to both Fritz and Jonquil (as well as to Leiber's early collaborator Harry O. Fischer), although the duration of this correspondence was quite brief: perhaps no longer than the period from October 1936 to March 1937, when Lovecraft died at forty-six. Neither Fritz nor Jonquil could know that Lovecraft was already in the final stages of intestinal cancer; and it is poignant to read—given the near-certainty that bad diet was a significant cause of Lovecraft's illness and death—how Leiber and Fischer ruminated "that something must be done to provide Lovecraft with fresh vegetables" (FM 80).

But that brief association was enough to effect some permanent changes in Leiber's work. Leiber had sent the typescript of his novelette, "Adept's Gambit" (rejected by *Weird Tales*), to Lovecraft; in response, Lovecraft on 19 December 1936 wrote a letter of twenty sheets, written on both sides of the page—perhaps 10,000 words in length—commenting in detail on points of style and historical accuracy in the tale, and supplying a copious reading-list of works on Greek and Roman history for any future historical fiction that Leiber might do. Leiber is right to call this lengthy epistle "crazily generous by hard-headed standards," and he goes on to say that it "influenced me permanently toward greater care in the polishing and final preparation of manuscripts" (FM 79).

The version of "Adept's Gambit" published in *Night's Black Agents* is very likely quite different from what Leiber sent to Lovecraft, since Leiber confesses in "Fafhrd and Me" that the novelette went through "three or four recastings and rewritings" (FM 15) after its initial rejections. (One of these versions contained references to Lovecraft's Mythos, and Leiber was probably wise in excising them from the final draft.) Lovecraft's fundamental criticism was that the story exhibited a certain fuzziness in the historical setting. From his remarks it is possible to infer that the tale was more firmly set in the Hellenistic period than the version as we have it, and the ever-scrupulous Lovecraft did not fail to pick up on certain inaccuracies or anachronisms in the portrayal of the period. In the published version we are told that "it was hardly a year since the Seleucids had beaten the Ptolemies out of Tyre" (N 22); other hints of this sort—assuming they were in the version he read—led Lovecraft to conjecture a date of 250 B.C.E. for the tale's action; but a later mention of Alexander the Great (d. 323 B.C.E.) as living "more than a hundred years ago" would give a somewhat later period, say 220 B.C. Interestingly enough, Leiber was conceiving a future tale in which Fafhrd & the Gray Mouser would be reincarnated into the Julio-Claudian age (i.e., the 1st century C.E.) by means of an elixir; it was for this reason that he had asked Lovecraft to supply him a reading-list of works on this period of ancient history.

"Adept's Gambit" does not bear much resemblance to Lovecraft's own work; indeed, in its picaresque narrative, its vivid character portrayals, and its liberal doses of humour and buffoonery it is about as far from the bulk of Lovecraft's dark, brooding, non-humanocentric work as can be imagined. Lovecraft himself was aware of the fact, remarking in his letter that "the style & manner of approach are almost antipodal to my own." He was also at a loss for parallels, citing the possible influence of James Stephens (*The Crock of Gold*), Dunsany (he is perhaps thinking of Dunsany's own picaresque pseudo-historical novels, *The Chronicles of Rodriguez* [1922] and *The Charwoman's Shadow* [1926]), Cabell, and others. There is perhaps an accidental resemblance to Lovecraft's then-unpublished novel, *The Dream-Quest of Unknown Kadath*—Lovecraft remarks on the similarity himself ("This picaresque kind of writing has a strong fascination, & I once attempted it myself . . . in a long novelette")—but of course Leiber could not have actually been influenced by the work. In any event, Lovecraft was highly impressed with the story, addressing his long letter to Leiber as from "The Castle of Mist" and signing himself "The Old Man Without a Beard." One remark in the letter is worth citing:

> Certainly, you have produced a remarkably fine & distinctive bit of comic fantasy in a vein which is, for all the Cabellian or Beckfordian comparisons, essentially your own. The basic element of allegory, the earthiness & closeness to human nature, & the curious blending of worldly lightness with the strange & the macabre, all harmonise adequately & seem to express a definite mood & personality. The result is an authentic work of art . . .

He adds presciently: "Let us hope that your mental collaboration [with Harry O. Fischer] will give rise to a long sequence of tales about Fafhrd & the Mouser . . ."

If "Adept's Gambit" bears little resemblance to Lovecraft's work, another Fafhrd and Gray Mouser story is so dependent upon Lovecraftian conceptions that it can qualify as a pastiche, although even this tale is considerably more imaginative as a pastiche than other Lovecraft-derived works. "The Sunken Land" (1942) is another relatively early story in which Fafhrd catches a fish in whose mouth is found an object that is both a ring and a key. This object makes Fafhrd think of the legends of a land called Simorgya, whose inhabitants "'were mighty magicians, claiming power over wind and wave and the creatures below. Yet the sea gulped them down for all that'" (N 6). The ship on which Fafhrd and the Mouser are sailing is rammed by another ship, controlled by the evil Lavas Laerk, and after a fight with its crew Fafhrd is taken prisoner and made to serve as an oarsman. Lavas Laerk is seeking to attain the sunken land of Simorgya, and after a time he and his crew seem to do so, coming upon a vast mountain jutting out of the sea. But something seems to be wrong, and Fafhrd is the only one to be aware that "Simorgya had indeed sunk under the sea and only risen up yesterday—or yester-hour" (N 15). Lavas Laerk comes upon the treasure-house of Simorgya and his crew revels in the gold and jewels therein; but from behind a golden door a "strange, undulant blanketlike monster" (N 16) emerges and overwhelms Lavas Laerk's men, while Fafhrd escapes with the help of the Mouser, whose ship has arrived to rescue him. Simorgya then once again falls back into the sea.

This story is an amalgam of at least four different Lovecraft stories, although some of the borrowings are very slight. When the Mouser, seeing the ring for the first time, remarks that he "did not recognize the style" (N 4), we think of the bizarre jewellery of the Innsmouth denizens of "The Shadow over Innsmouth" (1931), which "belonged to some settled technique . . . utterly remote from any—Eastern or Western, ancient or modern—which [the narrator] had ever heard of or seen exemplified" (DH 311). Later, as Lavas Laerk's crew penetrate the treasure-house and note its eerie phosphorescence, we are perhaps meant to recall Lovecraft's early tale, "The Temple" (1920), which involves a German submarine commander who comes upon a similarly phosphorescent temple buried beneath the waves of the Atlantic. And that "blanketlike" monster is perhaps akin to Lovecraft's protoplasmic shoggoth from *At the Mountains of Madness* (1931).

But clearly the predominant influence on this tale is "The Call of Cthulhu" (1926), Lovecraft's prototypical account of a sunken continent that suddenly rises up from the waves and from which the shapeless monstrosity Cthulhu momentarily emerges to wreak havoc on a hapless crew of Norwegian sailors who come upon it by accident. Indeed, "The Sunken Land" is nothing more than a rewriting of "The Call of Cthulhu," transferring the setting from the real world of the South Pacific to an heroic fantasy realm and including rather more fisticuffs and swordplay than was Lovecraft's wont.

Another early Leiber tale—"Diary in the Snow," first published in *Night's Black Agents*—is less obviously derivative but still owes its very conception to Lovecraft. Here it transpires that a race of extraterrestrial entities, dwelling in a world of bitter cold, discover the existence of Earth and look with envy at its temperateness. As they dwell on a planet enormously distant from earth, mind-exchange with the inhabitants of Earth is the only feasible way to effect their removal from their world; and "Diary in the Snow" is the account of a writer in a remote snowbound cottage who unwittingly serves as the conduit for the creatures' advent to this planet, unaware that the science-fiction tale he is writing is in reality his subconscious mind's warning of how these entities are planning to usurp the human race.

There is, perhaps, no specific Lovecraft story which served as the model for "Diary in the Snow," although the conceptions broached in it are heavily Lovecraftian. The idea of mind-exchange over enormous distances of space brings "The Shadow out of Time" (1934–35) to mind, and this is perhaps the most direct influence. Lovecraft, of course, used mind-exchange in a number of other tales, notably "The Thing on the Doorstep" (1933) and "The Haunter of the Dark" (1935); but only "The Shadow out of Time" involves mind-exchange over vast galactic spaces. Also, the scenario of the writer and his colleague being besieged by alien forces—for after a time they develop a dim awareness of the true state of affairs—recalls "The Whisperer in Darkness" (1930), where Henry Akeley finds himself trapped in his lonely Vermont farmhouse as the fungi from Yuggoth seek to overwhelm him and take his mind on stupendous transcosmic voyages. One very telling tip of the hat to Lovecraft in "Diary in the Snow" is the narrator's description, at the outset, of the anomalous phenomena he notes around him as "a sense of strangeness, a delightful feeling of adventurous expectancy" (N 208). Lovecraft may well have used that latter phrase in a letter to Leiber, for it became a standard coinage in his own aesthetic of the weird: "What has haunted my dreams for nearly forty years is *a strange sense of adventurous expectancy connected with landscape and architecture and sky-effects*" (SL 3.100).

Other early Leiber tales are influenced by Lovecraft in less significant ways; indeed, in some cases the resemblance may be accidental. "The Inheritance" (N) also deals with personality-exchange, and was perhaps influenced by "The Thing on the Doorstep," where a woman with great hypnotic powers displaces the personality of her husband and occupies his body on occasion. "The Man Who Never Grew Young" (N) appears to reflect Lovecraft's fascination with time—recall his celebrated statement that "*Conflict with time* seems to me the most potent and fruitful theme in all human expression" ("Notes")—in its depiction of a man who somehow travels backward through time. The influence of "The Shadow out of Time"— in which a man's mind, displaced by that of an alien entity, travels back 150,000,000 years into the body of his displacer—may be conjectured, although the parallels are not very precise: Leiber's tale simply involves a man who himself is somehow doubling back upon the time-stream.

The uncollected tale "The Dead Man" (*Weird Tales*, November 1950) betrays—as Stefan Dziemianowicz has pointed out—a peculiar influence of "The Thing on the Doorstep" in its use of a series of three knocks followed by two more as a cue to bring a patient out of a hypnotic trance; Lovecraft used the identical three-and-two pattern as a secret code between two characters in his story.

A reading of *Night's Black Agents* makes clear the central lesson Leiber learned from Lovecraft: the need to update the horror tale to make it relevant to present-day concerns. Lovecraft, of course, did so by fusing horror and science fiction, replacing the fear of vampires, werewolves, and ghosts (all completely outmoded in the light of contemporary science) with that of the boundless cosmos. Antiquarian though he may have been, Lovecraft was keenly aware of such radical and potentially disturbing conceptions as Einsteinian space-time, the quantum theory, and Heisenberg's indeterminacy principle, and utilised them to give a distinctly modern cast to such stale conceptions as the vampire ("The Shunned House") and the witch ("The Dreams in the Witch House"), to say nothing of the possibility of extraterrestrial incursions in such tales as "The Colour out of Space," "The Whisperer in Darkness," *At the Mountains of Madness*, and "The Shadow out of Time."

Leiber went about it in a somewhat different way. In his belief that weird fiction must be made relevant to contemporary audiences by means of vividly realised human characters and realism of setting, Leiber melded supernatural horror with the very real horrors of urbanism ("Smoke Ghost," "The Hound"), crime ("The Automatic Pistol"), and the omnipresent anxiety of living in the modern world ("The Dreams of Albert Moreland"); anticipating in this regard the work of Ramsey Campbell and many other contemporary writers. In a few striking stories ("The Hill and the Hole," "A Bit of the Dark World") Leiber even attempts (successfully) to duplicate Lovecraft's harrowing cosmicism.

"Smoke Ghost" is Leiber's prototypical tale of the horror to be found in the city. The very title suggests a paradoxical union of the antiquated (a ghost) and the modern (smoke from factories). This ghost, however, in the eyes of the protagonist, Mr Wran, is "'a ghost from the world today, with the soot of the factories on its face and the pounding of machinery in its soul'" (N 109). The vista of slum roofs seen by Wran symbolises for him "certain disagreeable aspects of the frustrated, frightened century in which he lived" (N 112). When Wran's son sees the ghost and cries, "Black man, black man" (N 120), we are not to interpret the remark racially but as emblematic of the omnipresent filth—literal and moral—in modern society. We may also think of Leiber's discussion, in "A Literary Copernicus," of Nyarlathotep, who in "The Dreams in the Witch House" appears as the Black Man. In pondering what Nyarlathotep may "mean," Leiber conjectures that one possibility is that "Nyarlathotep stands for man's self-destructive intellectuality, his awful ability to see the universe for what it is and thereby kill in himself all naive and beautiful dreams" (FM 70). This is, to be sure, not exactly what is going on in "Smoke Ghost," but Leiber may still have learned from Lovecraft how to use a symbol something like Nyarlathotep to convey his own views on the state of modern man.

Leiber's "The Hound" exactly mirrors the title of one of Lovecraft's early tales, but this duplication may be accidental, as Leiber's tale appears to owe nothing at all to Lovecraft's lurid and consciously self-parodic story, in which two graverobbers who meet their comeuppance when they pilfer the tomb of an old ghoul whose soul is represented by a gigantic hound. Leiber's "The Hound" is grimly potent, but again we are to see in the hound of the tale a symbol for the horrors of urbanism: "this thing . . . was part and parcel of the great sprawling cities and chaotic peoples of the Twentieth Century" (N 187). Later the narrator's friend, speaking of the relentless march of technology, points to the inability of the human spirit to keep pace:

> "Meanwhile, what's happening inside each of us? I'll tell you. All sorts of inhibited emotions are accumulating. Fear is accumulating. Horror is accumulating. A new kind of awe of the mysteries of the universe is accumulating. A psychological environment is forming, along with the physical one. . . . Our culture becomes ripe for infection. . . . our culture suddenly spawns a horde of demons. And, like germs, they have a peculiar affinity for our culture. They're unique. They fit in. You wouldn't find the same kind any other time or place." (N 190–91)

"The Automatic Pistol" is a somewhat slighter but piquant tale that effects a union of the gangster story and the supernatural tale. A criminal's gun is explicitly compared to a witch's familiar (N 133), making us recall perhaps how Lovecraft brought the tale of witchcraft up to date in "The Dreams in the Witch House" by the incorporation of Einsteinian physics. There the ratlike creature Brown Jenkin, the familiar of the witch Keziah Mason, appears in hyperspace as a "polyhedron of unknown colours and rapidly shifting surface angles" (MM 273). In these tales Leiber pioneers the modernisation of the weird tale; but he does so not as Lovecraft did—by attempting to make the supernatural plausible by appeals to advanced science—but by placing it in the frenetic urban milieu that holds so many of us in its tenacious grip. Nevertheless, it is likely that Leiber found in Lovecraft's tales some suggestive hints of how such a modernisation might be effected.

Three tales in *Night's Black Agents* feature the cosmicism and the very intellectualised, philosophical horror that lie at the core of Lovecraft's best work. In "The Dreams of Albert Moreland" the central character dreams that he is playing a chesslike game on some enormous gameboard, con-

vinced that the fate of mankind depends on the outcome. The basic plot is
strikingly similar to that of "The Dreams in the Witch House," in particular
the tableau where a statuette from Moreland's dream-world is found in his
room, a scene identical to one found in Lovecraft's tale, and a confirmation
that the "dreams" in both tales bear some harrowing relationship to the
"real" world. (Leiber could not know that a further similarity exists in the
original title of Lovecraft's story—"The Dreams of Walter Gilman.") When
Moreland fancies that "some cosmic beings, neither gods nor men, had created human life long ago as a jest or experiment or artistic form" (N 174), we
are clearly meant to recall Lake's conjecture in *At the Mountains of Madness* that
the Old Ones had created all earth life as "jest or mistake" (MM 22). But
Leiber performs a brilliant union of social commentary and cosmicism by
attributing the "omnipresent anxiety" that Moreland sees on "each passing
face" as symptomatic of a broader evil:

> For once I seemed able to look behind the mask which every person
> wears and which is so characteristically pronounced in a congested city,
> and see what lay behind—the egotistical sensitivity, the smouldering irrita-
> tion, the thwarted longing, the defeat . . . and, above all, the anxiety, too ill-
> defined and lacking in definite object to be called fear, but nonetheless in-
> fecting every thought and action, and making trivial things terrible. And it
> seemed to me that social, economic, and physiological factors, even Death
> and the War, were insufficient to explain such anxiety, and that it was in
> reality an upswelling from something dubious and horrible in the very con-
> stitution of the universe. (N 179)

Later Moreland believes that he is "getting perilously close to the inner-
most secrets of the universe and finding they were rotten and evil and sardonic" (N 182), a common theme in Lovecraft's work.

"The Hill and the Hole" speaks of some anomalous survey readings
whereby a hill seems to be a pit, leading the narrator to reflect about "how
little most people knew about the actual dimensions and boundaries of the
world they lived in" (N 159). And later: "Once admit that the dimensions
of a thing might not be real . . . and you cut the foundations from under
the world" (N 165). Lovecraft speaks in "The Call of Cthulhu" of the ge-
ometry of R'lyeh being *"all wrong"* (DH 143) and of "an angle which was
acute, but behaved as if it were obtuse" (DH 152), exactly the sort of reversal that we find in Leiber's tale. The fact that a surveyor's instrument
confirms the anomalousness of the situation may point to the influence of
"The Colour out of Space," where a spectroscope is applied to the meteorite and reveals "shining bands unlike any known colours of the normal
spectrum" (DH 58). In both cases it is important that the weird phenomena not be discounted as a mere hallucination; and the utilisation of scientific instruments in perfect working order is the best means to suggest that
some genuine bizarrerie actually exists.

"A Bit of the Dark World" (1962) is a later story added to the revised (1978) edition of *Night's Black Agents*, probably because Leiber saw it to be thematically similar to the Lovecraftian tales in the volume. There is, of course, a passing reference to "Mountains of Madness near the South Pole" (N 246), but the relationship is deeper than this. This tale consists largely of an intellectual discussion of the foundations of fear. Whereas one character speaks of mundane horrors—"'Nazi death camps, brain-washing, Black-Dahlia sex murders, race riots, stuff like that'"—another character counters: "'I'm talking about supernatural horror, which is almost the antithesis of even the worst human violence and cruelty. Hauntings, the suspension of scientific law, the intrusion of the utterly alien, the sense of something listening at the rim of the cosmos or scratching faintly at the other side of the sky'" (N 245), a very Lovecraftian formulation. Later a character has a cosmic experience very similar to those of Lovecraft's protagonists:

> I looked up at the heavens. There was no Milky Way yet, but there would be soon, the stars were flashing on so brightly and thickly at this smog-free distance from LA. I saw the Pole Star straight above the dark star-silhouetted summit-crag of the hillside across from me, and the Great Bear and Cassiopeia swinging from it. I felt the bigness of the atmosphere, I got a hint of the stupendous distance between me and the stars, and then—as if my vision could go out in all directions at will, piercing solidity as readily as the dark—I got a lasting, growing, wholly absorbing sense of the universe around me. (N 263)

The tale goes on to relate exactly such an "intrusion of the utterly alien," an entity as incomprehensible as the creature (or creatures) in "The Colour out of Space."

Late in life Leiber finally broke down and produced an avowed Lovecraftian pastiche, writing "The Terror from the Depths" when invited by Edward Paul Berglund to contribute to his anthology, *The Disciples of Cthulhu* (1976). The result is an extraordinarily rich and complex novelette that, as Byfield (57–58) has shown, is a model for Leiber's incorporation of the mythic theories of Jung and Joseph Campbell in his later work. On a superficial level, "The Terror from the Depths" can be read as a vast in-joke: it would require a lengthy commentary to pinpoint all the tips of the hat to works by Lovecraft scattered through this story, including something so insignificant as the cry "Merciful Creator!" (TD 301), borrowed from "Pickman's Model" (DH 22). More interestingly, Leiber has written a loose sequel to some of Lovecraft's most celebrated later tales, especially "The Whisperer in Darkness," whose protagonist Albert N. Wilmarth plays a major role in the story. Wilmarth, amusingly enough, bears a striking physical resemblance to Lovecraft himself. Although Leiber of course never met Lovecraft, he had by this time read enough about Lovecraft's life and mannerisms to capture some of his characteristic behaviour-patterns:

> He [was] . . . a tall young man, cadaverously thin, always moving about with nervous rapidity, his shoulders hunched. He'd had a long jaw and a pale complexion, with dark-circled eyes which gave him a haunted look, as if he were constantly under some great strain to which he never alluded. . . . He'd seemed incredibly well read and had had a lot to do with stimulating and deepening my interest in poetry. (TD 290)

The narrator, Georg Reuter Fischer, even remarks to Wilmarth at one point: "'You know, . . . I had the craziest idea—that somehow you and he [Lovecraft] were the same person'" (TD 310). Lovecraft himself, indeed, plays a minor role in the tale. Conversely, Fischer (whose first and last names are derived from Leiber's friends Georg Mann and Harry O. Fischer, and whose middle name is Leiber's own) is clearly modelled on Leiber himself, so that the story's scenario—in which Wilmarth acts as a sort of mentor to Fischer in the pursuit of arcane knowledge—echoes Lovecraft's own brief tutorship to the young Leiber.

More than mere imitation, however, "The Terror from the Depths" strives both to recapture some of the textural richness of Lovecraft's best stories and, perhaps, to show that profound portrayals of human character are not incompatible with the general "cosmic" orientation of Lovecraft's work. To put it very crudely, Fischer finds himself simultaneously attracted and repelled by the cosmic forces dwelling under his Southern California home; and his first-person narrative reveals, entirely unbeknownst to himself, the degree to which these forces have throughout his entire life affected his mind and guided his actions to the final cataclysmic conclusion. Leiber here has drawn from many of Lovecraft's tales: Cthulhu's control of dreams ("The Call of Cthulhu"); the possible attractions of yielding to the non-human ("The Shadow over Innsmouth"); the compelling quest for scientific knowledge in the face of personal danger ("The Whisperer in Darkness," *At the Mountains of Madness*). And yet, the result is a story that features considerably more psychological analysis than Lovecraft ever included in his own work.

Accordingly, "The Terror from the Depths" can on one level be seen as Leiber's attempt to "rewrite" "The Whisperer in Darkness" so that it has more to say about the "real world" and "real people." Recall that one of Leiber's criticisms of Lovecraft's tale is that Wilmarth is presented as excessively gullible—a comment that may point to Leiber's overall dissatisfaction with the portrayal of character in Lovecraft's work generally. The same cannot be said of "The Terror from the Depths," where the slow absorption of both Fischer and Wilmarth into the physical and mental grasp of the cosmic entities is depicted with subtlety and psychological insight. In Lovecraft's tale Wilmarth is also momentarily attracted by the prospect of cosmic insights that might be made available to him: "To shake off the maddening and wearying limitations of time and space and natural law—to be linked with the vast *outside*—to come close to the nighted and abysmal secrets of the infinite and the ultimate—surely such a thing was worth the risk of one's life, soul, and sanity!" (DH 243). But in the end he draws back and flees to the safety of the human world. Leiber's scenario shows that the mere option to yield or not to yield to the non-human has become a moot point, since Fischer's mind has long ago been captured by the cosmic beings. What Leiber has done here—and, really, throughout his work—is to break down the simple dichotomy of external horror and internal horror, showing that both can be, and usually are, fused into an enigmatic and chilling union.

It cannot be repeated frequently enough that Fritz Leiber was one of the few writers of the "Lovecraft Circle" to have fully assimilated the Lovecraft influence and gone on to produce vital, original work that reflects his own (not Lovecraft's) themes, concerns, and philosophy. The same cannot be said for the Lovecraftian work of August Derleth, Frank Belknap Long, Brian Lumley, and even Ramsey Campbell. Campbell became an original writer only when he repudiated the Lovecraft influence that dominated his first volume, *The Inhabitant of the Lake* (1964), and went on to write the very different work for which he is now justly acclaimed. Leiber never had to make such a clear break, perhaps because his youthful conceptions were already pointing in a somewhat Lovecraftian direction (especially in the mingling of horror and science fiction), so that he could use Lovecraft's work less as the source of abject imitation than as a spur to his imagination. Leiber never attempted to imitate Lovecraft's distinctive style (save, as an homage, in "The Terror from the Depths"), and instead drew upon fundamental Lovecraftian themes, moods, and aesthetic principles—the impingement of vast extraterrestrial entities upon the earth; the focusing upon a hapless, solitary human being caught in the web of cosmic forces; the intellectual terror of a defiance or subversion of natural law; the need to modernise the weird tale by utilising modern science as a source of terror—as the foundation of his early work. *Night's Black Agents* is a testimonial to how much Leiber has learned from Lovecraft, but many other works could be cited to flesh out the picture.

In the end, however, Leiber remains a writer capable of expressing his own unique vision; the most important lesson he drew from Lovecraft was some clues on how best to express it.

IV. Contemporaries

Rod Serling: The Moral Supernatural

For the literary critic to assess the career of Rod Serling (1924–1975) is an unusually difficult task. Even if we restrict ourselves to his specifically horrific or fantastic work—chiefly "The Twilight Zone" and "Night Gallery"—the process of evaluation is complicated by the fact that the bulk of Serling's literary work (three volumes of "Twilight Zone" stories, two volumes of "Night Gallery" stories, and the three novelettes gathered under the title *The Season to Be Wary*) was initially conceived for television. How valid, then, is an analysis of his writing simply as writing? Ought we to read his stories with the television episodes in mind, or should we conversely strive to forget that the stories are—in genesis, at any rate— secondary to the teleplays and judge them on purely literary grounds? As a literary critic not entirely comfortable with television as an aesthetic medium, my inclination is toward the latter course; and I have a suspicion that Serling himself would be grateful for such an evaluation.

If there is anything that unites the whole of Serling's work—whether it be short stories or film scripts, whether it be fantastic or mainstream—it is an abiding concern with human feeling. T. E. D. Klein has stated bluntly that "his stories are not afraid to teach a moral lesson" (TZ x), and the same could be said for the best of Serling's non-fantastic works, principally the teleplays "Patterns" (1955) and "Requiem for a Heavyweight" (1956). This is something "Twilight Zone" viewers and readers hardly need be told, for at times the moralism becomes rather obvious and heavy-handed: we know too clearly whose side Serling is on. Indeed, this moralistic element may well be the key to understanding why and how Serling used the supernatural in his work: it becomes an oftentimes transparent prop for the conveying of the moral message.

I think, however, that Serling is not always adept in his use of the supernatural. "The Fever" is a gripping tale about a straitlaced man who succumbs to gambling fever on a trip to Las Vegas, staying up an entire night trying to defeat a slot-machine which, in his frenzy, he has endowed with human feelings and a human countenance:

> Everything that he'd used to sustain himself through his lifetime—his willfulness, his pettiness, his self-delusions, his prejudices—held whipped together like a suit of armor and this is what he wore as he battled the machine on into the morning. Slip in the coin, pull down the lever. Slip in the coin, pull down the lever. Slip in the coin, pull down the lever. Keep it up. Don't stop. Don't break the routine of hand and arm and eye and ear. This was the new chronology of his life function. Sooner or later the machine would pay off. It would surrender to him. It would acknowledge his superiority by suddenly spewing out eight thousand silver dollars. This was all

he thought about as he stood there, oblivious to the dawn outside, to anything except that he was alone in the world with a one-armed bandit that
had a face. (TZ 87)

This is a brilliant and mordant psychological analysis, but the effect seems
marred or confused by the conclusion, where we are led to believe that the
machine was actually animate and possibly filled with malevolence against
its opponent. This dilutes the message by partially absolving the man of
moral guilt in the matter. A cleverer use of the supernatural is "The Big,
Tall Wish," one of Serling's most poignant stories. Here a boy's fervent
wish that an ageing boxer win a fight appears actually to make the fighter
win: the boxer returns to his neighbourhood in glory, receiving the con-
gratulations of his friends. But when he meets the boy he cannot believe
that it was simply the boy's wish that raised him from the mat to victory:

> They stood there close together. Henry's voice, a plaintive, hopeful
> prayer; the fighter's, a hollow, empty rejection. The sick, thin yellow light
> from the bulb over the roof door held them briefly in a weak illumination
> and then time froze again. The light gradually changed until it was no
> longer on the roof. It was the white-hot orb of the ring light bathing the
> canvas of the roped-off area of a fight arena where a dark and bleeding
> fighter lay on his stomach, his face against the canvas and rosin of the ring
> floor. Above him a referee brought down his arm in measured sweeps.
> "Eight, nine, ten." (TZ 226)

The fighter's lack of belief ("'There ain't no magic. No magic, Henry. I had
that fight coming and going. I had it in my pocket. I was the number one
out there and there ain't no such thing as magic'" [TZ 225]) has caused his
defeat, because for the magic to work, everyone has to believe—and nowa-
days "'there's not enough people around to believe'" (TZ 228). In "Dust"
there is doubt whether the supernatural comes into play: a seedy conman in
the old West sells some common dust that he has scraped off the ground to
an ignorant Mexican whose son is to be hanged, claiming that the dust will
cause people to forgive; the Mexican showers the dust over the crowd, and
the rope on the gallows breaks, allowing the victim to go free. Did the dust
actually work or was the rope (sold by the conman) simply defective? We
never know, and it is better so.

What I think is not sufficiently emphasised in discussions of Serling is
the degree to which his vision of human life is dark, pessimistic, cynical,
and even misanthropic. One develops the impression that Serling was an
optimist and idealist who suffered such repeated failures and disillusions
that he reacted even more extremely to instances of human failing or petti-
ness than a born misanthrope like Bierce or a bland indifferentist like
Lovecraft. Serling's view of petty bourgeois married life is particularly
bleak, as the opening description of Franklin Gibbs and his wife in "The
Fever" demonstrates:

He and his wife lived on Elm Street in a small, two-bedroom house which was about twenty years old, had a small garden in back, and an arbor of roses in front which were Mr. Gibbs's passion.

Flora Gibbs, married to Franklin for twenty-two years, was angular, with mousy, stringy hair and chest measurements perhaps a quarter of an inch smaller than her husband's. She was quiet voiced though talkative, long, if unconsciously, suffering and had led a life devoted to the care and feeding of Franklin Gibbs, the placating of his sullen moods, his finicky appetite, and his uncontrollable rage at any change in the routine of their daily lives. (TZ 72–73)

Later, during an altercation as to whether they should play the slot machines, we get a telling insight: "The corners of Franklin's mouth twitched in a righteous smile, and for one fleeting moment Flora hated him" (TZ 78).

The misanthropy of Serling's worldview is no more evident than in "The Monsters Are Due on Maple Street," where all it takes is to "stop a few of their machines and radios and telephones and lawn mowers" (TZ 134) and people turn upon themselves in mutual recrimination and bloodshed. Klein draws parallels to "the Communist witch-hunt of the fifties" (TZ xi), and there is certainly this undercurrent in the story; but I would not want to restrict the message to one so purely political. Another story with the same basic framework—intelligent aliens toying with human beings—has a surprisingly similar message. "Mr. Dingle, the Strong" is the ostensibly comic story of a man endowed with enormous strength by a Martian; but all that Luther Dingle does with this power is to exact cheap revenge on a lout who has repeatedly bullied him and to make a spectacle of his strength through the media. The Martian is right in concluding: "We give him the strength of three hundred men . . . and he uses it for petty exhibition" (TZ 182). We will never become supermen because we are not worthy of it.

"The Shelter" may well be the best story Serling ever wrote, and it is one of his bleakest. Here the message is overtly political—the cold war and its chilling effect upon everyone in the fifties and sixties is harrowingly etched in this tale of a private fallout shelter that is destroyed by desperate neighbours who want to save themselves during what appears to be a nuclear attack—but one character draws a broader message:

> "The damages I'm talking about," he said, "are the pieces of ourselves that we've pulled apart tonight. The veneer—the thin veneer that we ripped aside with our own hands. The hatred that came to the surface that we didn't even realize we had. But, oh Jesus—how quick it came out! And how quickly we became animals! All of us."
>
> He pointed to himself. "Me, too—maybe I was the worst of the bunch. I don't know."
>
> He paused for a moment and looked around. "I don't think it'll be normal again. At least, not in our lifetime. And if, God forgive, that bomb

does fall—I hope we've made our peace *before* we suffer it. I hope that if it has to kill and destroy and maim, the victims will be human beings—not naked, wild beasts who put such a premium on staying alive that they claw their neighbors to death just for the privilege." (TZ 336)

This same misanthropy can be seen at work in those tales where a transparently evil person gets his comeuppance. These stories are somewhat less successful overall, because—as Serling ought to have realised—this sort of poetic justice rarely occurs in real life; but we can feel the author's relish at consigning his characters to some merited destruction. "The Rip Van Winkle Caper" is perhaps the most effective: this well-known story of four criminals who steal a huge quantity of gold and then seal themselves away in suspended animation for a century, only to find upon awakening that gold is no longer valued, is too well known for detailed description; but some touches are uncommonly fine. The absolute evil of one character who extorts from his parched and exhausted colleague a bar of gold for every sip of water is a masterstroke. Also, the clever plot device of having one of the four thieves die and turn to a skeleton, as the glass container in which he is reposing shatters during his century-long sleep, both proves that some long period of time really has elapsed and suggests the tenuous and anomalous nature of their existence in a century where they do not belong.

It becomes obvious that two of the "Twilight Zone" stories, "Walking Distance" and "A Stop at Willoughby," are patently autobiographical in their portrayal of a harried businessman longing for the simplicity and blissfulness of childhood. Both stories, especially the former, are very powerful, but the conclusion of the latter is ambiguous: Gart Williams debarks from his commuter train at the old-fashioned town of Willoughby, which exists on no map, but in reality he has leaped off the train to his death. Is Serling saying that death is the only hope for such sentimental misfits who appear to have no place in the modern world? "Walking Distance," of course, ends relatively happily in that Martin Sloan appears to gain new strength to face his life from the brief encounter with his hometown past, as a conversation with his father suggests:

"Is it so bad—where you're from?" Robert asked him.

"I thought so," Martin answered. "I've been living at a dead run, Dad. I've been weak and I made believe I was strong. I've been scared to death—but I've been playing a strong man. And suddenly it all caught up with me. And I felt so tired, Pop. I felt so damned tired, running for so long. Then—one day I knew I had to come back. I had to come back and get on a merry-go-round and listen to a band concert and eat cotton candy. I had to stop and breathe and close my eyes and smell and listen."

"I guess we all want that," Robert said gently. "But, Martin, when you go back, maybe you'll find that there are merry-go-rounds and band concerts where you are and summer nights, too. Maybe you haven't looked in the right place. You've been looking behind you, Martin. Try looking ahead." (TZ 68–69)

"Walking Distance" provides as good an opportunity as any for comparing Serling as a short story writer and as a screenwriter, for the original script was published in the first issue (April 1981) of *Twilight Zone* magazine. (Some dozen or so scripts which Serling wrote into stories were eventually published in the magazine.) The comparison is illuminating, and shows that—in spite of Serling's own doubts on the matter—he mastered short story technique in every way. In the first place, Serling realised that he would have to paint the setting, characters, and atmosphere by words rather than by images, and accordingly he begins his story with a lengthy description of Martin's unhappy life in New York and his yearning to get away—and one memorable phrase in this passage could never have been captured on the screen: "Some kind of ghostly billy club tapped at his ankles and told him it was later than he thought" (TZ 53).

The scene where Martin scans his hometown and awakens his memories of youth is much elaborated in the story. Whereas in the TV episode we simply see Martin gazing at the houses (and, of course, infer that he is thinking of his childhood), the story is more explicit:

He felt the bittersweet pang of nostalgia. He remembered the games he'd played with the kids on this street. The newspapers he'd delivered. The small-boy accidents on roller skates and bicycles. And the people. The faces and names that fused in his mind now. His house was on the corner and for some reason he wanted to save this for last. He could see it ahead of him. Big, white, with a semi-circular porch running around it. Cupolas. An iron jockey in front. God, the things you remembered. The things you tucked away in an old mental trunk and forgot. Then you opened the trunk and there they were. (TZ 58–59)

In other instances we find that Serling, while filming the actual episode, made significant changes that improved the overall thrust of the plot; these changes were then incorporated into the written story. In the screenplay, after encountering a boy playing marbles, Martin goes right to his own house and meets his still living father and mother, only to be rebuffed by them in confusion; he then goes to a park and meets a woman, with whom he chats nostalgically. In the TV episode these two scenes are reversed— the chat with the woman occurs first, then the encounter with his parents—much to the improvement of the logic and dramatic climax of the scenario. This alteration is reflected in the story.

All this shows the care with which Serling pondered the transformation of script into story. It is true that some tales appear to be more literal adaptations of TV scripts—even the touching "The Big, Tall Wish" seems to be a succession of episodes somewhat jerkily stitched together—but on the whole Serling is successful in endowing his tales with the vividness of imagery and the narrative pace required for prose fiction.

"Walking Distance" has a bittersweetly happy ending; other "Twilight Zone" stories go even further to become either whimsical ("The Night of the Meek" is the most celebrated example) or outrightly comic. Perhaps it is a temperamental flaw of my own that I do not appreciate such stories as much as the darker tales. There is no question that such things as "The Mighty Casey," "The Whole Truth," and, to a lesser extent, "Mr. Dingle, the Strong" are successful as comic fantasy, and, as Klein points out, much of the humour is a result of the imagery and narration and not the dialogue, hence is a good index to Serling's talent in prose narrative. A slightly different kind of humour is present in "Showdown with Rance McGrew," involving one of Serling's cleverest uses of the supernatural. A vain but incompetent cowboy actor named Rance McGrew appears to encounter the ghost of Jesse James during a shooting of McGrew's television show; James is displeased at the treatment of himself and his associates on the show, and exacts a promise from the petrified McGrew to rewrite the episode. McGrew wakes up from an apparent hallucination, but as he strolls to his car he finds James sitting in the car to make sure McGrew fulfils his promise. The whole story gives the impression of being a parody of itself, and perhaps a parody of the entire "Twilight Zone" series.

A few words—but no more—ought to be said about Walter B. Gibson's two volumes of stories associated with "The Twilight Zone," *Rod Serling's The Twilight Zone* (Grosset & Dunlap, 1963) and *Twilight Zone Revisited* (Grosset & Dunlap, 1964). In spite of their titles, they have almost nothing to do with the television series. The first volume does contain adaptations of two "Twilight Zone" episodes, "Back There" and "Judgment Night," but the other eleven stories, as well as all thirteen in the second volume, are simply tales written presumably in the spirit of "The Twilight Zone." They are not very successful, and in fact provide an insightful contrast to Serling's own work. These lifeless and routine stories entirely lack Serling's vivacity, piquancy, and brooding concern with human evil. For the most part they are conventional ghost stories; in a very peculiar foreword to the first volume, Gibson appears to be encouraging us to take them seriously as excursions into the paranormal. It is still more difficult to do this than to take them seriously as stories of any aesthetic value.

The three novelettes comprising *The Season to Be Wary* (1967)—"Escape Route," "Color Scheme," and "Eyes"—are among Serling's least known works, as the volume has been out of print for more than thirty years. Although the stories are slightly prolix—they stretch short story ideas into novelettes—Serling's mordant cynicism is at its height here, with some imperishable metaphors: the Nazi pursued by Jews in "Escape Route" is "some stale breath left over from a death rattle" (SW 60); and of the hapless ex-fighter Charlie Hatcher in "Eyes": "What a Goddamned and miserable shame it was that God said to some men the moment they were born—'You lose'" (SW 145). The portrait of the con artist Tony Petrozella is etched in vitriol:

> It never occurred to Tony Petrozella that the best part—the most merciful part—of his condition was his stupidity. He could never—and would never—distinguish between lechery and love. And in that hungering little brain of his, he would never know that at this stage of the game, it was his last dance—and the music was a litany of the floating crap game that had been his life. He would be buried—still kicking in time to the music—with fading visions of broads and "good, fast boys" and a cashmere topcoat. And he would never know that in all his second-rate, cheap grubbing years, he had never drawn a really happy breath or felt any kind of contentment. The shrewdness it took to pick out a particular patsy who would uncomplainingly put himself on a rack did not extend to an awareness of himself. He lived and he would die with his own ignorance. (SW 163–64)

This last story, "Eyes," is perhaps the only one that deserves its length, and each of its characters—the evil, manipulative blind woman Miss Menlo, who will walk over everyone simply for a few hours of sight; Charlie Hatcher, an ignorant, confused pawn; Petrozella, who will do anything to save his skin—is realised crisply. The plot focuses around Miss Menlo's desire to undergo an optic nerve transplant, even though it will mean she will have sight only for about twelve hours; she, her lawyer, and Petrozella manoeuvre Hatcher into being the donor, and when he commits suicide Petrozella himself is forced to give up his eyes in order to escape an even worse fate for debts he owes. The transplant is carried out, and Miss Menlo gains her sight—but it occurs during the New York City blackout of 1965. Accordingly, she feels that the long sought-for operation is a failure and in her hysteria falls out her apartment window to her death. Serling's biographer Joel Engel claims to find all sorts of "plot holes" in the story, but they don't stand up. "Why, for example, does the doctor come to visit her before the bandages are removed; why does he not remove them himself, and wouldn't she want to see him?" Why shouldn't the doctor visit his patient? And Miss Menlo had already told the doctor she does not want anyone in her presence when she gains sight. Given her selfish nature, this is entirely in character. "Why was she unable to see the headlights of the thousands of cars streaming by her Central Park South apartment?" (Engel 286). Serling has accounted for this also, by noting that road work had sealed off the two blocks of the street around her apartment (which, by the way, was not on Central Park South but on Fifth Avenue). This may be a suspiciously convenient ploy, but it is unfair to Serling to suggest that he has not accounted for it at all. The one true plot failing in the story, rightly pointed out by Engel, is the fact that the twelve hours of sight would occur at night, when it was earlier mentioned that among the things Miss Menlo wished to do was to visit museums that are open only during the day. Alas! the brute fact of the blackout occurring at night forced Serling's hand here; but surely we can overlook this flaw in the biting pungency of the story. The other two tales are similarly sharp and bitter, and only their verbosity prevents them from measuring up to the best of Serling's other fiction.

The two volumes of "Night Gallery" stories have also not seen print for decades, but there is every reason to think them at least as meritorious as the "Twilight Zone" tales. It may be true that the whole "Night Gallery" episode was a painful and humiliating one in Serling's life—he was afraid that the series would not emphasise his moral concerns (Engel quotes Serling's comment to Universal Studios: "I wanted a series with distinction, with episodes that said something; I have no interest in a series which is purely and uniquely suspenseful but totally uncommentative on anything" [Engel 328]) and the editorial control of the show was not in his hands but in those of Jack Laird. But I still maintain that some of the "Night Gallery" episodes had undeniable power and—what is perhaps more important—some of Serling's "Night Gallery" stories reveal him to be absolutely at the top of his form as a fictionist.

"Make Me Laugh" is certainly one of the bleakest things Serling ever wrote, and this tale of a wretched two-bit comic named Jackie Slater demonstrates Serling's power to etch, in a few vicious strokes, the meaningless lives of ordinary Joes who yearn for a talent they don't have. Slater's agent Jules Kettleman reflects on Slater's and his own wasted existence:

> Jules swallowed, sniffed again, pulled out his handkerchief, and looked at this weeping whale in the chair. He wanted to reach out and touch him, say something gentle . . . something kind. But in the back of his fifty-seven-year-old agent's mind, the thought came to him. Oh, God, but Jackie was right. He could break his balls for the next twenty years, lining up the one-nighters, counting out his ten-percent in nickels and dimes, and telling this poor, no-talent hippo that he was the greatest—when they both knew you could blow only so much smoke up anybody's butt until you had to acknowledge defeat and officially surrender. He thought of all this as he tiptoed quietly out of the room. Jackie was the last of the stable. Most of them gone. Some of them dead and buried. All of them either has-beens or never-wases. Maybe he could find some stacked broad who'd sing topless. Or maybe he could latch onto a magician who did dirty tricks. He'd have to find some kind of act. He'd just have to scrounge. And scrounging, Jules Kettleman had done all his life. It wasn't his fault, he thought, as he went out a side door into the alley, that he always unearthed dogs. Dogs, hambones, and fat Pagliaccis who planted their big asses on a wailing wall and wondered why they got carbuncles instead of laughs. (NG1, 28–29)

But when a swami endows Slater with the power of making people laugh at anything he says, he finds the gift a mixed blessing: it is now all too easy, and, although he makes millions as a comic, he fails in his attempt to become a serious actor. The message is not new—the attainment of a sought-for goal does not always bring the satisfaction we expected—but the handling is adept.

"They're Tearing Down Tim Riley's Bar" might rank as Serling's finest story—in poignancy, in atmosphere, in concision and crispness of style— were it not for two factors: one, the basic plot—an ageing businessman being pushed out of the way by a go-getter upstart—is very similar to Serling's early and non-fantastic "Patterns"; and two, an adventitious happy ending has been tacked on (at the command of Jack Laird, as Engel reports [327]). For Randy Lane, caught in a job that has left him behind and with the wife he loved long dead, the visions of the now-closed Tim Riley's bar—which he sees as it was in its heyday, when his family and friends held a party for him there as he returned from World War II—are fragments of a time and place that was significant to him because he was a genuine part of them:

> Just for a second . . . just for a single moment . . . he saw a banner stretched across the room which read, "Welcome Home, Randy." And in that moment the voices were loud and the faces recognizable. His father. Tim Riley. Even McDonough was there—a very young cop. And something surged inside Randy Lane. A joy . . . an excitement . . . a sense of satisfaction, being where he belonged. But as he turned toward his father, the room went dark and empty. Cobwebs and wires from dismantled fixtures and a cracked mirror were all he could make out in the darkness. He stumbled over a broken, overturned chair as he turned and moved back toward the front door. Before leaving he turned once again to survey the room. His loneliness had been a dull, formless thing, and held learned to carry it with him. But now he felt the sudden sharp, jabbing pain of something beyond loneliness; some overwhelming anguish almost impossible to bear. He suddenly felt lost and bewildered, as if something . . . something important and integral—had just eluded him. (NG1, 123–24)

The "Night Gallery" tales are, if anything, even grimmer than the "Twilight Zone" stories. Here we encounter a doctor who collects human specimens for the fun of it ("Collector's Items"); a man who cannot endure the fact that he is not the first man on the moon, a secret voyage having taken place more than a century before ("Does the Name Grimsby Do Anything to You?"); a brutalised son who hangs the head of his cruel father, a celebrated huntsman, on the wall of his trophy room ("Clean Kills and Other Trophies"). It is clear that Serling chose to write stories only of those episodes that meant something to him and that stressed a conflict of human wills (I wish, however, that he had written up the episode called "Cemetery," which appeared on the "Night Gallery" pilot and petrified me when I saw it). And the heart-rending "Messiah on Mott Street," where a young Jewish boy appears to find the Messiah to save his aged and ailing grandfather, is perhaps the best of Serling's "happy" stories.

I trust I have suggested that Serling, in addition to being a highly adept storyteller, also displayed great skill in writing teleplays and in directing his "Twilight Zone" and "Night Gallery" episodes. The mass media were certainly Serling's prime interest, and writing short stories was a decidedly secondary activity. If I still conclude that Serling's literary work may outlast all his other accomplishments, it is not merely on account of my bias toward print. It is a commonplace that such things as television shows and movies are collaborative efforts, even when—as in the case of "The Twilight Zone"—a single individual has editorial control. It becomes, therefore, problematical how many of the virtues (or failings) of a given episode or film are to be attributed to its "author," who is merely a cog in a very complicated machine. And even in the age of the ubiquitous VCR and the availability of "Twilight Zone" episodes in syndication and on videocassette, it will still be easier and, perhaps, more satisfying to gauge the power and skill of Serling as an artist from his tales than from his teleplays. Serling claimed to find the task of writing prose fiction almost excruciatingly difficult—something, curiously, that links him with the founding editor of *Twilight Zone* magazine, T. E. D. Klein—but we should be grateful that he took the time and effort to write the three dozen or so stories he did, for they have earned him a small but unassailable niche in the domain of modern weird fiction.

L. P. Davies: The Workings of the Mind

The work of Leslie Purnell Davies (1914–?) is, in its quiet way, some of the most remarkable weird fiction written during the 1960s and 1970s. In a string of some twenty novels Davies combined the elements of mystery, horror, and science fiction in a manner duplicated by no other writer. Moreover, Davies' work is united in a curious way by a single theme—a theme he himself has labelled "'Psycho fiction' . . . fiction based on the workings of the human mind" (Reilly 437). The prototypical Davies novel features a man (his protagonists are all male) who has lost his memory or, more harrowingly, who seems to have had the physical tokens of his past completely wiped out, leaving him adrift in the present with no way to prove his identity. Other Davies novels focus upon possible expansions in the powers of the mind—telekinesis, mind control or psychic possession, and elaborate hypnosis or brainwashing. Davies repeatedly emphasises the logical possibility of all these phenomena, and in only one or two novels is the suggestion of the supernatural not explained away by natural, if at times supernormal, means.

The Paper Dolls (1964), Davies' first novel, initiates the series of works dealing with the expanded powers of the mind. Here we are introduced to a set of quadruplet boys, joined at the arms and separated shortly after birth, whose minds appear linked: at times each knows what the other is doing, and each suffers sympathetic wounds when one or the other is involved in accidents. This itself would be nothing to strain credulity—linkages of this sort are commonly found to exist among children born from the same fertilised egg—but Davies expands the concept by suggesting that the boys (at least the one of them who seems to be their leader) can control other people's minds for a time, inducing hallucinations or even suicidal tendencies. Two of the quadruplets, at widely differing times and places, are found to have been involved in incidents where another boy who had been harassing them jumps from a building or otherwise injures or kills himself. One character remarks:

> "It would appear . . . that at least one of the children is possessed of extraordinary powers. Powers that again I am prepared to accept, assuming them to be some kind of development from certain thought-projectory faculties that one hears mentioned from time to time." (82)

Later the narrator wonders:

> Mutants, were they? I had read of plants that had become altered, mutated—was that the right word?—by radio-activity. If plants, then animals. And we were still animals ourselves. Man the mammal. The genus of Primates. With a brain that we still hadn't learned to use properly. Was that

the difference between the children and ourselves? Had they learned the use of that part of the brain that we left idle? (112)

In fact, the matter is revealed to be still more bizarre than this: the four boys are really a single mind in four different bodies. One of the boys, Rodney, tells the narrator: "Tony-me is sleeping. If I wake that part I will think it to Simon-me at the Pillory and to me at home, and then I will think it here so that I can go before it reaches" (135). The narrator, reflecting on this odd language, finally concludes:

> This was dual personality carried to its incredible extreme. Doctor Jekyll working in his surgery at the same time as the evil Mr. Hyde prowled the night streets. Hyde looking through Jekyll's eyes into a microscope at the same time that Jekyll was watching through Hyde's eyes the back-street slut marked down as his next victim. At the same time; that was the difference. Not one man with two interchangeable personalities, but one man with two separate personalities, each housed in a separate body. One man who was two.
> And four boys who were one. The Rodney-me part with a talent for writing; Simon-me—physics and chemistry, according to Bart; Peter-me who was an artist. And Tony-me, musician, and other things. The part responsible for the killings. The evil quarter of the multiple personality. The dominant part. . . . (142)

The only flaw in this novel, aside from the almost excessively restrained narrative tone, is the naive suggestion that all the "evil" is concentrated in the boy's leader Tony, leaving the others guiltless and thus free to carry on with their lives after Tony perishes in a fire at the end.

The notion of "dual personality carried to its incredible extreme" links this novel to a later one, *Psychogeist* (1966), marketed as a science fiction novel for no especially compelling reason. Here we are presented with a man, Edward Garvey, with a recurring dream of being a denizen of another planet named Argred the Freeman who has some mission that he must accomplish, if only he could remember it. All this sounds a trifle hackneyed—there are references to the Old People, the Mind-Healers, Old Lorr, the Wise Elder of the Freeman—but this turns out to be by design: Garvey's subconscious is living out the events of an old comic book he had read in youth. One character makes no bones about the comic's literary merit:

> "Hardly what one might call a literary gem. The anonymous author had made use of every stock situation with a scant regard for verisimilitude. One received the impression that he had dealt out the various stages like playing-cards from a pack, or from a list tacked for reference above his typewriter. He had included everything; mind-rays, torture, underground places filled with mummies, poison, strange machines, magic—the lot. But the story was, of course, only intended for a juvenile readership." (98–99)

At this point there is nothing particularly remarkable; and one might expect that the rest of the novel will be spent on diagnosing and treating Garvey's schizophrenia. But Davies introduces a fascinating twist. Garvey's subconscious seizes upon the body of a young transient who has died by accident and reanimates it; and this body becomes Argred the Freeman. One character explains:

> "There is nothing supernatural about it . . . Not when you come to consider. Schizophrenia taken to its ultimate logical extreme. There were two—what?—beings inside Edward's mind; himself and Argred. All that has happened is that the subconscious being has left him, taking up occupancy in a suitable vehicle.
>
> "It's nothing new. The 'possession' of the Middle Ages—to be possessed of an evil spirit. Hypnotism is another facet. One person's mind temporarily controls the body of another. And reincarnation. . . . A large slice of the world's population implicitly believes that the life-essence, the soul, leaves the dying body to take up residence in a new body. And many psychiatrists believe that the soul is merely another name for the subconscious." (100)

The protagonists must now prevent this putrefying corpse from wreaking havoc in the small community in which it is loosed.

The otherwise inferior novel *The Lampton Dreamers* (1966) continues the pattern. Here the inhabitants of an entire village appear to have the identical dream. Eventually this phenomenon is attributed to the power of a single individual's mind—"will projected by the power of thought" (66). As with several other novels, the suggestion is that this power is latent within us all, hence not supernatural in any real sense: "A diseased, distorted mind? But there was another way of looking at it. A mind that has learned to use itself to the full, employing those parts of it that had become dormant through countless centuries of unuse" (103).

Two novels that give the appearance of involving actual psychic possession are *Stranger to Town* (1969) and *Possession* (1976). These works in some senses are mirror-images of *Psychogeist*: rather than a living individual reanimating the body of a dead man, a dead man seems to have possessed the mind of a living one. In *Stranger to Town*, another not entirely successful novel, Julian Midwinter arrives at a small town—one he has apparently never visited before—and seems to know things he cannot possibly know: the name of the ticket agent, the configuration of the hotel he is staying at, and still odder things. There is a strong suggestion that Midwinter is being possessed by the mind of Josh Hardman, who died several years before. His wife Amy is a member of the Church of Life's Return, a sect that believes that the souls of the dead return in other people's bodies. Initially the interest in the novel focuses upon the possible truth of this doctrine and the rather harrowing way in which Midwinter is subtly pressed into taking over Hardman's life, such that his own life and personality are nearly extinguished: he is persuaded to reopen Hardman's business, joins Hardman's cronies for late-evening sessions at the pub, and so on. But the novel suffers a serious letdown when it is implausibly revealed that Midwinter is really a con man, and the conclusion of the novel—involving fraud, blackmail, and attempted murder—is merely routine.

Possession is considerably better, and introduces us to the Brazilian religion called Macumba, which again holds that the dead can reoccupy living bodies. All along, though, doubt is cast as to whether this Macumba mumbo-jumbo is simply being used as an elaborate fraud or hoax; the protagonist remarks: "Black magic and voodoo curses and all the rest have been used as weapons in politics and business before now. I think that what is going on here is something to do with very big business" (83)—the reason for this being the anomalous appearance of several enormously wealthy real estate tycoons in an otherwise sleepy English village. Nevertheless, there are chilling glimpses of an individual who seems to have adopted the characteristics of a man who died in a suspicious accident some weeks before. But when one of those who appears to be staging the whole series of events refers to "the Macumba cover" (136), we seem vindicated in suspecting a natural explanation to the whole thing; but the supernatural—or, rather, some radical advancement of science—is suggested from another direction. A doctor has written a thesis on *Physical Transference by Means of Cell Ingestion of Habit, Character and Memory Patterns in Anguis Fragilis*. The narrator ruminates on this:

> You take your specimen—that's what the notes and the diagram mazes were about—you take your wriggling little specimen and put it in a maze and you teach it by trial and error to find its way to the food. And when it's learned to do that, you put it in a more complicated maze, you give it harder obstacles to master, and when it's learned that, you move it on to the next. And at the end you have a wriggling little monster that is clever enough to find its way without hesitation through your most complicated maze. And then what do you do? You kill it and cut it into pieces and pound the pieces and feed the mash to a new worm, a fresh, ignorant worm. And you put that ignorant worm in the most difficult maze, and it goes straight to the food without any wavering.
>
> Because what you have done is give it, in the mash, the thoughts and memories and the knowledge, the learned knowledge, of the first worm. Even its habits and idiosyncrasies—for Boyle had written about that, had made notes about one specimen that had its own peculiar way of turning a corner, its own way of approaching the food from one side. And dead, passed on those mannerisms in the mash of its body to the new worm fed on that mash.
>
> Memories, knowledge, character, habits. A kind of immortality. No, not just a *kind*—it *was* immortality.

And what you can do to a worm, you can do to a man. (147–48)

Implausible as this may sound, coming at this point in the story it offers an uncannily precise explanation of events; it is a pity that this novel, like *Stranger to Town*, in the end reduces the notion to a hoax.

Davies' second novel, *Who Is Lewis Pinder?* (1965), introduces us to his most representative series of novels, involving amnesia, brainwashing, or some nameless wiping away of one's past. A man is found in a ditch, dressed in a suit but with no shoes; he has suffered complete amnesia, and cannot even remember how he came to be where he was. Davies quietly but poignantly etches the man's sensations:

> He was putting everything down on paper in case anything else were to happen to his memory. Next time the shadows swallowed the past he would have something to go on. He wondered who he was. He wondered if he had a wife and family. He wondered who his friends had been; where he had lived; what he had done for a living; what sort of person he had been. (36)

But as the police investigation proceeds, more and more anomalous facts are unearthed: the man appears to be identified conclusively (by means of a highly unusual birthmark and other characteristics) as four different men, each of whom has been dead and buried for more than twenty years. Davies' narrative skill in presenting this baffling mystery may never have been excelled in later works, and it would be criminal to reveal the ingenious and thoroughly satisfying solution to this novel.

The amnesia theme reaches its pinnacle in *The Shadow Before* (1970), perhaps Davies' best novel. Here a man has an extraordinarily long and complex dream following a brain tumour operation, and it is in the dream that he experiences amnesia. As Lester Dunn[1]—all within the dream—struggles to regain his memory, he must also account for his radically changed circumstances: several years have passed, he has changed his name, he appears to have wealth beyond his dreams, and he seems to have been involved in criminal activity. This turns out to be the case. Dunn had noticed that a jeweller's shop abutted the rear of his pharmacy, and that it would be possible to tunnel underground to the jeweller's vault. Dunn and his friends have done this and apparently gotten off scot-free. But trouble arises: the husband of Dunn's shop assistant learns of the robbery and begins to blackmail all the parties, and this leads to Dunn's transformation into a murderer and a fugitive.

At this point Dunn wakes up. Enormously relieved to find it all a dream, he attempts to return to his normal life as a struggling pharmacist. But he finds himself haunted by the dream: it seemed not merely lifelike but utterly plausible. Every detail seems to fit, and Dunn has to find a weak link:

Turn reality back into fantasy, reason told him. Chip away at its foundations as you chipped at that wall. Find the weak places where the stuff of the dream has no solid foundation in the reality of the present. There must be those places. One will be enough. Find one factor in the dream on which you can lay your finger and say: "This was not so in real life." Find that, and the whole fabric of the dream will collapse; your mind will be rid of its presence and the ghost will have been laid. (89)

But as Dunn checks on the various details of the dream in an attempt to dispel it, his actions are noted by his friends and they eventually piece together the substance of the dream; worse, they find the dream so plausible that they compel Dunn into acting it out with them. It is at this point— where dream and reality begin to mingle insidiously—that the novel becomes almost unbearably chilling as Dunn is led step by step toward the fatalistic accomplishment of his dream-scenario. The ending of this novel is too good to reveal here.

Some touches in *The Shadow Before* are uncommonly fine. The early portions of the novel carefully delineate Dunn's impoverished circumstances ("A [profit] margin that could be measured in pennies. Trade was bad" [6]), providing both the contrast to the wealth he experiences in the dream and its psychological justification. Indeed, the highly cynical underlying moral of the tale is the ease with which normally law-abiding citizens will take to crime if they feel they can come away unscathed. During the dream his friends notice that Dunn has changed after he came out of the hospital ("'No werewolf-at-full-moon stuff. Nothing you could really put your finger on. Unsettled—that's the word. Dissatisfied with life in general'" [45]); then, during his actual life after the operation, he is also observed to have changed, but precisely because of the dream: the sequence of cause and effect has become monstrously confused. All told, this novel—enormously rich in psychological probing, extraordinarily convoluted in narrative structure, and endowed with a sense of harrowing inevitability—can rank as one of the finest weird novels of its time.

Each of Davies' major themes appears to have both its "mystery" and its "science fiction" representatives, and the amnesia theme is no different. Here we are specifically concerned with *What Did I Do Tomorrow?* (1972). I have already suggested that the distinction between mystery and science fiction is on the whole an artificial one in Davies, and this novel seems to have been marketed as science fiction only because the lead character, a teenager named Howell Trowman, finds himself drifting from 1969 to a future five years ahead. One moment he is sitting in a chair in his room at school, the next moment he finds himself sitting in an office he does not recognise, and he seems aware that several years must have passed. Like Dunn, Trowman must first set about finding out what has happened to him in the five-year interval, and many disturbing things seem to have occurred: he is working for the chief rival to his father's company; he has done something so heinous that not merely his old friends but his family—even his mother—refuse to speak to him; and he finds a large suitcase of money in his apartment. Trowman's quest, after ascertaining his circumstances, is to discover whether he has actually suffered amnesia or has somehow travelled in time. He is inclined to accept the latter answer: as he was finishing school, he was undecided whether to enter college or go directly into his father's business, and perhaps he has been sent forward into the future to gauge the results of his decision. But a young woman who has befriended him rightly points out the fallacy of this position, enunciating the "determinism paradox":

> "Look at it another way. You say you've been given the chance of looking at what your future's going to be. So supposing you find it's not so hot, supposing you find you came to the wrong decision way back when you were at school—well, don't you see, you can't go back and unchange it all, because it's all already happened. You see what I'm getting at? What's the use of showing you the future when you can't do anything to change it? It's just pointless." (39)

Again, it would be unfair to reveal the resolution of this situation, but Davies manages to make it both suspenseful and satisfying.

A sort of mirror-image to the amnesia theme is the theme of an individual's past being apparently wiped away. Here a character knows who he is and has suffered no lapse of memory, but finds that the physical relics of his past have been absolutely annihilated. What could possibly have caused this state of affairs? The characters are inclined to think that there is some vast conspiracy to obliterate their pasts and, hence, their very identities; but those around them more plausibly put forward the notions of brainwashing, schizophrenia, or some other psychological motivation. Since we see events through the eyes of the characters experiencing this "identity crisis," we ourselves are cut adrift: we know who the protagonists are, but how can they prove it?

In *The White Room* (1969) Axel Champlee, a wealthy businessman, flees his mansion when he is faced with the fact of his brother-in-law's embezzlement of funds and finds that his sister is urging him to kill him. But in fleeing he has only made matters worse: in the outside world he finds that it is not 1969 but 1979, that the parliamentary district he resides in does not exist, and that a popular writer he had just had dinner with died five years before. Has Champlee also been flung into the future? Or is there some elaborate conspiracy to delude him? If so, why? One of the most powerful scenes in all Davies' work occurs when Champlee attempts to return to the place where he believes his house to be:

He took out his keys and used the light of a street lamp to sort out the one for the front door. Better to have it ready than to have to waste time fumbling in the semi-darkness of the mews.

They were almost there. Another massive gate, a short stretch of blank wall, and they had reached the corner.

"The house is only a short way down on this side," Axel said in a low voice. "It's the only one on this side."

They turned the corner.

There was no house on the right-hand side, no sign of one, nothing but bleak towering wall with neither window nor doorway to relieve its stark ugliness. And there were no trees on the other side to be glimpsed through their branches. And this was no cul-de-sac, no narrow, dimly lighted mews. This was a wide modern thoroughfare with glaring overhead lights that reached far away into the distance. (72)

This is an almost archetypal moment in Davies: nothing could be more shattering to your sense of personal identity than the sudden awareness that the house you have lived in all your life has vanished and seemingly never existed. Does this mean that your whole life is a lie or a phantasm?

Give Me Back Myself (1971) develops the theme. Stephen Dusack, who has left his native South Africa to pursue his fortunes in England, is in a train accident and finds upon recovering that everyone believes him to be one David Orme, a wealthy industrialist: he is found with Orme's wallet in his pocket, and he has enormous difficulty proving that he is in fact Dusack—or even that such an individual ever existed. The hostel he was staying at no longer exists, his place of employment has turned into some other establishment, and even a call to one of his closest friends in South Africa reveals that the friend barely acknowledges him. Dusack wryly comments on the difficulty of proving his own existence:

"It's frightening in a way just what they've managed to achieve. If anyone were to ask me to prove I was Stephen Dusack, do you know, Fran, I couldn't. I haven't a single solitary thing to show. Even the very clothes I'm wearing must belong to David Orme. And while I couldn't produce a scrap of evidence to prove I am myself, I'm damn sure they could produce a whole mass of it to prove I am David Orme." (82)

But because we have, in the opening chapter, been introduced to the real David Orme, we know that Dusack really is Dusack; but if we adopt the theory of a conspiracy, as Dusack at one point does ("A conspiracy of a kind? But it was a stupid, ridiculous idea that anyone would want to conspire against him, for there was nothing they could hope to achieve by so doing. But what other explanation was there?" [61–62]), we are forced to conclude as Dusack does: "'I'm just a clerk, just an ordinary sort of person'" (94). Why would someone want to do this to him? Some of Dusack's existential reflections are very poignant:

"It's almost as if I'd already started to lose myself. I have to keep stopping to think who I am. It's like part of me is slipping away and something else is taking its place. That's what I'm afraid of—not of being killed—of suddenly finding out that the change is complete, that I'm not the me I've always known, but someone else, a stranger. Someone I don't know wearing me like it was a coat." (115)

The "science fiction" versions of the vanished-past theme are somewhat more conventional, but can still be on occasion very powerful. *The Artificial Man* (1965)—actually marketed as a mystery story, although it is far more clearly a science fiction novel than other of Davies' works so labelled—actually predates the first "mystery" novel on this theme by several years, and seems to have been written close to the time of Davies' first novel on the amnesia theme generally, *Who Is Lewis Pinder?* (1965). The science fiction element in *The Artificial Man* takes some time in manifesting itself: for the first third or so of the novel we appear to be concerned with Alan Fraser, a struggling writer residing in a placid English village in the year 1966 who hits upon the idea of writing a science fiction novel set in the year 2016. Gradually we understand that it actually is the year 2016 and that Fraser, whose real name is Arnold Hagan, is a spy who suffered an accident and lost his memory before he could reveal some vital piece of information learned while behind enemy lines. An artificial past is therefore implanted in his brain, and the novel he is to write will, his superiors feel, reveal the secret buried in his subconscious without driving him mad, as other methods of extracting the information might. In this sense *The Artificial Man* combines the amnesia and vanished-past themes: the latter comes into play as Hagan escapes from the village and encounters a young woman who has never heard of it, even though she lives only a short distance away (it has, of course, been artificially created for Hagan's benefit). Hagan suffers the same jarring sense of dislocation and lostness that Axel Champlee does in *The White Room:* "'If I wasn't born in that house down there, where did I come from? And who am I? Am I Alan Fraser?'" (72).

Twilight Journey (1967) is one of the best of Davies' novels in its rich texture and constant alternation between dream and reality. The opening is highly bizarre in its incongruous incidents and dialogue. Richard Worbey, having forgotten much about himself except his name, wanders about what appears to be a run-down section of London in the year 1967. He meets the owner of a cafe who treats him to the following discourse:

"This is a cafe. It is larger than a snack-bar, smaller than a restaurant. A restaurant is often part of a hotel. A hotel is a larger and better-class place than a lodging house. The customers who frequent this cafe are mainly long-distance lorry drivers and workmen. The lorries carry industrial components, foodstuffs—" (14)

We learn eventually that all this is happening in Worbey's mind as a result of "senduction," a new process developed in the twenty-second century whereby information is converted into electrical impulses and fed directly into the brain. The technique was invented by one Clayton Solan as a means of education: an individual can select a given historical epoch—here Late Twentieth Century Urban—and actually appear to experience it while in a sort of hypnotic trance. But it transpires that Worbey is Clayton Solan himself (hence his amnesia, since his subconscious is rejecting the false identity he has adopted), and a crisis is at hand because Solan must be brought out of the trance without driving him mad, as had occurred in a previous case some years before. The novel therefore oscillates between Solan's wanderings in his mind and the efforts to save him.

Solan's dream goes through several stages: at first he experiences the senduction as an ordinary man in the late twentieth century; then his mind transforms the scene to his recent past, replaying the invention of his system; finally, and most fascinatingly, his mind begins to probe into an extrapolated future where senduction has become a tool in the hands of the powerful for purposes of political indoctrination, with a small handful of rebels—including Solan and some of his friends—refusing to submit and living as outcasts, constantly hunting for scraps of food and fleeing from the authorities. It is difficult to bear in mind that all this is taking place simply in Solan's mind: Davies' writing has rarely been as vivid or as carefully crafted. Indeed, the premise of senduction is that it is "more real than real life"; a colleague of Solan's relates his account of why this is so:

> "He said it was because our waking senses are so inefficient. Our hearing is poor, our senses of taste and smell deficient. Our eyes are the worst of all, sending back distorted messages to the brain. Optical delusions . . . vistervision and television are only possible because the eyes can't move fast enough to follow a moving dot of light. Clay called our senses the weak link between life and the mind. Take that link away, put information straight into the brain, and we are able to see reality. And because it all happens in the subconscious, the memory of the dream remains vivid and complete without any fading of the memory." (58–59)

And, of course, this is why it is so difficult to bring Solan out of his trance: if he is simply woken up, then he will think that real life is merely a dream, from which he will eventually awaken.

The Alien (1968), like *The Artificial Man*, is also set in 2016, but of course an entirely different set of conditions obtains. John Maxwell emerges from an accident not merely with much of his memory gone but with all his senses subtly disturbed: food tastes peculiar to him, people smell odd and faintly revolting, and he experiences a sensation of foreignness to everything around him. Medical tests (not made known to him) reveal that there is something other than blood in his veins. Two competing alternatives are

eventually offered him: he is either a human being who may have sabo-
taged a medical research establishment two years before or, in fact, he is an
alien from another planet. Maxwell, attempting to retrace his past, oscillates from the one to the other, actually resolving on the second until at
last he is shown to be a product of elaborate brainwashing. At the beginning a scientist conjectures on the possibility of life on other worlds:

> "It has to be assumed that on a planet such as ours, based upon the
> carbon, hydrogen, and oxygen molecules—I think those were the three—
> life could be expected to develop much along the same lines as life on our
> world. But perhaps with minor differences. And it also has to be assumed
> that there are planets where civilisation is much older than ours—their
> technologies accordingly more advanced. Their means of propelling space
> vehicles would be far in advance of ours, not confining their exploration to
> their own planetary system as we are still confined to ours." (9–10)

The first part of this utterance is, of course, preposterous, since even the
existence of carbon, hydrogen, and oxygen on another planet would not be
remotely sufficient to trigger the evolutionary stages leading to life-forms
similar to those on earth; one can only hope that Davies intends this notion to be seen as the absurdity it is.

The bulk of Davies' work falls into the above patterns, but some cannot
well be encompassed in them. A few novels can be dismissed fairly readily:
although they are entertaining, they do not in any way add to Davies' otherwise systematic explorations of the anomalous workings of the mind. *Dimension A* (1969) and *Genesis Two* (1969) are two competent science fiction
novels, some of whose features may be observed later. The former is of interest in being a sort of science fiction variant of the locked-room mystery,
as a scientist who disappeared from a locked laboratory is found to have
discovered another world coexisting with our own, "although occupying
different vibratory planes" (9). Less interesting is *Adventure Holidays, Ltd.*
(1970), a tale of suspense and espionage whose only merit lies in the evocation of Davies' adopted homeland of Wales, where he moved in the mid-
1960s. It was marketed as a young adult novel, although it is scarcely different in tone or style from his other works; if anything, the narrative tone is
still more subdued and phlegmatic than in other novels. *A Grave Matter*
(1967) is similarly ineffective, being a fairly orthodox detective story involving the discovery of the graves of two long-dead children in a small country
town. By focusing almost exclusively upon the police investigation of the
matter, Davies fails to probe thoroughly the psychological dimensions of
the plot, which remain nebulous and unconvincing.

Assignment Abacus (1975) calls for some notice. Here we have a man,
Boyd Maskell, flown by helicopter to a remote mansion in Scotland for
what he believes is a high-level business meeting, who quickly finds himself
alone and virtually cut off from the rest of the world. Here the psychologi-

cal interest is in seeing whether Maxwell can retain his sanity in this isolated position, where bizarre, irrational, and sometimes supernatural-seeming incidents are occurring, and whether he can ascertain why he has been put in this anomalous position in the first place. The seemingly fortuitous appearance of a hiker, Bernard Fairfield, adds to the confusion: has Fairfield in fact stumbled into the situation by accident or has he been planted there? Much of the novel is harrowing in its depiction of the physical and psychological isolation of the protagonist and of his steadily weakening self-control and grasp of reality. At one point he is close to snapping:

> His one thought now was to get away from this place while he was still capable of rational thought and behaviour. Half of him knew that what had been happening was reality made to appear unreal and impossible. But the other part was already beginning to accept that he had been experiencing hallucination. There was no way of telling just how much more his divided self could take. (77)

Two other novels by Davies are what might, for lack of a better word, be called quasi-occult. *The Reluctant Medium* (1966) is structured more like a conventional detective story than other of Davies' novels: David Conway, although not a detective but an "industrial consultant" (11), is urged by a friend to investigate some strange happenings at the home of Matthew Rawson, since on the surface it seems that one of Rawson's business enemies has come back from the dead to harass and possibly kill him. Conway finds himself grudgingly and unwillingly accepting the supernatural until a car nearly kills him and other attempts are made on his life; this odd mix causes Conway to reflect:

> "It can't be a mixture; it's got to be one thing or the other. That's how I see it. If there was proof that just one of the natural accidents wasn't an accident, then we'd be dealing with some sort of criminal activity. You know what I'm trying to say. Or if there was proof that one of the supernatural incidents wasn't faked, then we'd know we were up against—" (110)

The conclusion is obvious. This reminds me of one of Dr Fell's reflections in a radio play by John Dickson Carr:

> Let me make it clearer. Suppose you tell me that the ghost of Julius Caesar appeared to Brutus before the Battle of Philippi and warned him of approaching death. All I can say is that I know nothing about it. But suppose you tell me that the ghost of Julius Caesar walked into the cutlery department at Selfridge's, bought a stainless-steel knife, paid for it with spectral banknotes, and then stabbed Brutus in the middle of Oxford Street. All I shall beg leave to murmur, gently, is: rubbish. You cannot mix the two worlds like that. . . . This was a human crime, planned by a human being. (Quoted in Joshi 116)

Sure enough, the events of *The Reluctant Medium* are finally explained by natural means, and the séances and other spiritualistic oddities are accounted for by elaborate trickery. But Davies—inexplicably to my mind—feels the need to tack on a supernatural "out" (perhaps he was thinking of Carr's much better effort of this sort, *The Burning Court*), and the novel ends meretriciously on a note of portentous mystery.

If we do not feel inclined to take this supernatural denouement very seriously, we are obliged to do so in Davies' late novel *The Land of Leys* (1979). It is odd that, after a series of some twenty novels in which (with the exception of *The Reluctant Medium*) all seemingly supernatural events are emphatically explained either as sleight-of-hand or as possible (and plausible) extensions of our current knowledge, Davies concludes his fictional work[2] by resolutely embracing a fairly conventional occultism. A survey of Davies' work will show how anomalous this sudden reversal is:

The Paper Dolls: "The four children were abnormal but not supernatural" (169).

The Artificial Man: "'You must understand that what is happening to him is in no way supernatural'" (201).

Psychogeist: "'There is nothing supernatural about it'" (100).

The Lampton Dreamers: "'We have to assume that it [mind control]'s an ability inherent in all of us'" (67).

The Shadow Before: "Nothing—he didn't want to use the word, but there was no other—nothing supernatural" (104).

Assignment Abacus: "Nothing supernatural, nothing hallucinatory" (39).

But all this changes in *The Land of Leys*. Here we have a conventional psychic detective trying to get to the bottom of some weird goings-on in a little English country town. Amnesia is also involved—Andrew Leigh is jolted to find that for months after his brother's death he has apparently been leading another life for half of every week—but it is dispelled very quickly, as Leigh discovers with little difficulty what he had been doing in his other life; and once this is resolved it plays no especial role in the matter. The focus of the novel is the attempt of Kale Manfred, the ponderous psychic authority, to probe the mysterious occurrences in and around the lavish home of Dr. John Harvester. All the old standbys are unearthed: crucifix, holy water (a little sheepishly, it must be admitted: "'I am going to ask you now to humour me and do as I ask without wanting to know why'" [111]), pentacles drawn on basement floors, the works. And of course Manfred sophistically argues for the equivalence of science and magic: "'I believe that every manifestation of what people call the 'supernatural' can be explained in terms of science. If not today, then tomorrow'" (100). This is an old argument, and I suppose we shall be waiting a long time for an explanation of how a crucifix and holy water can be efficacious against phenomena that are acknowledged to predate Christianity and even the human race. And when Manfred says, "'A printed circuit, something we are all familiar with, is able to create, intensify, and store power. This is magic we all accept'" (101), he falls into another elementary trap: the "magic" of the circuit has been explained scientifically and can be understood with sufficient training, whereas no amount of training can allow one to understand how or whether pentacles drawn on the floor have any effect. There are a certain number of mundane natural events in *The Land of Leys*—Leigh and others again undergo various attacks on their lives, obviously caused by a human agency—but the novel is designed to lead up to a grand supernatural climax, complete with the near-sacrifice of an innocent and tempting virgin. It is neither a satisfying nor representative end to Davies' fictional oeuvre, and one can only hope that the later *Morning Walk* (1982) is a return to his old manner.

Some general features of Davies' work can now be observed. His primary virtue is narrative drive. In the skilful manipulation and execution of a convoluted plot, in pacing, in the gradual revelation of the climax Davies has few equals. In *The Paper Dolls*, for example, we learn first that the odd boy Rodney Blake is one of twins, and only later the more remarkable fact that he is one of quadruplets. Analogously, in *Who Is Lewis Pinder?* the succession of Pinder's different identities is slowly revealed one after the other, and through Pinder's own eyes, so that doubt becomes impossible. It is adeptness in narration that is the principal feature in Davies' two best novels, *The Shadow Before* and *Twilight Journey*. The power of his work is all the more surprising in that his prose style is merely workmanlike, tending toward the glib and facile at times. In other words, it is purely the incidents—and their clever articulation—that produces his intense readability. Robert H. Waugh has remarked on the number of fantaisistes—as opposed to science fiction writers—who have developed a rich, perhaps eccentric prose style to augment or even create realism and believability (Waugh 1), but Davies is a notable exception. He relies upon the inherent fascination of his conceptions, as well as an atmosphere of utterly mundane reality as a backdrop for them, to lull the reader slowly and imperceptibly into belief. Perhaps only Algernon Blackwood has achieved such powerful effects with so undistinguished a style. But in a few notable instances Davies can create horrific scenes of great intensity. The image of the rotting corpse of Clive Murchison calmly going about his business as Argred the Freeman in *Psychogeist* is not soon forgotten:

> The head was hairless, the flesh—what had once been flesh—drawn tightly over the naked skull, gleaming dully like polished brown leather. The face—what had once been a face—was dead, the cheeks hollowed, chin and nose grotesquely elongated, only the deeply sunken eyes alive, glittering points in dark pools. And the body—bones—nothing more than the skeletal shape it seemed—encased in that same dried, brittle brown parchment as the head. The fiction of a living mummy. . . . (173)

In *The Artificial Man* Arnold Hagan's metabolism speeds up hideously as a result of the tinkering that was done to his brain, until he becomes nearly all brain:

> There were limbs at the base, almost hidden by the grass, thin, spidery arms and legs, shriveled, shrunken almost out of existence, matching the hideous mockery of features, the eyes, ears, nose, and mouth that were little more than indentations in the yellow-white, blue-veined parchment flesh. A being—a thing that was a brain and little else. A brain that had no need to see, to hear, to eat. Progression. They had said. Into the future. And was this ultimate man? (244)

In *Dimension A* we encounter a mistlike entity—a combination of "animal cells, plant cells, dust. All stirred together in a gigantic test-tube and acted upon by forces beyond our comprehension" (125)—that proves to be one gigantic cell. And yet, these instances themselves confirm that it is purely the vigour of Davies' ideas that produces the sense of awe and wonder in his work, not any skilful mastery of prose.

In some of his early work Davies was regrettably given to introducing an adventitious love element, so that his protagonists were safely married at the end of the novel. Davies restrained this element of conventionality in his later work, although he was still fond of creating a mild sexual tension by the inclusion of females accompanying the male protagonist. These protagonists are all cut from the same mould—quiet, reserved, rather meek except when compelled by circumstances into action—to such a degree that one cannot help supposing they are reflections of the author.

Davies' settings are also somewhat repetitive, and occasionally we grow tired of all the charming little English country towns we constantly find ourselves in. But he can paint the scene both realistically and, now and again, almost lyrically, as in *The Lampton Dreamers*:

> The hamlet at its foot, indistinguishable from here—for it must be two miles away across the fields—was Lampton. He had been there once, to visit Francis Quain; and Francis, with a great air of ownership, as if he had lived there with his sister for all his life instead of barely two years, had walked him along the lane, pointing out landmarks. Past the church and the handful of thatched cottages that clustered tightly in the shadow of its squat Norman tower; past the cluttered, faded fronts of three tiny shops and the Green Man of Lampton that, for all the dignity of title and white benches on cobbled forecourt, was nothing more than two cottages joined into one; past the small building that was an odd mixture of new blue bricks and old russet-red and had once been an open-fronted smithy but was now, so Francis had said, the home of Lampton Ware souvenir pottery; then over the toy bridge that spanned a stream that usually dried up in the summer, and then along the lane that led upwards, past more cottages and a farm, towards the slopes of the Pike. It had been a grand tour that

had lasted all of fifteen minutes. A village of perhaps three-score people—pretty enough, hardly picturesque, just one like a thousand others. (9–10)

Nevertheless, it is refreshing when the scene varies to a slightly futuristic London in *What Did I Do Tomorrow?* or, more grippingly, a hideous dystopian future envisioned by the mind of Clayton Solan in *Twilight Journey*.

A recurring image of Davies' amnesia novels is the protagonist's sudden and seemingly irrational sense that his face is somehow different, unrecognisable, or subtly changed. This obsessive image is found time and again:

> The face that stared back at him was suddenly that of a stranger. (*The Artificial Man* 8)

> For some obscure reason, he found no satisfaction—no assurance, even—in the sight of his own face. (*The Alien* 18)

> A man's face is the most familiar thing to him there can ever be. He knows every small crease, the exact shade of flesh, every infinitesimal blemish. And because he shaves almost every morning of his life, he knows exactly the feel and texture of the beard to be removed. Something was wrong . . . (*The White Room* 47)

> Hurriedly he retraced the few steps to the window of gaudy shirt-pyramids to stare with a mixture of fascination and disbelief at the stranger in the blue suit that was his own reflection in the background mirror.
> Certainly older—teenage gawkiness replaced by a kind of maturity—no doubt now about this being the future—no taller, but broader, with features that if taken singly were pretty much as they had always been, but if taken collectively, produced a face that was markedly different from the one that had looked back at him from the locker-room mirror only a couple of hours ago. (*What Did I Do Tomorrow?* 20)

> . . . that face in the oval glass. Not shrunken, distorted, as he had feared by its feel, but as it had always been—narrow features; soft, almost feminine lines—a visionary face, not that of a hard, knife-edge, on-the-ball executive. There had been times when that deceptive appearance had served him in good stead. Soft wing of dark-bronze hair silky on poet's white brow. And here he was wasting time gazing Narcissus-like at his own face . . . (*Assignment Abacus* 87)

As a strategy for unsettling the reader, this image is potent: not only is "a man's face . . . the most familiar thing to him there can ever be," but it is our preeminent token of identity; so that if our face is not as it should be, then there is nothing in our personality or identity that cannot be lost or disturbed.

In the course of his work Davies probes, without providing or attempting to provide any definite answers, certain fundamental questions about human identity: What is a human being if his memory has been erased? What are we if our pasts have somehow been eradicated? How do we go about proving that we are who we say and think we are? Could we at some time have undergone some sort of indoctrination or brainwashing such that we think we are someone else? These are the most interesting questions we find in Davies' work, although it becomes obvious that other, lesser matters also concern him: in several novels the ultimate culprit is money or big business, as wealthy industrialists engage in elaborate hoaxes—including toying with people's minds or ruthlessly killing them—for the sake of gain; and several of the futuristic novels elaborate the notion of political indoctrination by a ruling oligarchy. These lesser themes are presented too bluntly and obviously to be effective—we know too clearly whose side Davies is on—but the general amnesia theme that both brings Davies' work into a curious unity and distinguishes that work from all others in the field will remain his signal contribution. Perhaps, beyond his narrative skill and his powerful conceptions, it is the way in which he unites the three normally disparate genres of mystery, horror, and science fiction—or, rather, how he displays the complete artificiality of such distinctions in the face of compellingly original conceptions that draw a little from each but are the property of none—that is Davies' greatest achievement.

Notes

1. One wonders about the possible autobiographical connexions here: Lester Dunn has the same first and last initials as Davies, and is a pharmacist, as Davies was for many years.

2. Davies has written one other novel after *The Land of Leys, Morning Walk* (1982), but this has been published only in England and I have not been able to consult it. Nor have I read any of Davies' hundreds of short stories published under a wide variety of pseudonyms.

Les Daniels: The Horror of History

Many writers of weird fiction do not appear to be sufficiently aware of the conceptual and aesthetic difficulties of writing a "horror novel." How is such a novel (whether supernatural or not) to maintain the dramatic intensity of a short story? Should it attempt to do so? Conversely, how is a horror novel to succeed *as a novel* if it entirely forgoes such apparently essential features of novelistic writing as conflict and development of character? Is it, indeed, possible to write a "horror novel" at all?

Les Daniels (b. 1943) appears to be cognisant of these difficulties and has met them in an unusual way: he has openly renounced the supernatural as the exclusive focus of his work. The hallmark of his five novels—*The Black Castle* (1978), *The Silver Skull* (1979), *Citizen Vampire* (1981), *Yellow Fog* (1986; rev. 1988), and *No Blood Spilled* (1991)—is the intermingling of genres, notably the supernatural tale, the historical novel, the mainstream novel, and the detective story. This may not be a solution that would please everyone, but the result is a series of works that probe many questions other than the role of the supernatural in life and history.

If Daniels has any model for this mixture of genres, it may be the detective writer John Dickson Carr. In his treatise *Living in Fear: A History of Horror in the Mass Media* (1975), Daniels refers to Carr as "the modern master of the macabre story" (LF 86), making note of Carr's penchant for a quasi-supernatural atmosphere in an otherwise highly orthodox "fair play" detective story. It is Carr's most distinctive innovation in detective fiction, although Carr also wrote many successful "historical mysteries"—detective stories set in some historically vivid or dramatic period—and therefore effected a union of the detective story and the historical novel. Some of these "historical mysteries" are even nominally supernatural in involving time-travel, the appearance of the Devil, and so on.[1] But whereas Carr's emphasis is always on the detective element, Daniels stresses either the historic or the horrific. I am not certain that Carr has demonstrably influenced Daniels, but he appears to have been a suggestive model in the fusion of seemingly disparate genres.

The most important thing to realise about Daniels is that he was already a thorough student of the field before he began to enrich it with his own novels. *Living in Fear*, although on the surface a "popular" and non-scholarly account, is a remarkably comprehensive history of horror in all its forms—literature, drama, film, comic books, even rock music—from antiquity to the present. It is encyclopaedic, accurate, and written with obvious relish. It may have a few weaknesses—toward the end Daniels becomes so caught up with the ever-increasing number of horror films that actual literary contributions are somewhat slighted—but it could virtually serve as a sort of fifty-year update of Lovecraft's *Supernatural Horror in Literature* (1927)—if, of course, one can imagine Lovecraft discussing E.C. Comics and Alice Cooper. And like Lovecraft's work, it provides a valuable index to Daniels' own predilections in the field.

Daniels' boldness in choosing one of the most frequently used themes in horror—the vampire—and the additional burden he has shouldered in making his vampire a recurring figure, in the manner of a fictional detective, are a direct result, I believe, of his thorough familiarity with the horror field. He is aware of most of the permutations of the vampire trope—from LeFanu's "Carmilla" and Prest's *Varney the Vampire* through Stoker's *Dracula* to the many literary and film versions throughout this century, including Richard Matheson's highly innovative science fictional treatment, *I Am Legend* (see LF 204)[2]—but has evidently felt that the vampire still retains sufficient vitality for a further series of adventures. Daniels is also aware of the dangers of the serial character—principally, the issue of how to retain sufficient interest and variety from one work to the next—and has solved the problem both through diversity of setting (in place and in time) and through the dynamic evolution of his central character, the vampire Don Sebastian de Villenueva.

Living in Fear testifies to Daniels' perception that certain themes have not received adequate treatment in the history of the field. When he remarks early in his treatise that "It seems a pity that comparatively few writers have drawn material from the . . . fascinating American cultures of the Aztecs and the Mayas" (LF 3), one senses that the kernel of *The Silver Skull* may already have been in his mind. Daniels' curious and lengthy digression on the modification of Tarot cards by A. E. Waite (LF 78–80) is a significant precursor to his own use of the Tarot in *Citizen Vampire*. In dismissing the film *Rasputin, the Mad Monk* as a "bizarre combination of history and horror" (LF 210), Daniels may be suggesting that his own future combinations will be more harmoniously joined.

It is clear that Daniels draws upon prior works in literature and film in his own writing; but, in truth, he does not do so as much as one might have thought—or feared. His novels are not a succession of pastiches or tips of the hat to celebrated literary forbears. True, we know (and are meant to know) the origin of a passage such as this:

> Martinez looked toward the window. He saw the purple sky, the cold shimmering of stars, and the flat white disc that cast its glow upon the floor. Then he saw the long fingers that groped over the sill. It was the upper sill. Something was crawling down the side of the palace and into the room, something that moved as no mortal man could ever move. Now there were two hands, each silhouetted against the sky. The head hung down, and long black hair streamed toward the floor. Martinez burrowed into his corner as Montezuma's visitor slithered through the window like some gigantic snake. (SS 59–60)

Who cannot think of Dracula's descent down the side of his castle as seen by Jonathan Harker? In a more general sense, when Sebastian tells a new convert to vampirism of the dangers of their state—

> "There are so many things I must teach you. You must beware of the second death, from which there can be no awakening. You must be warned against the sun and against fire. They can destroy a vampire, as can a shaft of wood through the heart. Except for these, we are all but invulnerable. There are certain other limitations. You must return to your coffin before the morning comes and sleep in your native soil. You must beware of running water and of several herbs." (BC 146)

Daniels is aware that he is producing an amalgam of the previous literary tradition. Stoker laid down many of the rules governing the vampire's conduct:

> [Dracula] is so well known that it has become the authoritative source on the care and feeding of vampires; Stoker's decisions regarding the legendary attributes of these lecherous leeches have been accepted as gospel truth. Unlike most of the vampires described in the purportedly factual manuscripts of olden days, Dracula can transform himself into a mist, a wolf, or a bat. He has a marked aversion for symbols of Christianity and a chauvinistic fondness for female victims. Other debatable points include Stoker's declaration that this cursed condition is contagious and that the proper cure is a wooden stake through the monster's heart (vampires were most commonly burned by those who believed in them). At any rate, Stoker's deviations from tradition were dramatically sound, and they helped ensure his book's success. (LF 63)

The film *Nosferatu*, according to Daniels, introduced the innovation "that a vampire could be destroyed by sunlight . . . although Stoker's Dracula could walk abroad at noon without ill effect" (LF 109). By adhering to the most rigid conceptions of the vampire's behaviour, Daniels is increasing the difficulty of the task he has set himself of breathing new life into this seemingly exhausted legend.

It is worth pondering to what degree the very creation of such a figure as Sebastian—a ruthless and pitiless vampire who nevertheless elicits the reader's sympathy (or, at any rate, respect) by the cynical dignity of his bearing and his quest for knowledge—has been inspired by some of the prototypical characters of Gothic fiction. Ambrosio, the protagonist of M. G. Lewis's *The Monk*, is described by Daniels as "half-saint and half-Satanist" (LF 17), a description that could also apply to Sebastian; and Sebastian's worldweariness—throughout *Citizen Vampire* he resents being resummoned to the flesh after his disembodied soul spent centuries traversing the stars—brings the hapless Melmoth to mind. (Recall that both *The Monk* and *Melmoth the Wanderer* feature vivid scenes of the Inquisition, as does Daniels' *Black Castle*.) More mundanely, Daniels may have seen a possibility to improve over the title character in the film *Dracula's Daughter*, "a reluctant leech who spends most of her time bemoaning her condition and seeking medical advice" (LF 142). In Daniels' hands this same basic premise is shorn of its ludicrousness and results in the poignant depiction of Felicia Lamb, who in *Yellow Fog* refuses to drink blood after Sebastian has turned her into a vampire and literally wastes away to nothing.

Daniels knows that some variations in the standard vampire myth are necessary in order to sustain interest in such a well-used formula. One of the most interesting of these is the function of religion in his work. In a confrontation between Sebastian and his brother Diego, the Grand Inquisitor, we read the following:

> The Grand Inquisitor bridled. . . . "You came out of the darkness to kill me and you would have, if I had not been wearing a cross."
>
> "Do not depend too much upon the cross, brother. I admit it startled me a bit at first. I don't like the look of the thing, somehow. But I could bear it if I had to." (BC 63)

This is the first indication we have of Daniels' attempt to do away with— or at least modify—the religious substructure of the vampire myth. Sebastian himself has his doubts as to the existence of Satan (BC 128), and a scene in *Citizen Vampire* vividly underscores the uselessness of the cross for unbelievers as a defense against the vampire:

> "You would have done better to stay at home," Sebastian said.
>
> "I think this cross will protect me."
>
> "It means nothing to you," Sebastian said, "and so it means less to me. Such protection is only for the faithful."
>
> Madeleine held the cross aloft, but her full lips twisted when it began to crumble in her hands. The dry wood turned to dust and scattered into the air. (CV 92)

This scene is suspiciously similar (one hopes coincidentally) to one in Stephen King's *'Salem's Lot* (1975), but it nonetheless harmonises with Daniels' vision of a quasi-secular vampire. In effect, Daniels is attempting to present a counter-argument to the statement he puts into the mouth of the Marquis de Sade, who doubts the existence of vampires because "'if I believed in such things, I would be obliged to believe in God'" (CV 60).

This transition is, of course, never completed: Sebastian had earlier admitted that the cross appears to harbour some sort of power (see BC 146), and the climactic scene of *The Black Castle* provides some further clues. Pursuing a young woman through the streets, Sebastian is alarmed to find that she has run into a cathedral. He attempts to enter it, but cannot:

> The cathedral was as radiant as the gates of Heaven.

He had dreamed of such a night before. The cross had seemed to him a sorry thing, and he never doubted that he could surmount it. The idea that two sticks of wood could repel him was ridiculous; he was not that weak. But this golden edifice was strong.

It was not that he could enter it but that its presence saddened him. The images of martyred men and women rose before him and he pitied them. He pitied the young woman who had fled from him and the beautiful child in his arms. He thought of Margarita, her body pierced and bleeding, of himself, groveling toward a pool of blood, and he was ashamed. (BC 230)

I am not entirely sure what this passage is meant to suggest; perhaps the idea is that religion's power over a vampire now operates on a purely moral, not metaphysical, level. In any event, if Sebastian doubts the existence of Satan, he is cynical to the point of flippancy about godhead in general: "'What is a god?' asked Don Sebastian, seating himself on the stone slab where he had found another incarnation. 'Only a being with more power than its followers. And one who gains strength from their devotion. In short, a creature very much like a vampire'" (SS 95). And later:

"Then you think these gods came from the stars?"
"The documents suggest it. And the idea makes more sense than the story we were told as boys, of one force in the clouds and another buried in the bowels of the earth. The universe is infinite, Martinez. Dimensions beyond dreaming lie around us. Who knows what powers careen through the vast gulfs that spin around this ball of earth we stand on? You could speed among the stars for eternity, Alfonzo Martinez, and never reach your journey's end. Somewhere in those endless reaches there must dwell forces of such magnitude that they would shatter our poor human visions. Perhaps all the gods of men are such—titanic entities that pass us on their travels through unknown realms. Gods beyond good and evil, gods who long to find strong souls to join them in their cosmic dance." (SS 118–19)

This appears to be Sebastian's—and Daniels'—final word: the "cosmic," Nietzschean religion expressed here is Daniels' answer to all those crosses whose efficacy in regard to vampires—or anything else, for that matter—so many of us have come to doubt.

In a somewhat analogous manner, Daniels is more broadly seeking to downplay even the supernatural element in his novels. He does this not merely by the mingling of genres but more generally by the entire moral thrust of his work. What Daniels wishes to convey is the all-encompassing power of *human* evil in the world. It is true that Sebastian and his disciples cause the blood to flow very copiously; but they are no match for the ordinary human beings who, through self-righteous fanaticism, insist upon the brutal imposition of their will upon others. Daniels states this clearly in the introduction to the original version of *Yellow Fog:*

The theme that seemed to be emerging was an examination of the different shades of evil. What we are accustomed to fear is what Sebastian represents: the rebel, the monster, the other. But have these figures ever done the harm represented by those in authority, the ones who follow blindly because they claim to know better? No vampire in fact or fiction has ever made as much of a mess as an army can.[3]

But he need hardly have been so blunt, for the message is hammered home in each of his novels. *The Black Castle* is not simply a vampire novel set in 1496, in the midst of the Spanish Inquisition: the historical "background" ultimately comes to dominate the work, and the real horror becomes the Inquisition and not Sebastian. Why else do we have such lengthy and painfully precise depictions of the Inquisition's dungeons and torture procedures, and finally a spectacular *auto-da-fé* where living heretics are burned and dead ones exhumed and their rotting skeletons put to the torch? All through the novel Daniels suggests adroitly that the real source of terror is the living Diego de Villenueva, not his undead brother. At one point Sebastian casually makes reference to "'a monster like me or my brother Diego'" (BC 128); and later Sebastian confronts Diego on his deeds: "'Come, Diego. I am your brother, not one of those superstitious souls in the city below us. Do not preach to me. How sure are you of Heaven, you, who have spent your life creating Hell on earth? I believe—and you believe it too—that you have only enough faith in your theology to become one of the damned'" (BC 159).

When Daniels later writes, "Fear of the unknown is not always the most powerful: the Grand Inquisitor knew only too well what the Inquisition might do to him" (BC 183), he is deliberately reversing Lovecraft's standard affirmation of the power of the supernatural ("'The oldest and strongest emotion of mankind is fear, and the oldest and strongest kind of fear is fear of the unknown'"[4]) to suggest the greater "power" and horror of the human and the real. The conclusion of the novel leaves no room for doubt: in an sardonic effort to tie up all loose ends, Daniels makes it clear what image we are to carry away with us: "The castle fell in a few hours. Torquemada took two years to die, and Columbus was carried back in chains from his third voyage; but the Inquisition endured for another three hundred and thirty-eight years" (BC 241).

Similarly, the horror and barbarism of the Aztec rites, and the savage fighting between Aztecs and Spaniards, leave a far greater impression in *The Silver Skull* than Sebastian's intermittent feasting. A scene toward the beginning is riveting:

> He heard a scream, and against his will he looked back across the room. The flames from the braziers cast gigantic shadows on the wall, and the biggest of them was the image of the priest who held the knife aloft in both his hands. The black blade dropped down and ripped into the body

of the man, who writhed and squirmed in the grip of his captors. His gasp was cut off as the knife tore into the flesh below his ribcage, and he was nearly dead when the priest reached into his chest and pulled out his heart. (SS 39–40)

This ritual, admittedly, is part of the ceremony leading to the resurrection of Sebastian, but it is matched by others just as bloodthirsty that have no connexion with him. Sebastian, indeed, makes it clear that his interest lies not so much in drinking blood as in absorbing knowledge: "'I am less concerned with the health of these people than with their knowledge. The magic that brought me here exceeds anything I have ever experienced, and I would know more of it'" (SS 92). The Aztecs take Sebastian to be the incarnation of their god Smoking Mirror; Sebastian is inclined to accept this belief provisionally: "'I am a horror. Why do you think I seek to solve these mysteries? Because I must. There is no other hope for me. I can never turn back, and never be human again. I must go forward, wherever it takes me. This god, this force, this power may be the one thing in the universe with strength enough to lift me out of this decaying shell and set me free'" (SS 133). What is the freedom Sebastian is seeking? It is clarified in a dramatic passage toward the end where he confronts Cortez:

> ". . . we do not choose the roles we play. And yet I think you crave divinity, or at least the power you think it brings. In that, at least, we are much alike. But you are too much of this world; your ambitions do not extend beyond this life. I have been a soldier, like you, and I learned that conquest comes to nothing. What matters is what the mind conceives for the future. Not the next battle, but the next life. And so I cling to belief in Smoking Mirror, however alien it may be, in the hope that I may achieve his incarnation and be free at last of this accursed planet." (SS 190)

In the course of this novel, therefore, Sebastian gradually adopts that worldweariness that reaches its pinnacle in *Citizen Vampire* and *Yellow Fog*. The state of being a vampire is tiresome and fatiguing: it is not that Sebastian, in some recrudescence of conventional morality, regrets his state and the killing he must perform to maintain it; rather, it is simply that the narrow confines of a vampire's life begin to chafe upon him, and he misanthropically finds no virtue in preserving his quasi-existence upon the earth.

Citizen Vampire continues the contrast of real vs. supernatural horror. Sebastian, irked at being recalled from his wandering of the heavens to the chaos of the French Revolution, takes a decided back seat to such grisly realities as the invention of the guillotine, the storming of the Bastille, and the vicious revenge of the working classes upon the hapless and outraged aristocracy. The debate over the manufacturing details of the guillotine provides Daniels with the opportunity for considerable deadpan humour of the Biercian variety:

"You should study the edge of a blade through a microscope, my boy, so that you could see exactly what it is. No matter how carefully honed, it is still in reality a saw, and it is the sideways motion which does the job. The spine is easy enough to snap, but very difficult to sever. A curved blade, as it penetrates, has the same effect as a saw."

Andre swallowed his wine in one gulp, and Dr. Louis rose genially to pour him another glass from Dr. Guillotin's decanter.

"Of course the blade need not be convex like a sword," continued Dr. Louis, "although that is the design I suggest. It could just as well be concave, or slanted, or even pointed. The important thing, Dr. Guillotin, is that it must not be flat. Such a blade, even if it were heavily weighted and dropped from a great height, could do no more than smash the neck into a bloody pulp. And that, I assume, is not what you have in mind." (CV 86)

Sebastian, speaking to a lady's maid who seeks nothing but the destruction of her hated mistress, sums up his view of the Revolution: "'To me, you are the revolution. Impulsive, angry, vengeful, rushing righteously toward a destiny that even you cannot imagine'" (CV 173).

In *Yellow Fog*, the most vivid and horrific scene is not Sebastian's bloodsucking but Reginald Callender's vicious murder of his mistress, Sally Wood. He pummels her in anger with his walking stick, breaking it in the process. Having fled, he is appalled to discover that he has left the fragment of the stick behind; returning to Sally's apartment, he hears a curious sound—a song that Sally used to sing: "Could this be a ghost? Another trick of that damned spiritualist? He didn't believe it. He couldn't. It had to be a trick of his own mind" (YF 252). In fact, Sally had not completely perished, but is wandering about in a bloody daze. The contrast between the supernatural ("Could this be a ghost?") and the real (the reality of a brutal murder) could not be more explicit.

Yellow Fog is, indeed, probably Daniels' most successful attempt at the intermingling of genres. Here we have a little of the historical novel (the bulk of the work takes place in 1847), a little of the supernatural novel (the ubiquitous Sebastian), a little of the detective story (the ex-Bow Street runner Samuel Sayer, who is on the track of Sebastian as a private detective, as is the newly formed Scotland Yard),[5] and a little of the mainstream novel in its careful delineation of character. But it is the historical novel that, aside from supernaturalism, dominates this novel and Daniels' work generally; indeed, Sebastian's anomalous and unwilling traversing of the centuries allows him to gain a unique perspective on history, as he discusses the matter with the ardent revolutionary Madeleine:

[Madeleine:] "Now I have my liberty, and I want to share it with you. I can make a place for you in the new world we are building."

"The new world. I have heard those words before, centuries ago when men sailed west; but the new world proved to be much like the old, nothing but a scramble for power and gold. There are no new worlds, Madeleine, only those who proclaim them to disguise a viciousness that puts the old worlds to shame." (CV 93–94)

A final component we may study is the very idea of having a serial vampire. Daniels announced in the introduction to the original version of *Yellow Fog* that, when he killed off Sebastian at the end of *The Black Castle*, "I imagined that was the end of him."[6] The aesthetic motives behind resurrecting a figure like Sebastian for an entire series of novels are not intuitively obvious: he does not play the role of a detective, and in the end his principal function appears to be that of a sardonic observer of the inexorable march of history. Among the challenges Daniels faces in this whole procedure is contriving a plausible means to effect Sebastian's revivification, since he is apparently destroyed at the conclusion of each of the first three novels. The elaborate Aztec ritual that effects Sebastian's return at the beginning of *The Silver Skull* is certainly shuddersomely convincing, as is the Tarot card ceremony at the beginning of *Citizen Vampire*. At the end of that novel Sebastian, in the midst of a fight, drinks a fellow vampire's blood, and it becomes obvious that his motive in so doing is a sort of suicide ("'I came here to die'" [CV 196]). His demise is impressive:

> Beams of pure radiance stemmed from the sockets of his eyes, and Sebastian's features turned to crystal. His face and hands shone with a light of blinding brilliance, and his clothing began to smoke.
> Madeleine covered her eyes and turned away just before the final devastating flash. Still, minutes passed before she could see clearly again, and her life was not long enough to help her forget the ghastly sound of something shattering, or the mingled notes of triumph and terror in Sebastian's final cry. (CV 197)

This method of vampiric suicide (drinking another vampire's blood) is entirely Daniels' invention: other vampire novels are silent on the effects of this act, and certainly Anne Rice's vampires drink one another's blood with insouciance. But for Sebastian it is—or seems—fatal. Unfortunately, his resurrection in *Yellow Fog* is not well accounted for. Daniels' flippant remark in his introduction—"Sebastian, like most vampires, just won't stay dead"[7]—is not very helpful and is really an evasion of the whole issue. Only once in the novel itself is the question addressed, as the aged Madame Tussaud strives to recall what she heard of Sebastian as a young girl in the French Revolution: "The old woman thought for a moment. 'A girl was found, driven quite out of her wits, who said she saw him shatter like glass, or vanish in a puff of smoke, or some such thing, so I suppose he is dead. Then again, a master of the black arts might be capable of such tricks if he found it convenient to disappear for a time . . .'" (YF 141). This too is an evasion, because there is no indication in *Citizen Vampire* that Sebastian was merely planning to "disappear" for a shorter or longer time. This is the one major flaw in Daniels' entire work: it is as if he suddenly decided that he no longer wished to adhere to the rigid rules (whether laid down by others or invented by himself) concerning the "care and feeding of vampires" that he maintained throughout the rest of his work. It is certainly good that Sebastian is back for more adventures, but Daniels owed it to his readers to exercise some ingenuity both in effecting Sebastian's physical return and in accounting for his evident change of heart from the suicidal misanthropy he exhibited at the end of *Citizen Vampire.*

Yellow Fog presents itself as the first of a trilogy of novels, of which *No Blood Spilled* is the second component. As the final novel has not yet appeared as of this writing (and may never do so), it is difficult to know exactly where this trilogy is proceeding; but it certainly does appear as if these three novels will be much more closely linked than his first three. This, in fact, is part of the problem with *No Blood Spilled,* which came out three years after its predecessor: this middle novel has difficulty standing by itself as an independent aesthetic entity. The plot meanders, the characters seem rather one-dimensional, and the book fails to build to a suitable climax at the end. It is as if Daniels has decided arbitrarily to cut off his novel at a certain point and start the next one from there.

No Blood Spilled takes us to India, where Sebastian has gone to pursue his quest for knowledge—specifically, knowledge of the nature of death. We have seen how, in the first three novels, Sebastian has become increasingly weary of suffering the indignity of periodic resurrection, and begins to devote himself to the pursuit of utter extinction. Here, as a result, he comes to Calcutta to penetrate the mysteries of Kali, the Hindu goddess of death. He is pursued by the maniacal Reginald Callender, who escapes from the madhouse in which he has been confined and vows to hunt down Sebastian and dispatch him for causing the death of his fiancée. Callender actually becomes a little more interesting than Sebastian here: the latter, in fact, does not even make much of an appearance in the novel, while the former wavers between cringing sycophancy and a surprisingly dogged tenacity.

No Blood Spilled continues the now well-established Daniels formula of contrasting natural and supernatural horror, with a subtle suggestion that the former may perhaps be the more loathsome of the two. While Sebastian's thirst for blood is certainly described with verve, the many natural horrors usurp our attention: nightmarish accounts of the madhouse in which Callender is placed (reminiscent of Maturin's *Melmoth the Wanderer* but actually derived—as many of Daniels' historical details are—from thorough research[8]); the savagery of the Indian rite of suttee—the burning alive of a man's wife after his death; the vileness of teeming and impoverished Calcutta, where beggar children are intentionally mutilated by their family so as to appear more pitiable; and the viciousness of the Thugs, those assassins and worshippers of Kali who have been almost eradicated by the British but who can still be found on the underside of Anglo-Indian society. And yet, some of the supernatural episodes are of considerable interest also, although curiously enough many of these involve Sebastian not as perpetrator but as victim. Even he has difficulty dispensing with a rubbery, pale-white ghoul who gnaws off most of the flesh from his leg; and in probably the most striking visual image in the book (and perhaps in the whole of Daniels' work), we find the following resurrection of Sebastian after he has been left for dead (assuming that word has any meaning as applied to him) in a monsoon puddle after being repeatedly bitten by a cobra:

> And from one of these little lakes a human hand emerged, its pale fingers groping toward the sky like the tendrils of a plant in search of nourishment. A face floated up beside it, plastered with wet black hair that obscured all of its features but an open, hungry mouth. Sloping shoulders hunched out of the water, and in the ghastly glare of the next lightning bolt the figure of a man emerged, his lean body encrusted with mud, small stones, and crawling creatures of the earth. (NBS 156)

It is passages like this that make *No Blood Spilled* the entertainment that it is; but I miss the searching philosophical reflections of Sebastian on his anomalous state, reflections that make the Sebastian novels far more than mere exercises in bloodletting.

The complex and enigmatic figure of Sebastian is clearly Daniels' greatest accomplishment, although praise must also be extended to the richness of historical setting, the elaborate interweaving of genres, and in general the whole conception of a vampire stalking through history, something he accomplishes rather more satisfactorily than his contemporary Anne Rice. What further innovations we may look for in subsequent works, it is difficult to tell. Will Sebastian in fact reach the contemporary world? If so, what will he make of a time when bloodletting has reached proportions even he has never seen in his trek across four centuries and two continents? A more significant query, perhaps, is whether Daniels himself can avoid repetitiveness in the somewhat narrow and confining subgenre he has created for himself, and whether he becomes so typecast as a "vampire novelist" that he does not allow himself to direct his talents to other weird themes. Whatever the case, Daniels' steady production of satisfying—and short—novels is so refreshing a change from the pretentiousness and verbosity of his bestselling confrères in the field that one cannot help feeling his work will age rather better than theirs.

Notes

1 See further my *John Dickson Carr: A Critical Study* (Bowling Green, OH: Bowling Green State University Press, 1990).

2. Daniels makes no reference in LF, however, to Theodore Sturgeon's quasi-realistic treatment in *Some of Your Blood*.

3. "Introduction" to YF (1986), p. 11.

4. H. P. Lovecraft, *The Annotated Supernatural Horror in Literature*, ed. S. T. Joshi (New York: Hippocampus Press, 2000), p. 21.

5. This whole detective element was added in the revised version of *Yellow Fog*. I would not be surprised, given his appreciation of John Dickson Carr, if Daniels were influenced by Carr's novel *Fire, Burn!* (1957), set in 1829 and similarly depicting the early days of Scotland Yard.

6. "Introduction" to YF (1986), p. 10.

7. Ibid., p. 8.

8. See Les Daniels, letter to the editor, *Studies in Weird Fiction* No. 10 (Fall 1991): 35.

Dennis Etchison: Spanning the Genres

The work of Dennis Etchison (b. 1943) exemplifies in a particularly satisfying way a dominant tendency in modern weird fiction: the avoidance or subtilisation of conventional supernaturalism by a spanning of genres, in particular the neighbouring genres of mystery fiction and science fiction. To be sure, other writers could be cited for this same tendency, and we have already seen it embodied (from the mystery side) in the work of Robert Bloch; writers prior to Etchison—Fritz Leiber, Ray Bradbury (whom Etchison claims as a powerful early influence [FF 58]), Richard Matheson, and Charles Beaumont—also melded science fiction and weird fiction in a distinctive and piquant way. Etchison's weird writing consists of four collections of short stories—*The Dark Country* (1982), *Red Dreams* (1984), *The Blood Kiss* (1988), and *The Death Artist* (2000)—along with three novels, *Darkside* (1986), *Shadowman* (1993), and *California Gothic* (1995). Etchison is a distinctly uneven writer, but at his best he presents so magnificent and poignant a unification of genres that his work deserves at least cursory consideration.

Etchison has, moreover, made his genre-spanning tendencies a conscious goal of his writing, enunciating it most emphatically in interviews and in some of the anthologies he has compiled. The clearest statement is in an interview of 1985:

> I have never thought of myself as a horror writer. Someone said that there are two kinds of writers, those who find out what the market is and write to fill it, and those who write and then find a market that will take their work. And I think I'm the latter kind of writer. I've always tried to write whatever I wanted most to write and then send it out, usually starting with the top-paying markets and working my way down. And if the story ended up in a girlie magazine or a science-fiction magazine, that was essentially accidental. (FF 52)

A more curious declaration is in the first volume of *Masters of Darkness* (1986), in which Etchison supplies a rationale for including the work of authors predominantly known in the science fiction field:

> Since labels often function negatively by limiting an author's potential readership, I have attempted to cut across such boundaries by calling upon individuals whose darker works may not be as widely known as their more conveniently categorized writings. I have no interest in perpetuating the artificially imposed classes of commercial fiction. There are very few if any first-rate artists whose output falls neatly within the confines of a single camp. Science fiction, dystopian or otherwise, sometimes offers insights into our present condition that are not touched upon by the traditional horror story. On the assumption that there may be more frightening and

immediate threats to modern life than haunted houses, werewolves or tes-
taments secreted in musty attics, I have invited some of today's most gifted
science fiction writers to participate . . . (MD xii)

This is interesting for several reasons. Firstly, Etchison's attack on what he
fancies to be the "traditional horror story" is sadly misplaced: it would be
very easy to jeer in an exactly similar fashion at some elements of the traditional science fiction story (space ships, ray-guns, beautiful Martian prin-
cesses), but this would say little about the true merits of science fiction.
Secondly, Etchison implicitly alludes to publishers (or, perhaps more specifically, their marketing departments) and booksellers for perpetuating or
even creating the rigid categories against which he chafes. These groups are
certainly popular whipping-boys of unconventional writers, and probably
they should in fact take some of the blame for the fossilisation of certain
genres; it is exactly this tendency that Etchison is battling. Thirdly, although
Etchison here and elsewhere emphasises the horrific potential of science
fiction, his own work more often tends to mingle elements of the mystery
story, the *conte cruel,* or the non-supernatural horror story with traditional
supernaturalism; only a relatively small number of his stories can be classi-
fied as science fiction, even though these are among his most affecting. Indeed, as early as 1985 Etchison was already declaring that "I have an interest
in contemporary science fiction that approaches absolute zero" (FF 56).

Etchison's most unrestrained statement on the state of contemporary
imaginative fiction occurs in the introduction to *Cutting Edge* (1986), in
which he lashes out at every conceivable form of writing save that of his
own brooding, atmospheric, and cheerless work: conventional science fiction (which has "retreated to the less ambiguous ray guns and rocket ships
of its space opera past" [CE xi]), imaginary world fantasy ("booksellers became convinced that their customers were more interested in pseudo-
historical pastiches about attractive role models engaged in quests for grails
beyond mysterious forests, aided by gnomes with crossbows, elves in chain
mail and magic" [CE xi–xii]), "hard" science fiction (which "went retro-
grade and began eating itself, excreting shiny but sterile wet dreams of a
Fourth Reich in space" [CE xii]), and, most virulently of all, the standard
horror best-seller:

> Supermarket racks continue to stock a never-ending farrago of flashy
> paperbacks, their lurid covers competing with *The National Enquirer* and
> *People,* each one promising to render previous best-sellers about unruly
> children (possession!) or suburban unrest (poltergeists!) as passé as last
> week's *TV Guide.* Like fad diets and astrological predictions of disaster,
> such pandering seeks to exploit middle-class unease with the latest pre-
> packaged devil theory. Those old standbys the Communists (or Terrorists,
> now) may or may not be lurking just around the corner and up your street
> this month, according to the editors of *Time* and *Newsweek,* but Something

Not from Around Here is surely behind the ubiquitous disintegration of the American family, and an endless supply of facile excuses is being marketed to housewives hungry for answers at $3.50 a shot. . . . (CE xiii–xiv)

All this is great fun and pretty much on the mark; it would be churlish to suggest that any sort of personal resentment lies behind this diatribe, even though Etchison himself perhaps unwittingly leaves himself open to such a charge by remarking ingenuously: "My work was too soft for what sf had become by then, too speculative for the mainstream markets, too hard-edged and disquieting for the slicks, and too downbeat for the fantasy field" (CE xvi).

For the fact of the matter is that Etchison is right—at least as far as his own work is concerned. It really is an unclassifiable and, hence, a somewhat unmarketable product, and he has preceded Thomas Ligotti in gaining a word-of-mouth reputation that has raised him to prominence amongst the *cognoscenti* in the field without his being a spectacular commercial success. Etchison's work is not always as good as he thinks it is, but at its best it really is very good.

Consider "On the Pike." This story bears affinities with Robert Aickman's "The Swords" but is in the end a purely non-supernatural tale of sadistic voyeurism. A woman, Sherron, persuades her fiancé, Geoff, to visit a carnival featuring all sorts of faintly repulsive freak shows. One especially versatile individual first swallows a sword, then eats fire, then eats a phonograph record, then puts out a cigarette in his mouth. Each time a woman's voice is heard daring the man to go on and asking if it hurts ("'Sure it hurt.' The sword swallower stepped up to the curtain. 'Sure I feel it. *Wouldn't you?*'" [RD 69]). Finally the couple go to see an old man who bills himself the Human Pin Cushion. Someone asks him to stick a pin through his ear:

> The old man stared her down. He folded his upper ear and pressed with a slow, trembling force, driving the tip through the cartilage in a tiny stirring motion.
> He stepped to the edge, the needle penetrating his ear in two places. He looked down past his chins at the girl. At Sherron.
> "You are satisfied now?" he asked.
> "How come you don't bleed?" she said defiantly.
> The old man stepped back. He grasped the ball on the end of the needle. "This show," he said, "is over." And then, to Sherron alone, he said:
> "What do you think I am? Don't you think we are human?
> *"Of course we bleed."* (RD 71)

It was Sherron who had been baiting the sword-swallower, Sherron who wanted to "'see some more'" (RD 70), wanted to see people bleed for her entertainment. It is she who is the horror, not the freaks of the carnival.

Now consider "A Walk in the Wet," which displays Etchison's ability to write what appears to be an orthodox science fiction story (it appeared in the *Magazine of Fantasy and Science Fiction*), but which is in fact potently horrific. An astronaut tries to reorganise his shattered life after a spectacular accident in space; it is the worse for him because he was born with telepathic ability—the ability to perceive the sensations of others as if they were his own—and he continually relives the accident:

> He winced in pain, remembering for a mercifully brief but vivid flash just what it had been like, swinging free of the *Deneb*, his lifeline drifting out and away with the torn shard of his arm still gripped to it as his suit sealed itself off and his eyes bulged behind his faceplate in unimaginable horror; and all the while he was sinking into unconsciousness, the seconds impaling him for eternities on the rays of the glaring twin suns, hearing across the soundlessness of space the soul-deaths of 130 others, screaming silently the agony of the dying, screaming inside his own mutant skull. (BK 51)

He encounters a young boy who has the same telepathic ability, and he reflects keenly on his fate:

> Every day that there is a fire, a crash on a nearby highway, the agony of a drunken lovers' quarrel that ends in a knifing or worse, every time a man is beaten and dumped bleeding in just such an alley as this . . . or a baby dies screaming in a scalding tub, or is born . . . every time, every time he will be that person. He will know what it feels like for a man to suffer so much that he begs to be killed so there can be an end to it. And he will not be able to stop it. He might one day teach himself to shut his mind, but that would take years and years and years. And by then he may have gone mad. (BK 55)

This tale is authentically science fiction—not merely a horror tale masquerading as such—because its premise is based upon some future development of human consciousness. But Etchison is interested not so much in the mechanism as in the horrific effect it can have upon human emotions.

A more conventionally supernatural tale is "The Late Shift" (DC), whose premise—reanimated corpses employed to work the night shift in 7-Eleven drugstores—might on the surface appear ludicrous but whose execution is exceptionally suave. Etchison has commented upon the symbolism of the tale:

> If I were really talking about dead people working at the 7-Eleven, I would write an essay about it. But if I am writing fiction about dead people at the 7-Eleven, obviously I am more concerned with the meaning of it than the possibility of the event itself. So I don't really think that there were dead people at the 7-Eleven on Pico and Twenty-sixth in Santa Monica. But I do think that it is a way of getting at questions of exploitation under capitalism, which is what that story was really about. (FF 62)

No clearer statement on the supernatural as metaphor could be found.

But it is those tales of Etchison's that nebulously defy all neat categori-sation which cause him to be classed as a writer who somehow writes weird fiction but doesn't write "horror fiction" or "science fiction" or "mystery fiction" or anything else of the sort. "It Only Comes Out at Night," the first story in The Dark Country, is paradigmatic. A man driving late at night on the highway turns off at a rest stop and finds a row of cars in the dark parking lot. Are they vacant? They appear to be, but then the man detects some figures within each car. Perhaps they are asleep—but if so, why do there appear to be cobwebs over the bodies? And what is the significance of the "dark brown" (DC 11) stain that covers one figure's neck? This whole scenario could conceivably be accounted for non-supernaturally—perhaps some madman came along and murdered all the people at the rest stop—but explanations like this matter less than the nightmarish inversion of an utterly commonplace and seemingly harmless facet of American life that emerges from the few pages of this chilling story. Then there is "Daughter of the Golden West," about a strange girl who turns out to be a preternatural survival from the cannibalistic Donner Party. This tale is nominally supernatural, but its elegance of exposition makes such issues entirely subordinate to the atmospheric intensity of the story.

Later stories continue the pattern. In "When They Gave Us Memory" (DA), we are uncertain whether a successful actor's parents have gone mad or senile in failing to recognise him or whether the actor himself is living in some kind of fantasy world he has invented for himself. "The Detailer" (DA) is about what a young employee in a car wash discovers in an expen-sive car he is asked to clean; and "The Dog Park" is about what happens to dogs (and people) if they venture too close to a gorge near the edge of a park. From the simplest, most ordinary situations, Etchison can fashion a scenario that slides with exquisite subtlety from the prosaic to the disturb-ing to the appallingly horrific.

Three stories in The Dark Country—"The Machine Demands a Sacri-fice," "Calling All Monsters," and "The Dead Line"—are thematically linked in their recounting of the potential physical and ethical horrors of a medical profession in which technological skill has outpaced moral re-straints. These stories are all nominally science fiction in that they appear to take place in the future and are extrapolations upon contemporary so-cietal issues. The first tale grimly speaks of unscrupulous private ambu-lance outfits who attempt to be the first on the scene of fatal accidents in order to obtain bodies so that parts of them can be sold later. The second is a magnificently hypnotic tale in which medical technology performs the surgical removal of bodily organs while the brain is still alive. Stream-of-consciousness is used to superb effect:

For the love of God I can't feel but I can hear it slicing away. Why can't I feel? They must use anesthetic now but even so I know what fiends they are. I think I always knew. O now the obscene sucking sound growing fainter even as my hearing dissolves, wet tissue pulling apart. They suction my blood, the incision clamped wide like another mouth a monstrous Caesarean and I hear the shiny scissors clipping tissues clipping fat, the automated scalpels striking tictactoe on my torso and I know they are taking me, the blood in my head tingles draining down down and I am almost gone. (DC 96–97)

"The Dead Line" returns to this same theme, telling of "Neomorts," brain-dead patients who are kept alive after a fashion so that their organs can be used when needed. Etchison becomes rather hysterical at this point—the whole idea is obviously a source of great loathing to him:

"They will take him organ by organ, cell by cell. And it will take years. As long as the machines can keep the lungs and heart moving. And finally, after they've taken his eyes, his kidneys and the rest, it will be time for his nerve tissue, his lymph nodes, his testes. They will drill out his bone marrow, and when there is no more of that left it will be time to remove his stomach and intestines, as soon as they learn how to transplant those parts, too. And they will. Believe me, they will." (DC 108)

But in spite of Etchison's furious attempt to instill the conception with horror, I honestly find myself rather indifferent to such a state of affairs. Etchison seems to be infected with a somewhat primitive and superstitious belief in the sanctity of the human body after death, a belief that perpetuates the staggeringly wasteful practice of burial rather than some more rational disposition of human remains. I suppose the general issue of human beings losing control of their bodies is well enough taken, but Etchison seems to be straining a little here. These three tales, incidentally, can be related also to the purely supernatural "The Late Shift," which also tells of the callousness of using human beings as "objects, commodities" (DC 124).

Even those tales that appear to be wholly non-supernatural can occasionally be stirring solely on account of deft technique and execution. "Drop City" (RD) is the convoluted story of a man who has suffered amnesia and becomes framed for a murder; but this relatively mundane plot is enlivened by some of the most powerful and affecting dreamlike prose outside the pages of Ramsey Campbell and Thomas Ligotti. "Call 666" (BK) also appears to be a tale of psychological horror—although I am not entirely clear what exactly happens in the story—but the fragmented style again creates eerily hallucinatory effects. "Talking in the Dark" (RD) is a more orthodox *conte cruel* about a celebrated writer who turns out to be a psychopath, but its wry exposition and stunning climax redeem it.

Several of the stories in *The Death Artist* are not weird, nor even tales of mystery and suspense; but they are fine works for all that. "The Last Reel" is a poignant account of a young woman lured inexorably into the pornography industry by ruthless, uncouth entrepreneurs preying upon her loneliness and yearning for stardom. "Call Home" grippingly depicts what appears to be a little girl lost on a California street, but who turns out to be something quite different. "No One You Know" is the tale of a love triangle, made complex by a spare narration relying almost entirely on transcripts of telephone conversations.

Stylistically Etchison seems to see himself as a sort of James M. Cain or James T. Farrell of the weird tale, etching his tales with clipped and dour realism but with moments of prose-poetic impressionism:

> Yesterday in Ensenada, the car horns talking and a crab taco in his hand, he had wanted to buy a pair of huaraches and a Mexican shirt. The best tequila in the world for three-and-a-half a liter. Noche Buena beer, foil labels that always peel before you can read them. Delicados non Filtros cigarettes.
> Bottles of agua mineral. Tehuacan con gas. *No retornable.*
> He smiled as he thought of churros at the Blow Hole, the maid who even washed his dishes, the Tivoli Night Club with Reno cocktail napkins, mescal flavored with worm, eggs fresh from the nest, chorizo grease in the pan, bar girls with rhinestone-studded Aztec headbands, psychoactive liqueurs, seagulls like the tops of valentines, grilled corvina with lemon, the endless plumes of surf. . . . (DC 173–74)

But realism—the realism of brand names, of kids going to school, of parents shopping for groceries and cooking dinner, of watching a movie, of going to the hospital—is the core of Etchison's work, and he enlivens his native Southern California as piquantly as Ramsey Campbell does his Liverpool and T. E. D. Klein his New York:

> Traffic moved up Beaumont Canyon at an impossibly sluggish pace. Cars bearing the names of swift and exotic animals—Impala, Lynx, Jaguar, Cougar and the like—surrounded Doug's sedan, trapping him in their uphill fight as though to some doomed roundup in the sky. From time to time a renegade Maverick, Mustang, Colt or some such would cut loose from the herd and charge ahead impatiently, only to be shouldered back into line by the boundaries of the trail. Mufflers grumbled sullenly in a steady processional of misery, broken by the occasional lowing of a complaining horn, but the mass of dusty bodies continued to press homeward at a regulated pace under the watchful eye of a blood-red sun. In the southbound lanes reckless workers from the Valley raced back to the Westside in their Dashers, Demons and Hornets in an untrammeled flow.

Doug observed them enviously, gritted his teeth and wondered how much he had gained, after all, by moving to beautiful Beverly Hills. (D 103)

"Deadtime Story" (DA) features this crisp glimpse of the landscape:

> The gas station on the corner fired a volley of soft bells at him as cars wheeled past the pumps, their lights wavering coronas through a descending mist. At the Apple Pan customers were lined up three deep behind the stools for pie and hot coffee. He smelled the warmth blowing out the open door as he passed, thought of eating but knew he wouldn't be able to hold it down, not now. He cut left at the first side street and pressed north through a residential neighborhood, moving away from the open boulevard and the traffic.
>
> He crossed Olympic, then the tracks at Santa Monica Boulevard, moving up Glendon so fast that his ankles began to hurt. As he drew closer he felt less protected than ever despite the darkness, with the Mormon Temple to his right as brightly lighted as a movie set, its golden angel with trumpet raised as if to announce his passage. By the time he hit the alley behind the Club he could no longer be sure that he was not being followed. (DA 69)

These richly textured passages display to the full Etchison's keen observation, evocative imagery, and apt metaphor—skills that can vivify even the most mundane events into a sort of prose-poetry of urban life.

Etchison's first novel, *Darkside*, is a modest success, even though he himself speaks of toiling laboriously over it for many months (FF 55). But he is not content to speak of his own difficulties in novel writing; like Thomas Ligotti, he lashes out at the form as a whole:

> . . . I think the novel is an outdated form. It was a moribund form that was created in centuries past for people who had no other entertainment during long winter nights than to sit by the fire with these huge thick books. In our time, the novel is a curiosity. Occasionally someone will do something brilliant with the form, but the idea that we should all have to write stories that run 350 pages is as absurd as saying that all films should run between 90 and 120 minutes. . . . I wish that we could all write books that went on for however long they needed to be and then stopped. We would have 78-page novels, 122-page novels, and 10,000-page novels or however long it took. But if it's too short or too long, it won't be bought and published. What I am saying is that it's because we live in a capitalist culture. We are victims of the dictates of the marketplace. (FF 55–56)

Whatever validity Etchison's remarks on the history of the novel have, I think his account deserves serious attention. It is, indeed, even more wide-ranging than Ligotti's, since the latter has only noted the difficulty in writing *horror* novels, whereas Etchison here is speaking of the novel generally; but then, he does not have much faith in the future of the mainstream short story either ("It seems to me to be essentially dead except in the genres" [FF 56]). Nevertheless, Etchison's own novel is a worthy contribution which we are certainly glad to have, although it cannot be said to rank among the masterworks of the form.

The atmospheric prologue to *Darkside*—in which a youth named Shaun suffers some loathsome fate—suggests the supernatural, as does the novel proper, with its talk of a strange group of children or young adults named "The Lost Ones" and some realm or state of being called "The Darkside" toward which they appear to be striving; but, unlike many works of this type, there is no appreciable letdown when the events turn out after all to be non-supernatural. This is because the social message presented by the entire scenario so perfectly captures and accounts for the seeming listlessness and disregard for life and death that typify the youth movement of the mid-1980s. The focus of the novel is a teenager named Erin (she, as well as her entire family, is resurrected from a story in *The Blood Kiss*, "The Olympic Runner" [1986], although I do not know what if any relation there is between the story and the novel) whose apathy and alienation from her parents and her whole society impel her to participate in some nebulous event which even she cannot clearly recall but which leads to her death about halfway through the novel. The rest of the novel is occupied in her family's various attempts to account for her death, in the course of which both her stepfather Doug Carson and her sister Lori nearly lose their lives as they penetrate the drug-infested youth culture of southern California. In the end Gil McClay, a friend of the family, discusses with Doug the true state of affairs: the Lost Ones are a band of youths who are experimenting with the very borderlands of life and death:

> "The s&m crowd I told you about, they use the same neck rigs, plastic bags, anything that cuts off the normal intake of air long enough to cause a blackout. *But.* Suppose you want to take it one step further, to the limit, beyond that? Interrupt oxygen exchange and it doesn't take long for the pulse, the metabolic processes to stop, and clinical death occurs. As long as you revive before somatic death sets in—within about six minutes—then you're one of the lucky ones. You were medically dead, but you made it back. You survived the biggest thrill ride of them all."
>
> "You mean they do it *voluntarily?* Why would anyone want to die like that, least of all kids?"
>
> "You've hit it. They're kids. They don't have a firm idea of death in the first place. When they did it they convinced themselves that they were seeing 'the other side,' the which than which there is no whicher. They always came back with a story to tell. When they came back. The ones who did were out to spread the word." (D 210–11)

Etchison is intent on not taking a narrowly moralistic view of the situation: he not only contrasts it with the experimentation of the 1960s—

"Why wasn't booze enough?" said Doug. "Or pot, acid, *anything* else? PCP, for God's sake? Why did they have to go that far?"

"Those were the old ways, the ways of their parents. Our ways." (D 212)

—but even holds out the possibility that the entire enterprise might actually have had some benefits: "'The only other explanation,' [Gil] went on, 'is that they really were seeing another place, a better place than this one. If you can accept an idea as crazy as that . . .'" (D 212).

Whatever sociological value Etchison's tale may have, it is in any event enlivened both by careful, atmospheric writing—including a spectacular pseudo-dream sequence wherein Doug deprives himself of oxygen and enters some hallucinatory realm in order to save his daughter Lori—and a conclusion that seems to promise a naive "happy ending" but which unexpectedly does the very reverse. *Darkside* is certainly nothing Etchison—or anyone else—should fail to be proud of, and in many ways it completes his brooding picture of contemporary American life.

Etchison's long-awaited second novel, *Shadowman*, continues the probing of social concerns by means of the horror tale, but does so in a rather less compelling fashion. It is, to be sure, enlivened by the same crispness of prose that we have come to expect from the author; consider two descriptions of a homeless woman: "Her eyes were inconsolable, like those of someone who has awakened from a nightmare only to find that her house has burned down. . . . Something had happened to her somewhere down the line, something too fierce for her to talk about, and she had landed here, discarded, tossed into a far corner like a set of keys to a house that no longer exists" (S 223, 239). But the novel is dragged down by diffuseness, prolixity, and a failure to come to terms with the social and personal issues raised by the scenario. We are here concerned with the small suburban California community of Shadow Bay, where a series of child-murders had occurred some years previous and are now unexpectedly beginning again. All through the novel there are suggestions that the killer—whom some traumatised surviving children can only describe as "The Man With No Face"—is a supernatural entity, but in the end we learn he is nothing more than an ordinary human being interested in the sexual exploitation of children. This devolution from the supernatural to the non-supernatural comes as much more of a letdown here than in *Darkside* because Etchison has not dealt in any coherent or compelling way with the issue of the role of children in our society; instead, the novel reduces to a suspense or adventure story in which the seemingly invincible killer is tracked down by a motley band of adults and children and dispatched in a surprisingly easy manner. There are random references to a group of homeless people who have consciously withdrawn from American society and hope somehow to lead a sort of quiet revolution whereby everyone simply walks off their jobs and reverts to nature; but the conception is never worked out intelligibly nor is it shown to have any vital connexion with the main narrative.

California Gothic, Etchison's third novel, is also, sadly, his worst. In this novel we are introduced to Dan Markham, apparently a loving husband to his wife Eve and a devoted father to his thirteen-year-old son Eddie. But the family's placid life in the San Fernando Valley is disrupted when Dan receives a letter from Jude, a woman with whom he had been involved years ago and who held left him to join a radical group, CSR (the Church of Satan the Redeemer). Dan believes that she had died in a fire, but the letter indicates either that she did not so perish or that she is a revenant or that someone else is attempting some morbid joke. Dan attempts to adopt the last hypothesis, but the reader has already learned that Jude has viciously murdered a forest ranger in the remote cabin where she had been living and then paid an enigmatic visit to Eve at the Markhams' house when Dan was away.

Etchison strives to portray Jude as a vaguely supernatural figure who is both sexually alluring and potentially dangerous; but her prominent feature seems to be her amoral blandness. When Eddie and his friend Tommy Oshidari go to a nearby junkyard and, in their devotion to shlock horror movies, pretend that they are filming a grisly horror film, Jude appears, having already killed the owner of the junkyard. The place goes up in flames; and, although Tommy appears to escape unscathed, Eddie remains within, to be rescued by his mother in a rather confusingly narrated action sequence. Later Jude comes to the Markhams' house, where she reveals herself to Dan as Jude's daughter; her real name is Susan. In an ensuing scuffle between Susan and Eve, Eddie (apparently) disposes of the former by finding a gun in her backpack and shooting her. The Markhams' life returns implausibly to normal afterwards.

California Gothic is both too long and too short. It is too long by being padded with a vast amount of excess verbiage in a bootless attempt to engender suspense. In particular, several sequences dealing with the movie, *American Zombie III*, which Eddie and Tommy are visualising in their minds and which are written in the form of a screenplay, take up much space but bear little relation to the central events of the novel. Another incident—where Dan falls from a ladder and, after suffering a head injury, appears to lose his memory, only to regain it pretty nearly intact in the very next chapter—similarly plays no integral function in the text. And the novel is too short because its emphases are misplaced. We are never given sufficient background on the characters for them to seem at all real, and their activities throughout the work seem wooden and unmotivated.

Even Etchison's customarily prose-poetic style departs him in *California Gothic*, to be substituted by flat declarative sentences interspersed with unconvincing and flatulent sociopolitical diatribes about life in California. And at critical moments in the narrative Etchison's prose lapses into a kind of coy indirectness that produces only confusion rather than enticing ambiguity. *California Gothic* is a near-total failure on Etchison's part, and one can only hope that it may persuade him to abandon the novel form—a form to which his impressionistic style is manifestly unsuited.

I have not felt the need to comment on the rather large number of Etchison's tales that fall flat either because of their excessive obscurity or their less than inspired conceptions. This is because, amid the mass of mundane or routine work he has produced, he has a core of enormously powerful tales that would rank him with a Campbell or a Klein if his work were more uniformly meritorious. His best tales could perhaps form one slim but brilliant volume that would exhibit not only his genre-spanning abilities but his bleak and unflinching vision, a vision that is bitterly antipodal to the cheerful optimism so uniformly if implausibly evident in even the most physically extreme modern weird fiction. If Etchison's subtlety and restraint link him with an older weird tradition, his aggressively contemporary themes and his occasional innovations in style and execution place his work emphatically in a vibrant and modern mode that contrasts sharply with the flabby sentimentalism of Stephen King or the hypertrophic pyrotechnics of Clive Barker. Etchison's continuing devotion to the weird short story may also reward him—as it will reward Campbell, Klein, and Ligotti—with a permanence and endurance which the more pretentious best-selling novels of today are not likely to achieve. One can only hope that Etchison will remain faithful to the relentlessly unconventional principles of weird writing he has enunciated so vigorously.

David J. Schow and Splatterpunk

The term splatterpunk was coined by David J. Schow at the World Fantasy Convention in Providence in October 1986. The word itself seems to be a not very felicitous adaptation of "cyberpunk," a brand of science fiction—noted for its dark portrayals of a world overrun by computer technology—that has really very little to do with the type of literature written by the splatterpunks. But if the term is nebulous, then so is the philosophy behind it. Its proponents like to fancy that it is the most daring, confrontational, loud, and generally innovative brand of weird fiction currently being written, and that it is about to put into the shade all the musty old writers who are only interested in mood, suggestion, and restraint. Even Schow, the most talented by far of the splatterpunks, falls into this fallacy: "And here come those nasty old Splatterpunks, their hair is strange, their clothes are weird, their fiction is often noisy, and they do things like cross over to films, to music, to a whole audience uninterested in haunted New England towns besieged by the Old Ones and malignant, demonic children coming through the doorway to Hell and making deals with the Devil" (W 24).

Paul M. Sammon, self-appointed guru of splatterpunk, has compiled a volume, *Splatterpunks: Extreme Horror* (1990), that gives a tolerably good picture of the scope of the movement, although we shall have occasion to note a number of anomalies and omissions in the book. He tries at the outset to characterise this mode of writing: "Imagine a new word for an old attitude, one which knows no restraints, bows to no god, recognizes no boundaries. Imagine energy, and imagination, and freedom from convention" (Sp xv). What this really boils down to is an unrestrained display of gruesome physical horror, frequently mingled with sex, drugs, and rock 'n' roll. Sammon gives a litany of what you will find in his anthology: "Incest, racism, rape, animal cruelty, serial murders, exploitation of the dead"—but then adds hastily and a little nervously, "But please, not only for the shock value. For these stories carry profound subtexts, harrowing insights into our own sick and shining twentieth century" (Sp xv). This is, however, exactly the weakest point in the whole splatterpunk movement. No reasonable person would have any *intrinsic* objection to the use of explicit violence in literature generally, much less in weird fiction; the issue is whether there is a true aesthetic purpose behind its use in any given instance. Mere declarations that the works "carry profound subtexts" will not be sufficient unless the texts themselves deliver on the promise.

In any event, all this theorising gives us some handle on what splatterpunk is or is trying to be. In effect, it purports to be simultaneously literary and philosophical: literary in its reaction to the whole school of artistically restrained weird fiction, whether it be M. R. James or Robert Aickman or

Ramsey Campbell or (and this seems to be a favourite whipping-boy of the splatterpunks) the "quiet horror" propounded by Charles L. Grant's *Shadows* anthologies of the 1980s; philosophical in its reflection of our chaotic and violent era. When we see so many horrible things happening in the world, how can we not write fiction that echoes or transmogrifies them? Seventy years ago Lovecraft had already written on this subject, speaking of how he could write weird fiction during World War I: "The physical horrors of war, no matter how extreme and unprecedented, hardly have a bearing on the entirely different realm of supernatural terror. Ghosts are still ghosts—the mind can get more thrills from unrealities than from realities!"[1]

There is also a certain problem with ascertaining who exactly the splatterpunk writers are. David J. Schow is being touted on the covers of his books as the "father of splatterpunk," but he refused to participate in Sammon's anthology; and Sammon is repeatedly forced into awkward confessions such as: "Ray Garton cannot really be called a splatterpunk, and like Joe R. Lansdale, he actively resists the label" (Sp 197). The collaborative team of John Skipp and Craig Spector seem to be prototypical splatterpunks, but only Skipp is included in Sammon's volume. And if Schow is splatterpunk's father, then surely Clive Barker, whose *Books of Blood* (1984–85) really ushered in the era of unrestrained grisliness, is a sort of granduncle of the field.

What is peculiar about most splatterpunk writing is that, in spite of its claims of being "unconventional," it is in fact conventional in every way except that pertaining to the depiction of gruesome physical violence and explicit sex. It always puzzles me how the splatterpunks—and Barker as well—can imagine that the mere harm that can be inflicted upon the human body is the culmination of horror or weirdness. This surely betrays an unusually limited imaginative range. Moreover, it never occurs to these writers that repeated doses of this sort of physical mayhem leads not so much to revulsion as to boredom.

While concentrating on "extreme" physical horror, splatterpunk writers fail to enunciate any novel *moral* approach or orientation. Once again I wish to cite Lovecraft:

> Popular authors do not and apparently cannot appreciate the fact that true art is obtainable only by rejecting normality and conventionality in toto, and approaching a theme purged utterly of any usual or preconceived point of view. Wild and "different" as they may consider their quasi-weird products, it remains a fact that the bizarrerie is on the surface alone; and that basically they reiterate the same old conventional values and motives and perspectives. Good and evil, teleological illusion, sugary sentiment, anthropocentric psychology—the usual superficial stock in trade, and all shot through with the eternal and inescapable commonplace.[2]

This could have been written as a review of *Splatterpunks*. I fail to find any sort of original perspective in the volume at all. It is symptomatic that Sammon, while repeatedly whining about the threat of censorship in the current conservative national temper, desperately wishes to defend his school from the charge of misogyny (Sp 282–84). I would almost welcome some sort of misogyny or misanthropy as a relief from the tired moral platitudes into which the splatterpunks so regularly fall. Joe R. Lansdale's "Night They Missed the Horror Show" portrays a vicious case of racism, but the treatment is obvious and superficial. Edward Bryant's "While She Was Out" extends obvious sympathy to a middle-class suburban woman who is set upon by a gang of street youths; and improbably, she manages to kill them off one by one! "Goodbye, Dark Love" by Roberta Lannes is a sort of feminist treatment of incest and necrophila, but again the tale fails to escape conventionality of sentiment. Sammon evokes Clive Barker's dictum about the "subversiveness" of splatterpunk writing, but neither he nor his stable of writers seem to realise that such figures as Bierce, Lovecraft, and Shirley Jackson are much more truly subversive than they in their scorn of bourgeois ethics and their blistering satire on middle-class conventionality.

It is a little odd that so many splatterpunk writers feel the need to affect a slangy, profanity-laden style to convey their gruesomeness. Even Barker can occasionally descend to this sort of thing, although on the whole his style, however slipshod from a purist's perspective, is a little more dignified than those of his followers. I suppose this sort of thing is a part of the splatterpunks' rock 'n' roll sensibility, but they seem utterly oblivious of the imaginative poverty of such an idiom. Here again, as in so many other areas, only Schow has distinguished himself by going beyond the mere adolescent hurling about of obscenities to write with a vigorous, arresting, richly metaphorical style that lays bare our hypertrophic, technology-choked, morality-vacant century. His compatriots seem, on the contrary, like schoolboys scribbling "fuck" on a wall.

This rock 'n' roll style of writing is a particular handicap in critical work, as displayed by Chas. Balun's painfully inept essay on splatter films in the *Splatterpunk* volume, "I Spit in Your Face: Films That Bite," or by Sammon's effusive concluding essay, "Outlaws," or even by Schow's ridiculous afterword to his anthology, *Silver Scream* (1988). None of this work can by any stretch of the imagination even be called genuinely critical, and Sammon's piece in particular is nothing more than a flatulent brief in support of the movement on whose coattails he hopes to ride. His outlandishly exaggerated claims for the importance of the movement ("The writers who comprise *Splatterpunks* haven't just brought horror up to date; they've brought literature up to date" [Sp 274]) make him sound like a pompous buffoon.

It is also of some interest to note that it is entirely irrelevant whether the work of the splatterpunks adopts or repudiates the supernatural: as with Barker (who, however, is predominantly supernatural), all such metaphysical questions are wholly subordinate to mere sensation—the sensation of horror, loathing, and disgust that the splatterpunks hope to inspire by their exhibition of mangled bodies and aberrant sex. Of the sixteen stories in *Splatterpunks*, all but three are non-supernatural. Two are supernatural—"A Life in the Cinema" by Mick Garris and "Goosebumps" by Richard Christian Matheson—but neither makes even the remotest attempt to give any plausible account of the supernatural phenomenon: it is simply a given, and its sole point is to serve as the foundation for a series of grotesque images and tableaux. The other tale, "Meathouse Man" by George R. R. Martin, is an unabashedly science fiction tale; and it is as good an indication as any that splatterpunk, if it is anything, is not so much a subgenre—much less a world view—as a mode of writing which all sorts of writers can employ when it suits their purposes.

But the sad fact is that the splatterpunks are, by and large, simply bad writers. They are incapable of deft plotting, keen characterisation, and true originality of conception. Their writing is all surface and no substance, and their desperate attempts to be hip and contemporary will doom them to oblivion once the transient social and cultural phenomena to which they allude are forgotten. I do not wish to be unkind, but I must single out two stories—"Reunion Moon" by Rex Miller, a moronic attempt at scatological humour, and "Full Throttle" by Philip Nutman, an interminable and superficial portrayal of the aimless life of British punks, concluding with a neatly tacked-on moral—for especial dispraise. It is not a good commentary on Sammon's skills as editor that these are the only two original stories in the volume. The only genuinely meritorious story is "Less Than Zombie" by Douglas E. Winter, at once a hilarious parody of Bret Easton Ellis' *Less Than Zero* and a harrowing portrayal of the physical and moral lassitude that has overwhelmed the yuppie generation.

On the whole, however, Chet Williamson has enunciated the situation succinctly:

> Fear is a very easy emotion to evoke. All you do is pull a knife on somebody and hold it to their throat, and they're going to be scared. And you can do the literary equivalent of that a half a dozen ways per page. It's easy to scare a reader. It's easy to gross out a reader.
>
> What isn't easy is to reach down inside the reader and hold the mirror up and get to the more serious subjects that horror writing can reach . . .[3]

The best one can do for splatterpunk is to express the hope that *Splatterpunks* does not represent the movement to best advantage. There is something to be said for this view—certainly the absence of Schow is cavernous, although Spector's absence is rather less devastating from a literary perspective—and Sammon concludes his volume with a list of about a hundred works which he identifies as splatterpunk, quasi-splatterpunk, or proto-splatterpunk, some of which are indeed substantial contributions to weird literature. There is a certain amount of posturing here, of course: to list *The Exorcist* in this context (Sp 334) is to list a work that has helped to spawn the entire range of modern weird fiction, while listing *Psycho* (Sp 340) is vaguely analogous to the attempts of old-time science fiction critics to see the beginnings of their field in Plato's *Republic* or of deconstructionists to enlist Nietzsche as their founder or mentor. Still, one hopes that in the future—assuming splatterpunk has a future and has not already petered out or fragmented or imploded from its own lack of a compelling *raison d'être*—a more representative anthology may be compiled that might display both the virtues and the limitations of this noisy movement.

But so long as there is a writer of the talent and skill of David J. Schow (b. 1955), splatterpunk cannot be wholly written off, although it is more likely that splatterpunk will be remembered because of Schow than that Schow will be remembered because of splatterpunk. Schow's publishing history is, to say the least, a little odd. Four books published under his name appeared in 1990: two collections of short stories, *Seeing Red* and *Lost Angels,* and two novels, *The Kill Riff* and *The Shaft* (the latter published, as of this writing, only in England). This sudden array of books disguises several facts: that Schow had been publishing short stories for the whole decade of the 1980s; that he had written many volumes of adventure novels (which he refuses to specify [W 18]) under a pseudonym or house name; and that he had written (and continues to write) novelisations of films and television shows, including some episodes of "Miami Vice." Another collection, *Black Leather Required,* appeared in 1994. But however prolific Schow has been, it is only the work published under his own name that merits consideration—and it merits a good deal of consideration.

The first point to note about Schow is that he is, quite simply, a good writer. While his subject-matter tends to be restricted to the variegated phenomena of modern-day urban life—crime, drugs, rock 'n' roll, vast wealth juxtaposed to desperate poverty—he has developed a gruff, raw, richly metaphorical style that can vivify anything, from a bum—

> One of the street denizens for which Union Square is infamous had stopped to stare at me. I stared back, head to toe, from the clouds of gnats around his matted hair to the solid-carbon crustiness of his bare, black feet. He caught me crying with his mad prophet eyes, and the grin that snaked his face lewdly open suggested that yes, I *should* howl with grief, I *should* pull out a Mauser and start plugging pedestrians. . . . The bum and I ceased to exist for each other the moment we parted. (SR 2)

to a drug dealer in his gaudy residence:

Hanging at Bauhaus' overblown wet dream of a bachelor pad held all the appeal of a Drano enema. Bauhaus was not merely a coke vendor; he was the dealer cliché loudly personified. He *played* at being a player, spending half the day with his ear in a mobile phone and the other half bragging and braying. The man was piggish, lethargic, overfed; in seconds Cruz had stockpiled a lifetime of hatred for Bauhaus' donkey laugh. He was the sort of spud who would huzzah his own stupid jokes with a half-assed chuckle designed to cue all brown-noses within range that they'd better laugh along, loud, or else. Bauhaus cut loose that laugh a lot in public, dropping five hundred on dinner, wasting good bubbly while parading his catch of the day from the teenybop coke whore zone. It was all smoke for his urban contacts—a bunch of beard-stubbled fucksticks wearing bolo ties. All smoke. (S 81)

This last passage may be full of violent and repulsive images, but that is because it is describing a violent and repulsive scenario. The subject-matter demands an imagery and a style that lays bare the true loathsomeness of the situation. It is not absurd to say that, on a purely linguistic level, Schow's style is as carefully crafted as Lovecraft's, Aickman's, or Ligotti's, and that the slang and obscenities are used not indiscriminately but exactly where they will have the most telling effect. And Schow's ability goes beyond mere landscape or character description to portray scenes of violence and horror: "Chiquita hit the pool apron and broke. Blood reddened the pool runoff gutter near what used to be her scalp. Her hair spread out like crimson seaweed in a shock corona around the disintegrated crockery of her skull" (S 26).

But don't be fooled. Although Schow manages this raw style without a single false step, and pulls it off with a dazzling verve and panache, he is no Johnny one-note. Consider now this passage from "Sand Sculpture," describing a man whose young wife has just died:

Hadn't he become just a bit overwrought? Obsessive? Hinged to the past, bereft of new emotions and stagnantly content to convert their home into a ghoulish shrine to her memory? Balance had been misplaced. In here, it was Lorelle who was favored, and as a consequence of an ailment he called love, he was now in mortal danger of being dragged under by the riptide of what she had meant to him. (BLR 194)

Here again are startling metaphors—"ghoulish shrine to her memory," "the riptide of what she had meant to him"—but it is all expressed in a clean, refined prose that is leagues away from the slipshod pyrotechnics of Skipp and Spector.

It should also be noted that Schow wields a surprising variety of tone and mood. While his work is unified by a generally grim, dark world view that sees little hope either for the social and economic underclass (what in *The Shaft* is called "anything that survives on the outskirts of polite civilization" [S 5]) or the middle class whose sole object is to avoid contact with the underclass and its zones of violence and despair, his tales themselves range from the brooding to the comical to the poignant. "Bunny Didn't Tell Us" (SR) is an updating of the graveyard humour of Bierce, while "Pulpmeister" (SR) is a hilarious send-up of Schow's own pseudonymous and anonymous hack writing, telling of a writer of pulp adventure novels whose lead character, irritated by his portrayal in the novels, comes to life and tries his hand at writing them himself, only to botch the job. Then there is "Monster Movies" (LA), a touching love story centring upon a man who recalls his boyhood love of horror films and the degree to which they have shaped his entire emotional life. This tale is in fact not merely non-supernatural but entirely non-weird. Schow has even mingled horror and science fiction in "The Embracing" (SR).

And yet, it is those dark tales of urban violence that seem most characteristic of his work. "Red Light" may be Schow's finest weird short story, telling of a model who gains spectacular success only to suffer a hideous fate. She broaches the idea of "psychic vampirism": "'What it always boils down to is, "Climb off it, bitch—who did you *really* blow to get that last *Vogue* cover?" They feed off you. They achieve gratification in a far dirtier way, by wanting you and resenting you at the same time. By hating your success enough to keep all the tabloids in business. It's a draining thing, all taking and no giving . . .'" (SR 10). "Coming Soon to a Theatre Near You" is the spectacularly horrifying tale of a dubious movie theatre teeming with vermin. One scene, depicting a derelict thrown into the orchestra pit of the theatre, tells the whole story:

> The dude and the new employee heaved Fatigue Coat over the lip of the orchestra pit into the riotous, churning sea of chitinous bugs. He seemed to hinge at the waist, like one of those backward-jointed dummies used for the big jump in the cheapest films. He did not look real. Neither did the sheer mass of waiting roaches—at least three vertical feet of them, swarming nearly to the rusted brass rail of the pit. They embraced the body hungrily. The last part of him to submerge into the attack of brown, bullet-like forms was his foot, toes protruding from a demolished sneaker wound with dirty friction tape. Then he was gone, gobbled up, and quickly. (SR 174)

I am not convinced, however, that this tale is anything more than a manipulation of our fear and loathing of cockroaches. "Not from Around Here" is rather more effective: although it is stylistically a little more "normal" than Schow's other work, it is in many ways a prototypical splatterpunk tale in its perfect mingling of sex and violence, telling of a monster that causes violent orgasms while dismembering his victims. This is a piquant conception, and so ably handled that we fail to notice its implausibility.

Seeing Red is a miscellaneous collection of tales; *Lost Angels* purports to be more unified, although, in the absence of any author's note, the unity must be inferred from the texts themselves. One imagines that the theme of loss, especially as it relates to human relationships, is the dominant theme in the five long stories in the book ("Red Light" is reprinted here); but, while these tales are less obtrusively violent in imagery, they also tend toward diffuseness and lack of focus. These flaws are particularly evident in a very long story, "Brass," which is founded upon unconvincing occultist presuppositions. Schow, indeed, has spun this tale to such length precisely in order to make the occultist mumbo-jumbo—which emerges fully only toward the end—vaguely plausible, but his abrasively modern and generally atmosphereless style does not make for persuasiveness on this matter. "The Falling Man" analogously involves the Tarot, and—aside from some uncharacteristic melodrama and maudlin sentimentality between the young couple who are the focus of the story—it is a little more effective in showing how an evil little man has been manipulating the couple's romance for his own aesthetic purposes.

But the one remarkable tale—aside from "Monster Movies"—in *Lost Angels* is "Pamela's Get," which presents one of the most bizarre conceptions in modern weird fiction. We initially witness what appears to be a series of reflections by various characters on the life and personality of a woman who has tragically died; but in the end it transpires that the woman had actually *imagined* all these friends. Such a plot summary cannot begin to evoke the fantastically convoluted structure of the story and the insidiously gradual way in which the final revelation dawns upon the reader.

Schow, like the splatterpunks generally, alternates between supernatural and non-supernatural scenarios at will. He is, however, not always successful in his use of the supernatural, which, in spite of his modernism of tone and setting, can be either curiously conventional (as in "Night Bloomer," in which a man uses a mysterious plant to dispatch his boss) or implausible (as in "Lonesome Coyote Blues," in which we learn of dead rock stars recording new songs for a remote radio station). "Incident on a Rainy Night in Beverly Hills" is non-supernatural, attempting to account for the manifold evils of Hollywood—and, consequently, of many elements of our popular culture—by conceiving of a secret group called The Conclave that has the power of manipulating events in the real world for the sake of their media potential. One supposes that "Coming Soon to a Theatre Near You" is, strictly speaking, non-supernatural, although it is a little hard to imagine that even the seediest theatre could have a yard-deep supply of cockroaches.

In many tales in *Black Leather Required*, however, we are presented with conventional vampires, zombies, werewolves, and the like; and Schow's flip tone causes these tales, perhaps unwittingly, to lapse into self-parody. Actually, Schow is rather good at treading the borderline between humour and horror. "Last Call for the Sons of Shock" puts Frankenstein's monster, Count Dracula, and the Wolfman on stage, and the scintillating mix of supernaturalism, B-movie references, and low farce produces an effect I have never encountered anywhere else. But when Schow attempts to give a "serious" treatment of the vampire myth ("A Week in the Unlife"), even he can't pull it off. Conversely, "Pitt Night at the Lewistone Boneyard" starts out as mere buffoonery—all the occupants of a family gravesite have somehow become zombies, and the one surviving member of the family encounters each of them in turn—but gradually turns serious and even poignant; for what this tale really is about is the effort of this one survivor to say and do the things he could not or did not say or do to his relatives when they were alive. By doing so, he relieves himself of the guilt he has felt at their passing and can now go on with his life.

Some of Schow's stories border on science fiction. "Sedalia" (BLR) is an entertainment about dinosaurs having come back to life in our day and the social and logistical problems this causes; the tale goes on a little too long, but is amusing enough. Rather more substantial is "Kamikaze Butterflies," a conscious tribute to Ray Bradbury's story "A Sound of Thunder," in which a man, going back in time, treads on a butterfly and thereby changes all future history. In his story, Schow displays a group of soldiers of fortune who go back in time and intentionally do as much damage as possible in an effort to wipe out entire future civilisations or perhaps all human life:

> The story went that the tiniest death, the soundless pulverization of a butterfly's fragile body in the past, could grow, in the future, to a thunderstroke, a palpable floodtide of sound that touched all, and changed all it touched. The payoff for death on a massive scale was therefore seductive to Masterson. Although the mission he proposed was a guaranteed one-way op, each member of Omega Team had volunteered. Each volunteer realized that each of their actions, even the tiniest, like Mendoza's smoldering cigarette butt, would yield results too large to be contained by any history book, ever. That power, savored briefly but equally guaranteed, was enough to recruit them. A story of people who never were, a fiction printed on dead trees in cheap black, could change the face of a world they scorned. (BLR 77)

Of Schow's two novels, *The Kill Riff* is non-supernatural, while *The Shaft* is emphatically supernatural. This fact alone is part of the reason why the latter is far more successful than the former. In *The Kill Riff* we encounter a man who has just emerged from a psychiatric hospital, having evidently recovered from the double trauma of his wife Cory's apparent death by suicide and, some time later, his daughter Kristen's death during a riot at a rock concert. Lucas Ellington appears to be on the way to regaining normalcy in his life as he returns to work, a little shaken but seemingly ready to face the world again. But it becomes rapidly evident that such is not the case, as he quietly and calmly makes plans to kill off the members of the rock band, Whip Hand, at whose concert his daughter died. It is at this point that the novel loses suspense and tension. In the absence of any supernaturalism, we are presented with nothing more than a long series of tableaux in which Lucas systematically kills off the first two or three of the rock musicians. There are also certain plot holes. The principal band member, Gabriel Stannard, whom Lucas is saving for last on his hit list, seems to have no doubt that Lucas is behind the killings of his associates; similarly, the woman psychiatrist who treated Lucas and who now has a romantic interest in him also immediately concludes that Lucas is the culprit. All this strains credulity, for there is no reason why either of these individuals should make such a deduction in the total absence of any visible evidence pointing to Lucas's guilt.

The evolution of Lucas's character is, however, well handled. We are initially led almost to sympathise with his murderous quest, since the rock musicians were all hastily absolved of any guilt in the riot or in the resultant deaths. But our tentative sympathy is emphatically withdrawn when Lucas, having befriended a young woman who has blundered into his mountain retreat, suddenly kills her after they have sex. We do not immediately understand the motives for this act, but then we learn that Lucas had been sleeping with his daughter and that the two of them had staged Cory's death to make it appear a suicide. Later we have yet another partial reversal, as Lucas's mania is generalised into a social philosophy: "Lucas represented what could almost be termed another evolutionary step—Psychopathic Man, possessing the mechanisms to cope with what living has become, to survive in this world" (KR 397). For his part, Stannard, like the model in "Red Light," has become the victim of his own macho image and is forced into a final violent confrontation with Lucas, as Lucas himself realises: "'To preserve the myth of what he is, he has to come. The cult of personality says so. Rules of promotion and publicity say so. . . . For him to cringe now is bad advertising'" (KR 358).

If *The Kill Riff,* while typically splatterpunk in its mingling of violence and rock 'n' roll, is not a complete success, *The Shaft* most emphatically is. This novel, about the drug culture that festers on the underside of Chicago's tenements, is perhaps the only genuine contribution of splatterpunk to weird literature. It embodies many of the central concerns in Schow's fiction—the pervasiveness of drugs and their corrosive effects upon society and human lives; the insidious melding of the normally separate worlds of grinding poverty and middle-class yuppiedom; and the emergence of the weird and the horrific from the mundanities of daily life.

The novel tells of the inevitable if fortuitous joining of Cruz, a low-level drug runner who has had to flee Miami for Chicago because he had inadvertently caused the death of a drug kingpin's concubine, and Jonathan, who has come to Chicago from Arizona on the breakup of his marriage. Both are forced by circumstance to put up temporarily in a hellishly decrepit rooming house, the Kenilworth Arms, in the dead of winter; but, for all their differences in background and temperament, they become friends after a fashion when Jonathan charitably helps supply bail for Cruz after he has been imprisoned on a minor drug charge. Cruz realises that the two of them occupy wholly different worlds:

> Jonathan was real people; he fit into the bourgeois world of people who drove Nipponese compacts and paid taxes. Cruz was a fringe dweller, a maverick virus; he slipped through the cracks and hung at the edge of proper civilization. Like a predator, he fed off the norm. Columnists wrote inept articles on what they called "the drug subculture." People like Jonathan read them in Sunday supplements, having one of two reactions: *How can people LIVE like that?* or *Jesus; must be goddamn nice.* (S 132)

Also involved is Jamaica, a whore on the payroll of Bauhaus, the drug lord for whom Cruz works in Chicago. Cruz and Jamaica are forced to drop two kilos of cocaine down a ventilation shaft when the police unexpectedly arrive at the building one night. Cruz imagines that they have come for him, but in fact they have been summoned because a child in a neighbouring apartment has disappeared and suffered some loathsome fate: a shoe, with her foot still in it, is found in the corridor. Jonathan, Cruz, and Jamaica seek to rescue the cocaine, thinking that by splitting the profits they can rearrange their lives and begin afresh—if nothing else, they can leave the vile building in which they are immured.

This mingling of a clearly supernatural horror with the very real dangers involved in drug-running creates a uniquely compelling atmosphere. Amid the inexplicable terrors of a building that seems weirdly animate and of some loathsome monstrosity lurking in the bottom of the ventilation shaft, the pursuit of Cruz, Jonathan, and Jamaica by Bauhaus and his minions seems by turns insignificant and chillingly immediate. But while Bauhaus in the end is dispensed with, the supernatural entity is not so easily escaped.

I am not, however, entirely clear on the nature or plausibility of that entity. *The Shaft* is a radical reworking of a short story of the same title (now included in BLR); and while the nebulousness of the entity is acceptable in the story, Schow's account of its origin and development in the novel is confusing and unsatisfying. We are asked to believe that, initially, a huge and loathsome tapeworm emerged from the stomach of the tenement's seedy landlord and stationed itself in the shaft. Fed by one of the kilos of cocaine, which burst from its wrapping and mixed with the standing water at the bottom of the shaft, the tapeworm grew to huge size and strength. All this is tolerably believable, but then a further metamorphosis occurs: somehow the building itself becomes animate, bleeding when its walls are damaged and able to enlarge and contract its rooms to trap some hapless tenant; on top of this, the human beings it dispatches come back to life as hideous zombies. This is a mighty tall order for a tapeworm to accomplish.

When, early in the novel, it is said that "Kenilworth Arms was like a latter-day House of Usher" (S 125), we are eventually led to understand that this is not a mere simile but a reality—that, like the House of Usher, it is a sort of living organism. Toward the end we are given a makeshift explanation:

> Kenilworth Arms weathers, and maintains itself. Its tenants have no idea that their own despair is a protein that helps to keep the building whole.
> Lately, more blood than usual has moistened the walls and carpet runners. The dosage is capacious enough for the building to experience the power of blood, and be transported by it.
> All this has come to pass thanks to the tapeworm. (S 322)

This whole conception allows Schow some highly pungent horrific effects—

> Stallis saw a moist visage awash in discharge and blood, looking peeled, or overbaked. Skinless sinews cuddled a good nine inches of jaw in which hundreds of pencil incisors were crookedly seated. At the crown was a pulsing wad of cauliflower brains topped by a froth of bloody white hair. The arms supporting him were naked bone enwrapped in hanks of muscle like a derelict's clothing held together by electrical tape. (S 232)

—but at the expense, perhaps, of the reader's credulity.

Nevertheless, *The Shaft* is a triumph for its keen character portrayals, its magnificent atmosphere of oppressive horror, its dismally effective etching of lives crushed by poverty and drugs, and the unrelentingly vivid evocativeness of its brash, tight-lipped, yet strangely poetical prose. Without either romanticising or moralising, Schow conveys the staggering human toll exacted in the drug culture, in which money, drugs, and sex are free for the taking but security is harder to come by. Toward the end Cruz finally realises that he "had to arrange a life that did not require him to constantly look back over his shoulder in unending fear" (S 250), and Jamaica comes to a similar conclusion: "Hadn't she swallowed enough fast-lane horseshit to know how superficial glitz was, and what the true costs were?" (S 272). I am, however, a little disappointed with Jamaica's final pronouncement on the entire state of affairs: "'Shit happens'" (S 326). This sort of bumper-sticker philosophy is not a very fitting conclusion to an otherwise rich and substantial piece of writing.

Schow's moral philosophy is not any more innovative than that of his splatterpunk colleagues, although it rarely descends to their levels of sophomoric platitudinousness. For all his tough-guy image, Schow's politics seem to be a fairly orthodox liberalism. His scathing depictions of police brutality (see S 126–31) are not a product of some knee-jerk hostility to authority but of an awareness of the cynicism, racism, and abuse of power exhibited by so many members of urban police forces overwhelmed by ferocious crime. Amid all the portrayals of sex in his work, his women are never objectified or portrayed misogynistically; indeed, Jamaica eventually emerges as the heroine of *The Shaft*, if for no other reason than that she has had either the luck or the toughness to survive the horrors, both natural and supernatural, to which both Cruz and Jonathan succumbed. The model of "Red Light" suffers a very different fate, and we are meant to sympathise with her, both as a successful model and as a victim of "psychic vampirism." Schow's depiction of street toughs or punks is at once sympathetic—he avoids easy moral condemnation of their acts of irrational violence, realising that these are a product of the youths' aimlessness and sense of alienation from bourgeois society—and brutally realistic, in showing the ease with which their lives can be snuffed out by the gyre of violence in which they have become entrapped. At the moment Schow sounds rather like an angry young man, and it shall be interesting to see if his work remains as loud and boisterous in his later years. As for his splatterpunk friends, they too are very loud right now, but I cannot help feeling that they will meet a fate enunciated in a charming utterance by Lord Dunsany: "What a noise we made! But it will all be forgotten."[4]

Notes

1. H. P. Lovecraft, "The Defence Reopens!" (1921), *Miscellaneous Writings*, ed. S. T. Joshi (Sauk City, WI: Arkham House, 1995), p. 150.

2. H. P. Lovecraft, letter to Edwin Baird (c. August 1923), *Miscellaneous Writings*, p. 509.

3. Chet Williamson, cited in Stanley Wiater, *Dark Dreamers* (New York: Avon, 1990), p. 204.

4. "The Policeman's Prophecy," in *The Man Who Ate the Phoenix* (London: Jarrolds, 1949), p. 95.

Poppy Z. Brite: Sex, Horror, and Rock-&-Roll

Child prodigies are tolerably common in horror fiction. Matthew Gregory Lewis was twenty-one when *The Monk* (1796) was published, as was Mary Shelley upon the publication of *Frankenstein* (1818). Edgar Allan Poe was twenty-two when he wrote his first significant weird tale, "Metzengerstein" (1831). All this might lend further fuel to hostile critics' claims that horror fiction is fundamentally juvenile; but it could as easily be maintained that the imaginative fire that leads to vivid, dynamic work in this field requires the stimulus of flaming youth.

In recent decades several writers in our field have been deemed (or have deemed themselves) prodigies, and it is worth studying the actual merits of their work to see whether such a designation is in fact justified. One of these is Poppy Z. Brite (b. 1967), who has to her credit a short story collection, two novels, and an anthology of erotic vampire stories, *Love in Vein* (1994). As the latter contains no work by her, I shall not discuss it here but rather turn to her own creative work.

It is perhaps best to start one's reading of Brite with the short story collection *Swamp Foetus* (1994; reprinted in 1996 as *Wormwood*), since this volume collects tales written prior to her novels. They are, certainly, a mixed bag. Brite can write, but in many cases she has nothing to write about. She can craft a fine descriptive passage like this vignette of New York City's now-vanished red-light district around 42nd Street:

> The light of the setting sun was as red as desire. X's paraded across every marquee. The poster girls' nipples and lipstick had long since faded to a dusty orange. The signs and lampposts and even the square of sidewalk we stood on seemed to vibrate silently in the hellish glow, as if some enormous city machine thrummed far below the pavement. "You've gotten us lost," said Robert, licking his lips nervously, and then we rounded a corner and saw the pinnacle of Chinatown's first gaudy pagoda rising above the city.

Let it pass that one does not get to Chinatown from the red-light district by rounding a corner. But it should be pointed out that, evocative as this passage is, it is entirely a description of a physical object or series of objects. There are many such word-pictures in Brite's work, but they never go beyond the level of physicality. She has much more difficulty describing mental states or things beyond the realm of the senses.

Most of Brite's stories are not so much stories as vignettes. Very few actually go anywhere, narratively speaking. The story "Xenophobia," from which the above passage was taken, is a case in point: it is really nothing more than a series of impressions about New York City and, to this former Manhattan resident, seems to be a rather naive and hyperventilated rant about the dangers of the city. "How to Get Ahead in New York" is similar. "Calcutta, Lord of Nerves" is better in that it does not pretend to be anything more than a prose poem (and a very fine one) about the city of Calcutta. But the best tale in *Swamp Foetus* is "The Sixth Sentinel." Narrated by a ghost, this tale skilfully uses the supernatural as a vehicle for the exploration of character, as the ghost has the ability to enter the mind of a haggard stripper who lives in his flat. This is what weird fiction is all about.

Brite has resurrected two characters who appear in several of her stories, Steve and Ghost, in her first novel, *Lost Souls* (1992); but the result is confusion, verbosity, and lack of focus. Here even Brite's usual virtues as a prose stylist are not on very good display: the language fluctuates wildly and jarringly between high-flown prose-poetry and grating colloquialism and slang, and the work shows how far Brite has to go to master that critical element in a fiction writer's arsenal called narrative drive.

We are here concerned with two intersecting tales. One involves the efforts of a trio of vampires, Zillah, Molochai, and Twig, to carry out their bloodthirsty activities as they drive somewhat aimlessly in a van across the southern United States. The other is the story of Steve and Ghost, two-bit rock stars who lead equally aimless lives until they finally become enmeshed with the vampires. The connecting link is a boy named Nothing, who turns out to be the son of Zillah and a sixteen-year-old New Orleans girl and who is fascinated with the music of Steve and Ghost's band, called Lost Souls.

This is an acceptable premise for a novel (at least, no less acceptable than that of many other novels in this field), but Brite's execution of it leaves much to be desired. The flaws in *Lost Souls* can be specified as follows: 1) implausibility of the supernatural phenomenon; 2) structural problems, especially the excessive use of coincidence; 3) lack of interesting or sympathetic characters; 4) lack of overall thrust or purpose.

Brite has chosen to utilise the vampire myth but to dispense with most of its features and "rules." This is her prerogative—certainly the standard vampire legend must be utterly played out by now, although one would never know it from the continual proliferation of books and stories about these wearisome entities—but what she has put in its place is confused and paradoxical. In Brite's metaphysics, vampires are a race or species separate from human beings altogether; they are also not "undead," but are born from the union of a male vampire with a human woman, and each vampire kills its mother by eating its way out of the womb. This is rather picturesque, and it allows Brite to dispense with the vampire's fear of crosses or of daylight and much other rubbish; but it causes significant conceptual dilemmas. If vampires are a different race, how did they become so uncannily similar to human beings? Where did they come from? Brite presents no "origin of species" for vampires here, as Anne Rice does in *The Vampire Lestat*. Also, Brite's vampires can live for hundreds of years unless they die by violence; but when do they stop "growing" outwardly? All the vampires in the novel seem to be of different (outward) ages, from Nothing (who is both fifteen and looks it) to Molochai and Twig (who seem in their early twenties, although clearly they are much older) to Christian, a 368-year-old vampire who looks middle-aged. Brite has one character say that "after a point they do not age"—but at what point? Writing a supernatural tale does not absolve an author of the duty of making the supernatural plausible—aesthetically if not scientifically.

Then there is the matter of the very frequent coincidences Brite uses to keep her plot moving. Nothing, feeling dissatisfaction with his sterile middle-class existence (Christian had left him as a baby on the doorstep of a family in the suburbs), runs away, and as a hitchhiker runs right into Zillah's van! A short time later they pick up another hitchhiker, who proves to be none other than a young friend from Nothing's town. Nothing persuades Zillah to go to Missing Mile, North Carolina (the home of Steve and Ghost), so that he can see his rock idols. Somehow or other Christian winds up there also. While in Missing Mile, Zillah bewitches and impregnates Steve's estranged girlfriend Ann. All the characters then uncannily find themselves back in New Orleans, where Steve and Ghost just happen to run into a man whose brother had been a vampire victim and who knows of a potion that might abort Ann's fetus before it kills her. This proves to be a vain hope, and Steve, enraged at Ann's death, wants to kill Zillah. Steve and Ghost track down the vampires, who just happen to be somewhat incapacitated because they drank the blood of a cancer victim and are suffering a type of blood poisoning; this allows Steve to kill Zillah with remarkable ease. They walk away and the book is over.

Brite makes efforts now and again to portray these coincidences as some sort of overarching destiny (of Nothing's hitchhiking encounter with Zillah and his crew it is said, "this had all been meant to happen"); but this is an evasion. Coincidences and conveniences of this sort are the author's way of cheating; it is like someone painting himself into a corner and then painting a door to walk out of it. It makes writing too easy; it allows the author to skirt the issues of how things actually happen in the world and how people actually behave.

Perhaps these things would not make a difference if the characters in *Lost Souls* were at all compelling, but they are not. We are presumably meant to sympathise with Steve and Ghost, but the former is a jerk who brutalises his girlfriend and then feels sorry for it afterward, while Ghost—who, to the convenience of several plot twists, is a "sensitive" who can read minds—seems merely colourless. Incredibly, we are also meant to sympathise with Nothing, even though he brutally sucks the blood of his best friend. As for the vampires—they give the term "banality of evil" a whole new meaning, although toward the end Brite coyly denies the possibility of passing a clear moral judgment on them ("Maybe they did what they had to do to live").

But the greatest problem with *Lost Souls* is simply a lack of focus. What is this novel about? Where is it going? What is it trying to say? Brite seems so intent on shaping individual scenes that she has given no thought to the effect of the whole. In the middle of the book we are told: "when you have too much faith in something, it is bound to hurt you. Too much faith in anything will suck you dry. In this way, all the world is a vampire." I hope to heaven that this supreme epitome of high-school philosophy is not the message we are to derive from this work, but in the absence of any other, I fear it will have to do.

It is debatable whether Brite's second novel, *Drawing Blood* (1993), is or is not an improvement over her first; my general feeling is that it is not quite as bad—or is bad in less pronounced ways—but it still reveals significant flaws in conception and execution and has even fewer countervailing virtues than its predecessor. We here return to Missing Mile, where in 1972 a troubled comic-book artist, Robert McGee, kills his wife, one infant son, and himself one night; his five-year-old son Trevor survives, and twenty years later returns to his hometown to see if by some means he can ascertain why his father left him alive when by all rights he should be dead. Trevor has himself evolved into an accomplished comic artist, and he seems to use his art both as self-expression and as a means for investigating his own psyche.

What begins, however, as a promising rumination on the nature and purpose of art quickly loses focus when Brite introduces a whole new set of characters centreing around one Zachary Bosch, a nineteen-year-old computer hacker, and his various friends. Zach finds himself compelled to flee New Orleans when he learns that he is about to be arrested by government agents for some entirely unspecified criminal activity related to his hacking. He heads northeast and just happens to end up in Missing Mile! He encounters Trevor brooding in his now abandoned house, and the two fall in love with a haste and intensity that is entirely unconvincing given how little we still know about either of them and how little they know about each other. But it allows Brite to engage in lavish descriptions of homosexual sex, even if it bogs her plot down woefully.

On top of this, a supernatural element is suddenly and incompetently introduced about halfway through the book. The house at which Trevor and Zach are staying begins inducing wild hallucinations in them; but instead of fleeing, they stay and take drugs (mushrooms, to be exact) to induce more hallucinations. As a result, they enter some nebulous fantasy realm which may or may not be the cartoon universe (Birdland) created by Robert McGee. Coming out of it more or less intact, although with sundry injuries, they are abruptly forced to leave Missing Mile when they find the government agents on Zach's trail again; they end up—happily ever after, one imagines—in Jamaica.

In *Drawing Blood* Brite has at least pruned her overly lush prose so as actually to carry the narrative forward a little more briskly than in *Lost Souls;* but in some ways she has gone to the opposite extreme by writing in a commonplace, slang-ridden idiom that repeatedly deflates any atmosphere of horror she has managed to create. At one critical juncture toward the end, when Zach and Trevor are in Birdland, Brite comes out with: "We're so fucked up, Zach thought. We could be the Dysfunctional Families poster kids if either of us lives long enough." Buffoonery of this sort is exactly what is *not* needed at this point.

Brite has erred seriously in the very introduction of the subplot about Zach's hacking and his pursuit by the government, which is really not very interesting and takes up valuable time away from the potentially compelling supernatural phenomena at the McGee house. It is, in fact, never made clear how the house suddenly gained its supernaturalism: Did it have it beforehand, so that it induced McGee to kill his family? or did the killing itself engender it? Trevor remarks toward the end, "This place preserves its dead"—but there is no telling how this could possibly have come about. Indeed, it does not even seem as if Trevor even finally learns what he came to the house to learn—why he remained alive when the rest of his family was killed. We are only told at the end:

> Sometimes Trevor thought about the house. Sometimes he dreamed about it, but remembered only frozen images from these dreams: the shape suspended from the shower curtain rod, slowly turning; the terrible dawning recognition in Bobby's eyes as he looked up from the bed of the sleeping son he had meant to kill after all, but could not.
>
> Had Bobby meant to die already, or had the sight of his elder son grown, in Birdland, driven him to his death? Trevor would never know. He no longer worried much about it.

Didn't worry much about it? The whole novel has been leading up to the resolution of this point—but now Brite is saying it doesn't much matter!

There are other problems in *Drawing Blood:* a lot of excess verbiage, both on the level of words and of entire scenes (including one long passage about Zach becoming a rock star for one evening, which has absolutely nothing to do with the thrust of the book); gaucheries such as the inclusion of an actual individual (the comic book publisher Steve Bissette) as a character and the caricature of Stefan Dziemianowicz (who had given Brite's first novel a poor review) under the transparent guise of a young hacker, Stefan Duplessis; absurdities in the conception of Birdland, including a talking saxophone ("Hey, cat—you in a cartoon, dig? Cartoons is s'posed to be silly"); and more owlish schoolgirl philosophy, this time placed in self-important italics: *"This isn't just about having someone to wake up next to,*

Trevor realized. It's about trusting someone else not to hurt you, even if you're sure they will. Its about being trustworthy, and not leaving when it gets weird."

I have already remarked that *Drawing Blood* is chock full of sex, mostly of the homosexual variety. This is itself an interesting phenomenon, indicating that straight women find homosexuality as fascinating as straight men find lesbianism; and Brite is to be praised for her loving and honest descriptions. We live in an age when too many self-appointed guardians of morality want to tell us what we can or cannot do. I think Brite does go on a little too long and a little too sentimentally about it, so that parts of her work begin to read like souped-up Harlequin romances; but only a hypocrite or a Republican (much the same thing, actually) could find such passages offensive.

I repeat that Poppy Z. Brite can write—she is probably a better prose stylist than many of the more commercially successful writers in our field, although this is not much of a compliment—but at the moment she has nothing to write about. I have been led to wonder whether this is simply a generational thing: maybe I simply cannot sympathise with all the young characters (almost no one in Brite's work is over the age of thirty) she so lovingly puts on stage. But maybe it is the case that Brite has not really figured out what she wants to say, or—worse—thinks she doesn't really have to say anything in particular so long as she keeps writing pretty sentences. Even Thomas Ligotti, a far superior writer, suffers occasionally from this problem.

What Brite lacks is discipline. If she is going to write supernatural fiction, she had better make sure that the supernatural is made to seem both real and plausible. Her work is also seriously marred by treacly sentimentalism, verbosity, and lack of direction. She takes herself too seriously. She is not as good a writer as she thinks she is. One does not wish to harp on her youth, but her general attitude to the world seems even younger than her years—teenage rather than twentysomething. It is conceivable that she may amount to something in the coming years, but she has a long way to go.

Bibliography

E. F. Benson

Benson, E. F. *The Collected Ghost Stories of E. F. Benson*. Edited by Richard Dalby. New York: Carroll & Graf, 1992.
————. *The Countess of Lowndes Square and Other Stories*. London: Cassell, 1920.
————. *Desirable Residences and Other Stories*. Edited by Jack Adrian. London: Oxford University Press, 1991.
————. *Final Edition: Informal Autobiography*. London: Longmans, Green, 1940.
————. *The Flint Knife: Further Spook Stories*. Edited by Jack Adrian. Wellingborough, UK: Equation, 1988.
————. *More Spook Stories*. London: Hutchinson, 1934. [MSS]
————. *The Room in the Tower and Other Stories*. London: Mills & Boon, 1912. [RT]
————. *Spook Stories*. London: Hutchinson, 1928. [SS]
————. *Visible and Invisible*. London: Hutchinson, 1923. [VI]
Lubbock, S. G. *A Memoir of Montague Rhodes James*. Cambridge: Cambridge University Press, 1939.

Robert Bloch

Bloch, Robert. "Black Bargain." *Weird Tales* 36, No. 5 (May 1942): 66–76.
————. "The Laughter of a Ghoul." *Fantasy Fan* 2, No. 4 (December 1934): 62–63.
————. *Mysteries of the Worm*. Second Edition. Edited by Robert M. Price. Oakland, CA: Chaosium, 1993. [M]
————. "Satan's Servants." In Lovecraft's *Something about Cats and Other Pieces*. Sauk City, WI: Arkham House, 1949. [S]
————. *Strange Eons*. Chapel Hill, NC: Whispers Press, 1978. [SE]
Lovecraft, H. P. *Letters to Robert Bloch*. Edited by David E. Schultz and S. T. Joshi. West Warwick, RI: Necronomicon Press, 1993. [L]
————. *Letters to Robert Bloch: Supplement*. Edited by David E. Schultz and S. T. Joshi. West Warwick, RI: Necronomicon Press, 1993. [LS]

Poppy Z. Brite

Brite, Poppy Z. *Drawing Blood.* New York: Delacorte Press, 1993.

———. *Lost Souls.* New York: Delacorte Press, 1992.

———. *Swamp Foetus.* Baltimore: Borderlands Press, 1994. New York: Dell, 1996 (as *Wormwood*).

Robert W. Chambers

Baldwin, C. C. "Robert W. Chambers." In *The Men Who Make Our Novels.* Rev. ed., as by "George Gordon." New York: Dodd, Mead, 1924.

Chambers, Robert W. *In Search of the Unknown.* New York: Harper & Brothers, 1904.

———. *The King in Yellow.* Chicago: F. Tennyson Neely, 1895.

———. *The Maker of Moons.* New York: Putnam, 1896.

———. *The Mystery of Choice.* New York: D. Appleton & Co., 1897.

———. *Police!!!* New York: D. Appleton & Co., 1915.

———. *The Slayer of Souls.* New York: George H. Doran, 1920.

———. *The Tracer of Lost Persons.* New York: D. Appleton & Co., 1906.

———. *The Tree of Heaven.* New York: D. Appleton & Co., 1907.

———. *The Yellow Sign and Other Stories: The Complete Weird Tales of Robert W. Chambers.* Edited by S. T. Joshi. Oakland: Chaosium, 2000.

Cooper, Frederic Taber. "Robert W. Chambers." In *Some American Story Tellers.* New York: Henry Holt, 1911.

Hughes, Rupert. "The Art of Robert W. Chambers." *Cosmopolitan* 65 (June 1918): 80–81, 116.

Kilmer, Joyce. "What Is Genius? Robert W. Chambers." In his *Literature in the Making.* New York & London: Harper, 1917.

Lovecraft, H. P. *Selected Letters II.* Ed. August Derleth and Donald Wandrei. Sauk City, WI: Arkham House, 1968.

Underwood, John Curtis. "Robert W. Chambers and Commercialism." In *Literature and Insurgency: Ten Studies in Racial Evolution.* New York: Mitchell Kennerley, 1914.

F. Marion Crawford

Crawford, F. Marion. "The King's Messenger." *Cosmopolitan* 44, No. 1 (November 1907): 89–93. Rpt. West Warwick, RI: Necronomicon Press, 1989.

———. *Khaled: A Tale of Arabia.* London: Macmillan, 1891.

———. *The Witch of Prague.* London: Macmillan, 1891.

———. *Zoroaster.* London: Macmillan, 1885.

Moran, John C. *An F. Marion Crawford Companion.* Westport, CT: Greenwood Press, 1981.

Les Daniels

Daniels, Les. *The Black Castle.* New York: Scribner's, 1978. [BC]
_____. *Citizen Vampire.* New York: Scribner's, 1981. [CV]
_____. *Living in Fear: A History of Horror in the Mass Media.* New York: Scribner's, 1975. [LF]
_____. *No Blood Spilled.* New York: Tor, 1991. [NBS]
_____. *The Silver Skull.* New York: Scribner's, 1979. [SS]
_____. *Yellow Fog.* West Kingston, RI: Donald M. Grant, 1986. Rev. ed. *New York: Tor, 1988. [YF]
Wiater, Stanley. "Les Daniels." In *Dark Dreamers.* New York: Avon, 1990, pp. 43–50.

L. P. Davies

Davies, L. P. *Adventure Holidays, Ltd.* Garden City, NY: Doubleday, 1970.
_____. *The Alien.* 1968. Garden City, NY: Doubleday, 1971.
_____. *The Artificial Man.* 1965. New York: Scholastic Book Services, 1968.
_____. *Assignment Abacus.* 1975. Garden City, NY: Doubleday, 1975.
_____. *Dimension A.* 1969. New York: Dell, 1972.
_____. *Genesis Two.* 1969. Chicago: Playboy Press, n.d.
_____. *Give Me Back Myself.* 1971. London: Barrie & Jenkins, 1972.
_____. *The Lampton Dreamers.* 1966. Garden City, NY: Doubleday, 1967.
_____. *The Land of Leys.* Garden City, NY: Doubleday, 1979.
_____. *Man out of Nowhere.* 1965. New York: Signet, 1968.
_____. *Morning Walk.* London: Hale, 1982.
_____. *The Nameless Ones.* London: Long, 1967 (as by Leslie Vardre). Garden City, NY: Doubleday, 1968 (as *A Grave Matter*).
_____. *The Paper Dolls.* 1964. Garden City, NY: Doubleday, 1966.
_____. *Possession.* 1976. Garden City, NY: Doubleday, 1976.
_____. *Psychogeist.* 1966. Garden City, NY: Doubleday, 1967.
_____. *The Shadow Before.* Garden City, NY: Doubleday, 1970.
_____. *Stranger to Town.* 1969. Garden City, NY: Doubleday, 1969.
_____. *Tell It to the Dead.* 1966. Garden City, NY: Doubleday, 1967 (as *The Reluctant Medium*).
_____. *Twilight Journey.* 1967. Garden City, NY: Doubleday, 1968.
_____. *What Did I Do Tomorrow?* 1972. Garden City, NY: Doubleday, 1973.
_____. *The White Room.* Garden City, NY: Doubleday, 1969.
Joshi, S. T. *John Dickson Carr: A Critical Study.*Bowling Green, OH: Bowling Green State University Popular Press, 1990.
Reilly, John M., ed. *Twentieth-Century Crime and Mystery Writers.* New York: St. Martin's Press, 1980.
Waugh, Robert H. "Horror: The Accuser of This World." *Studies in Weird Fiction* No. 8 (Fall 1990): 1–11.

Dennis Etchison

Etchison, Dennis. *The Blood Kiss*. Los Angeles: Scream/Press, 1988. [BC]

————. *California Gothic*. New York: Dell, 1995.

————. *Cutting Edge* (editor). 1986. New York: St. Martin's Press, 1987. [CE]

————. *The Dark Country*. 1982. New York: Berkley, 1984. [DC]

————. *Darkside*. New York: Charter, 1986. [D]

————. *The Death Artist*. Minneapolis, MN: DreamHaven, 2000. [DA]

————. *Masters of Darkness* (editor). New York: Tor, 1986. [MD]

————. *Masters of Darkness II* (editor). New York: Tor, 1988.

————. *Masters of Darkness III* (editor). New York: Tor, 1991.

————. *MetaHorror* (editor). New York: Dell, 1992.

————. *Red Dreams*. 1984. New York: Berkley, 1987. [RD]

————. *Shadowman*. New York: Dell, 1993. [S]

Stamm, Michael E. "The Dark Side of the American Dream: Dennis Etchison." In *Discovering Modern Horror Fiction I*, ed. Darrell Schweitzer. Mercer Island, WA: Starmont House, 1985, pp. 48–55.

Winter, Douglas E. "Dennis Etchison." In *Faces of Fear*. New York: Berkley, 1985, pp. 50–64. [FF]

L. P. Hartley

Hartley, L. P. *Collected Short Stories*. London: Hamish Hamilton, 1968. [C]

————. *Complete Short Stories*. London: Hamish Hamilton, 1973. New York: Beaufort Books, 1986. [C]

————. *Facial Justice*. London: Hamish Hamilton, 1960. Garden City, NY: Doubleday, 1961.

————. "Introduction" to *The Third Ghost Book*, ed. Cynthia Asquith. London: James Barrie, 1955.

————. *The Killing Bottle*. London: G. P. Putnam's Sons, 1932. [KB]

————. *Mrs. Carteret Receives and Other Stories*. London: Hamish Hamilton, 1971. [MC]

————. *Night Fears and Other Stories*. London: G. P. Putnam's Sons, 1924. [NF]

————. *The Novelist's Responsibility: Lectures and Essays*. London: Hamish Hamilton, 1967. [NR]

————. *The Travelling Grave and Other Stories*. Sauk City, WI: Arkham House, 1948. [TG]

————. *Two for the River*. London: Hamish Hamilton, 1961. [TR]

————. *The White Wand and Other Stories*. London: Hamish Hamilton, 1954. [WW]

Jones, Edward T. *L. P. Hartley*. Boston: Twayne, 1978.

Sullivan, Jack. "Ghost Stories of Other Antiquaries." In *Elegant Nightmares: The English Ghost Story from Le Fanu to Blackwood*. Athens: Ohio University Press, 1978, pp. 91–111 (esp. 100–107).

Rudyard Kipling

Kipling, Rudyard. *Actions and Reactions*. London: Macmillan, 1909. [AR]

————. *A Diversity of Creatures*. London: Macmillan, 1917. [DC]

————. *Life's Handicap*. London: Macmillan, 1891. [LH]

————. *Many Inventions*. London: Macmillan, 1893. [MI]

————. *The Mark of the Beast and Other Horror Tales*. Edited by S. T. Joshi. Mineola, NY: Dover, 2000.

————. *Mine Own People*. New York: United States Book Co., 1891. [MP]

————. *The Phantom 'Rickshaw and Other Tales*. Allahabad: A. H. Weeler & Co., 1888. [PR]

————. *Plain Tales from the Hills*. Calcutta: Thacker, Spink & Co., 1888. [PT]

————. *Traffics and Discoveries*. London: Macmillan, 1904. [TD]

Fritz Leiber

Byfield, Bruce. *Witches of the Mind: A Critical Study of Fritz Leiber*. West Warwick, RI: Necronomicon Press, 1991.

Dziemianowicz, Stefan. "Dead Ringers: The Leiber-Lovecraft Connection." *Crypt of Cthulhu* No. 76 (Hallowmass 1990): 8–13.

Leiber, Fritz. *Fafhrd & Me: A Collection of Essays*. Newark, NJ: Wildside Press, 1990. [FM]

————. *Night's Black Agents*. 1947. New York: Berkley, 1978. [N]

————. "The Terror from the Depths." 1976. In *Tales of the Cthulhu Mythos*. Rev. ed. Sauk City, WI: Arkham House, 1990, pp. 267–312. [TD]

Lovecraft, H. P. *At the Mountains of Madness and Other Novels*. Sauk City, WI: Arkham House, 1985. [MM]

————. *The Dunwich Horror and Others*. Sauk City, WI: Arkham House, 1984. [DH]

————. Letter to Fritz Leiber (19 December 1936). Ms., John Hay Library, Brown University.

————. "Notes on Writing Weird Fiction." In *Miscellaneous Writings*. Ed. S. T. Joshi. Sauk City, W: Arkham House, 1995, pp. 113–16. ["Notes"]

————. *Selected Letters*. Ed. August Derleth, Donald Wandrei, and James Turner. Sauk City, WI: Arkham House, 1965–76. 5 vols. [SL]

Mosig, Dirk W. "H. P. Lovecraft: Myth-Maker." 1976. In *H. P. Lovecraft: Four Decades of Criticism*, ed. S. T. Joshi. Athens: Ohio University Press, 1980, pp. 104–12.

Tierney, Richard L. "The Derleth Mythos." In *HPL*, ed. Meade and Penny Frierson. Birmingham, AL: Meade and Penny Frierson, 1972, p. 53.

Frank Belknap Long

"The Body Masters." *Weird Tales* (February 1935). Rpt. (as "The Love-Slave and the Scientists") *Avon Fantasy Reader No. 13*, ed. Donald A. Wollheim. New York: Avon, 1950, pp. 3–12.

Escape from Tomorrow. Ed. Perry M. Grayson. West Warwick, RI: Necronomicon Press, 1995. [ET]

The Eye Above the Mantel and Other Stories. Ed. Perry M. Grayson. West Hills, CA: Tsathoggua Press, 1995. [EM]

The Horror from the Hills. Weird Tales (January–February 1931). Sauk City, WI: Arkham House, 1963. In Long's *Odd Science Fiction.* New York: Belmont, 1964, pp. 7–99. [HH]

"The Horror in the Hold." *Weird Tales* 19, No. 2 (February 1932): 259–64.

The Hounds of Tindalos. 1975. New York: Jove/HBJ, 1978. [HT]

"Johnny on the Spot." *Unknown* (December 1939). Rpt. in *Rivals of Weird Tales*, ed. Robert Weinberg, Stefan R. Dziemianowicz, and Martin H. Greenberg. New York: Bonanza Books, 1990, pp. 223–25.

The Rim of the Unknown. 1967. New York: Condor, 1972. [RU]

"The Sea Thing." *Weird Tales* 6, No. 6 (December 1925): 751–57.

H. P. Lovecraft

Barzun, Jacques. "Introduction." *The Penguin Encyclopedia of Horror and the Supernatural.* New York: Viking Penguin, 1986.

Burleson, Donald R. "The Mythic Hero Archetype in 'The Dunwich Horror.'" *Lovecraft Studies* No. 4 (Spring 1981): 1–9.

Elliot, Hugh. *Modern Science and Materialism.* London: Longmans, 1919.

Leiber, Fritz. "A Literary Copernicus" (1949). In *H. P. Lovecraft: Four Decades of Criticism*, ed. S. T. Joshi. Athens: Ohio University Press, 1980.

Lovecraft, H. P. *At the Mountains of Madness and Other Novels.* Sauk City, WI: Arkham House, 1985. [MM]

———. *Dagon and Other Macabre Tales.* Sauk City, WI: Arkham House, 1986. [D]

———. *The Dunwich Horror and Others.* Sauk City, WI: Arkham House, 1984. [DH]

———. *Miscellaneous Writings.* Ed. S. T. Joshi. Sauk City, WI: Arkham House, 1995. [MW]

———. *Selected Letters.* Ed. August Derleth, Donald Wandrei, and James Turner. Sauk City, WI: Arkham House, 1965–76. 5 vols. [SL]

Mackie, J. L. *Ethics.* Harmondsworth: Penguin, 1977.

Nelson, Dale J. "Lovecraft and the Burkean Sublime." *Lovecraft Studies* No. 24 (Spring 1991): 2–5.

Russell, Bertrand. *Human Knowledge: Its Scope and Limits.* New York: Simon & Schuster, 1948.

Wilson, Edmund. "Tales of the Marvellous and the Ridiculous" (1945). In Joshi, *Four Decades.*

W. C. Morrow

Morrow, W. C. *The Ape, the Idiot and Other People.* Philadelphia: J. B. Lippincott Co., 1897.

———. *The Monster Maker and Other Stories.* Edited by S. T. Joshi and Stefan Dziemianowicz. Seattle: Midnight House, 2000.

Moskowitz, Sam. "W. M. Morrow: Forgotten Master of Horror—First Phase." In *Discovering Classic Horror Fiction I,* ed. Darrell Schweitzer. Mercer Island, WA: Starmont House, 1992, pp. 127–73.

Sir Arthur Quiller-Couch

Brittain, F. *Arthur Quiller-Couch: A Biographical Study of Q.* Cambridge: Cambridge University Press, 1948.

Quiller-Couch, Sir Arthur. *Corporal Sam and Other Stories.* London: Smith, Elder & Co., 1910. [CS]

———. *The Horror on the Stair and Other Weird Tales.* Edited by S. T. Joshi. Ashcroft, BC: Ash-Tree Press, 2000.

———. *I Saw Three Ships and Other Winter's Tales.* London: Cassell, 1892. [IS]

———. *The Laird's Luck and Other Fireside Tales.* London: Cassell, 1901. [LL]

———. *Merry-Garden and Other Stories.* London: Methuen, 1907.

———. *News from the Duchy.* Bristol: Arrowsmith; London: Simpkin, Marshall, Hamilton, Kent & Co., 1913.

———. *Noughts and Crosses.* London: Cassell, 1891. [NC]

———. *Old Fires and Profitable Ghosts.* London: Cassell, 1900. [OF]

———. *Q's Mystery Stories.* London: J. M. Dent, 1937.

———. *Two Sides of the Face: Midwinter Tales.* Bristol: Arrowsmith, 1903. [TS]

———. *Wandering Heath.* London: Cassell, 1895. [WH]

———. *The White Wolf and Other Fireside Tales.* London: Methuen, 1902. [WW]

David J. Schow

Sammon, Paul M., ed. *Splatterpunks: Extreme Horror.* New York: St Martin's Press, 1990. [Sp]

Schow, David J. *Black Leather Required.* Shingletown, CA: Mark V. Ziesing, 1994. [BLR]

———. *The Kill Riff.* New York: Tor, 1988, *1989. [KR]

———. *Lost Angels.* New York: New American Library, 1990. [LA]

———. *Seeing Red.* New York: Tor, 1990. [SR]

———. *The Shaft.* London: Macdonald, 1990. [S]

———. *Silver Scream* (editor). New York: Tor, 1988. [SS]

Warren, Bill. "*Weird Tales* Talks with David J. Schow." *Weird Tales* No. 296 (Spring 1990): 17–25. [W]

Rod Serling

Engel, Joel. *Rod Serling: The Dreams and Nightmares in the Twilight Zone.* Chicago: Contemporary Books, 1989.

Serling, Rod. *More Stories from The Twilight Zone.* New York: Bantam Books, 1961.

———. *New Stories from The Twilight Zone.* New York: Bantam Books, 1962.

———. *Night Gallery.* New York: Bantam Books, 1971. [NG1]

———. *Night Gallery 2.* New York: Bantam Books, 1972. [NG2]

———. *The Season to Be Wary.* Boston: Little, Brown, 1967. New York: Bantam Books, 1968. [SW]

———. *Stories from The Twilight Zone.* New York: Bantam Books, 1960.

———. *Stories from The Twilight Zone* [omnibus of the three "Twilight Zone" volumes]. Introduction by T. E. D. Klein. New York: Bantam Books, 1989. [TZ]

Edward Lucas White

Lovecraft, H. P. *The Annotated Supernatural Horror in Literature.* Ed. S. T. Joshi. New York: Hippocampus Press, 2000.

Wetzel, George T. "Edward Lucas White: Notes for a Biography." *Fantasy Commentator* 4, No. 2 (Winter 1979–80): 94–114; 4, No. 3 (Winter 1981): 178–83; 4, No. 4 (Winter 1982): 229–39; 5, No. 1 (Winter 1983): 67–70, 74; 5, No. 2 (Winter 1984): 124–27.

White, Edward Lucas. *Lukundoo and Other Stories.* London: Ernest Benn, 1927.

———. *The Song of the Sirens and Other Stories.* New York: E. P. Dutton, 1919.